English Churchyard Memorials

Frederick Burgess

The Lutterworth Press
Cambridge

Published by
The Lutterworth Press
P.O. Box 60
Cambridge
CB1 2NT
England

e-mail: **publishing@lutterworth.com**
website: **http://www.lutterworth.com**

ISBN 0 718 89140 6 paperback

British Library Cataloguing in Publication Data:
A catalogue record is available from the British Library.

First published 1963
reprinted 2004

Contents

CONTENTS

List of Plates

Introduction

DURING THE PRESENT CENTURY the work of various scholars has firmly established the artistic importance of our English heritage of stone carving. Such research has brushed away certain myths woven by former prejudice and ill-formed opinion. Romanesque sculpture has lost its stigma of being thought uncouth and barbarous; medieval building and carving have been established as the work, not of monks, but of professional craftsmen who have shed much of their former anonymity; while post-Reformation tomb-makers and architects have been rescued from Victorian obloquy and shown to form a part of this same tradition. Within the last ten years this mass of information has been summarized in three individual indices, compiled by John Harvey, Rupert Gunnis and Howard Colvin, which are standard works of reference forming a roll of honour of English craftsmanship.

One branch of stone-carving, however, has received scant attention: our native monuments set out in the open air in burial grounds, church-yards and cemeteries, commemorating not so much the rich and the great, but the rank and file of humanity—the common man. The present book attempts to supply this lack and give not only a general account of such memorials from prehistoric until recent times but more particularly introduce the results of new research on those of the post-Reformation period which have suffered most from neglect.

Although tombstones previous to this historical turning-point have been individually described in learned papers or collectively under separate art-styles by authorities who have made such periods their special study, comparatively little has been done in the way of their overall assessment. In some respects, due to archaeological fervour, our knowledge of prehistoric has outstripped that of historic monuments; the bulk of Anglo-Saxon carving, although certain of its aspects have received minute attention, still awaits the completion of a survey initiated by Sir Thomas Kendrick; and information on medieval memorials is mainly imbedded in the reports of county antiquarian societies. For any reader, other than the specialist, the available data is therefore widely dispersed, and difficult of access; for this reason, its essentials are here presented in a form which, it is hoped, is lucid and reasonably impartial, although the reader should bear in mind that the greater proportion of space is devoted to the post-Reformation period as this material is presented here for the first time. This point has largely determined the choice of illustrations.

Several reasons may account for the general apathy towards these latter monuments. Most important may be a subconscious unwillingness to acknowledge anything that reminds us of our own irrevocable destiny and, springing from this, there may be a certain satisfaction that lichen, weeds and ivy should be their shrouds; perhaps there is too a certain snobbery or class-consciousness which inhibits appreciation, or it may be the physical fact of their position out-of-doors, which permits their detail to be clearly seen only for an hour or two about mid-day. For these stones are indeed vulnerable, subject to the quixotic changes of English weather, to air pollution since the days of industrial progress, and to man's charity, as fickle as a vane. However well-chosen the stone (and much of it has lasted for centuries in spite of all these hazards) it cannot last for ever, and a monument no longer performs its function when it becomes unintelligible. Every churchyard contains a few monuments which time has defaced in this way.

Advantage has been taken of this fact by a specious logic and without discrimination, and many wholesale clearances of churchyard memorials have already been made (often in the teeth of safeguards initiated by church and diocesan authorities). Such vandalism, which masquerades as tidiness, has increased since World War II, and there is a very real danger of its becoming a regular practice. This insidious change from neglect to destruction makes the work of record an urgent and immediate duty.

It would seem that such a task (which involves a knowledge of local conditions and the minutiae of parish documents) could best be done by county archaeological societies, making systematic surveys in their own areas. Their main interest, however, has been confined to the genealogical data of inscriptions, which are such useful supplements to parish registers. Unfortunately, with the exceptions of Surrey, Sussex and Herefordshire, nothing has yet been done to initiate county photographic records and, apart from a few instances performed through the auspices of the Georgian Group and the Central Council for the Care of Churches, little to restore or preserve monuments of distinction. In most legitimate cases of clearance headstones at least are usually preserved by lining them up against the churchyard wall; but there can surely be little objection to retaining a few of the finest under cover in the church porch or interior? Rubbings and plaster casts of noteworthy details could also be made at little expense and housed in the county museum along with photographs for display and reference, while additional prints of the latter could be sent to the National Buildings Record to enlarge the material already contained in its files.

As well as the monuments themselves it is one of the aims of this book to rescue their carvers from an ill-deserved oblivion. These craftsmen can be identified either by personal memorials, or by their habit of signing work, usually at the base of the design. Through individual examination of monuments in this way, some adequate idea of a mason's output and range of influence can be obtained and, when such first-hand evidence is followed up by research into parish documents, wills, directories, etc., the jigsaw of his life can be assembled. Such signatures, however, were rarely cut before the middle of the eighteenth century, the oldest being visible on the hard-wearing slates of the West Country and Midlands; but the majority, being of softer freestone have seldom remained legible before the early years of the nineteenth century. Actual proof of identity is thus limited in scope and period, although comparative analysis can distinguish not only regional, but individual styles with some degree of probability. On the other hand, many masons are known from documentary evidence to have produced gravestones, although in the absence of signatures they will forever remain mere names.

While the present index of craftsmen at the end of this book, owing to pressure of space, has been condensed to a list of names and dates, it presents a foundation at least on which others may be inspired to build. For it must be emphasized that the present work is mainly the result of personal research, yet, owing to the increasing tempo of iconoclasm, future investigation needs to be both co-operative and co-ordinated. Presumably the immediate solution would be the election by county learned societies of working committees to investigate the available material in their own localities. The writer will feel his own patience to have been rewarded if this book leads to such practical steps being taken. In the meanwhile he would be very grateful to receive and acknowledge any data or photographs relating to churchyard monuments and their makers, or notice of any errors or omissions that are unavoidable in a work of this kind which refers to many persons, places and sepulchres. Indeed it is more than likely that, in spite of careful checking, some of the items described in the following pages have since ceased to exist. The task is urgent, yet there are many thrills and pleasures involved in its field-work. Like Mr Landor's precept for happiness, it offers an object of unending pursuit. In his own course the writer has re-experienced the excitement of those early topographers who discovered our landscape and antiquities with fresh vision, it has led down roads unfolding to Pisgah-sights of unknown churches, and to long, quiet hours of content.

And in a larger sense what else is this inquiry—whereby these glyphs of the paradoxical English temperament become articulate—but a tribute from the living to the dead, an act of faith in man's posterity?

Most of my field-work during the past twenty-five years has been achieved on solitary visits during summer vacations. Pleasant exceptions have been excursions spent with my friend Birkin Haward of Ipswich (who has photographed many monuments throughout East Anglia), and later with my wife, whose eagle eye let no signature escape her. I owe much to the help and advice of my late step-father, John Newnham of Billingshurst, and the inspiration given by my former school-master, Edward Kirby of Kettering. I am grateful for help given by the late Mrs Katherine Esdaile and Mr Walter Godfrey (former Director of the National Buildings Record), and to Mr H. M. Colvin and Mr Rupert Gunnis for generously sharing information when they were producing their own records; for the loan of photographs by Miss Innes Hart, Miss M. Wight, Mr M. W. Barley, Mr E. Brown, Mr Lindsay Fleming, Mr G. L. Remnant, and Mr Philip Rogers (who single-handed has made an important photographic record of churchyard monuments throughout the county of Kent), and also to Mr Alan Ludwig, of Rhode Island (who recently visited this country in the attempt to find sources for the sepulchral art of New England). To the Central Council for the Care of Churches, the Society of Genealogists, to Mr F. W. Steer, and Mr M. P. Statham (respective archivists of

Sussex and West Suffolk), and to many secretaries of local archaeological societies, my thanks are due for the loan of documents, and the circulation of inquiries among their members; and to Mr P. F. Bridgman, Messrs. Gilliam and Son, Mr A. S. Ireson, Mr E. Jenkins, and Mr J. B. Witcombe for the loan of account-books relating to their forebears in the craft of stone-masonry. Many correspondents have patiently answered my queries and volunteered data at various times during the past years and, while it is impossible to name them all, I would especially like to thank Mr D. Bircher, Mr B. Bailey, Mr G. Broderick, Mr Felix Erith, Mr John Harvey, Mr R. Hawkins, Mrs M. U. Jones, Mr E. K. Roberts, the Rev. Charles Steer, the Rev. E. V. Tanner and Mr W. H. Whitehead.

To Mr F. Measom and Mr D. Fiford, its past editors, and to Mrs Helen Whittick, the present editor of *Monumental Journal*, I am indebted for the opportunity given me during the last twenty years of making regular contributions on monumental design old and new to this craft periodical, and in conclusion to my present publishers for allowing me to crystallize this research in the span of a single volume.

1

Churchyards and Cemeteries:
their Origins and Development

BOTH Tertullian and Origen mention the existence of Christians in Britain during the third century. Certainly during the Diocletianic persecution in the early years of the fourth century three martyrs were yielded to this holocaust: the canonized Alban, and the lesser-known Julius and Aaron of Caerleon; while immediately following Constantine's declaration of religious tolerance, the British church was represented by three bishops at the Council of Arles, and later in the century at Ariminium.

Although our own pious heretic Pelagius left his native country c. 380 to wander with his friend Caelestius through Italy, Africa and the East, some of his followers, exiled from Italy, returned to spread his doctrine in Britain. When the native church appealed for Roman help, presumably through force of habit, the Pope sent Germanus and Lupus from Gaul to restore orthodoxy in 429. However, obdurate backsliders made necessary a later mission, when one former cleric is said to have fought at the head of local militia against barbarian invaders, teaching them the battle-cry of Alleluia.

While the political and military ties between Britain and Europe became weaker, a spiritual liaison gained strength. Romano-British clerics—trained in such important monastic schools as Lerins near Marseilles, where St Victor was introducing the principles of Egyptian monasticism, at Tours under St Martin, or Auxerre under the militant Germanus—established their own mission-stations in remote un-Romanized regions of the West. In 397 Ninian founded at Whithorn in Pictish Galloway his Candida Casa, the white-washed stone monastery which was the first of its kind in Britain; Illtud, disciple of Germanus and teacher of St David, founded the first Welsh community at Llantwit Major; and Patrick, fellow-student of Illtud at Auxerre and created bishop in 432, devoted his life to the conversion of Ireland.

The archaeological evidence for Christianity during this period has revealed the remains of small churches at Silchester and Caerwent, and a number of household goods from various parts of the country marked with the Chi-Rho monogram.[1] The occurrence of this emblem on a mosaic floor at Frampton (Dorset) and painted on the walls of a private oratory at Lullingstone (Kent), both villa-sites, shows that Christianity had gained converts among the wealthier classes by the middle of the fourth century. Tombstones have been discovered at Lincoln, York, Chesterholm, Carlisle and Brougham Castle in the Border country, the latter group showing that Ninian's evangelists had blazed a trail which two centuries later the Irish missionaries were to follow from Iona to Tyne.

At the time of the official Roman evacuation in the first half of the fifth century Christianity could be considered as firmly established, but increasing Teutonic raids along the East coast and the occupation of the Lowlands cut off European influence. With headquarters perhaps at Glastonbury, the western districts of Cornwall, Wales and Strathclyde became the stronghold of the British faith, until Columba founded Iona in 563, and sent from its centre evangelists to convert North Britain and Pictland.

The Roman mission, following Augustine's conversion of Kent at the end of the sixth century, established its headquarters at Canterbury, sending emissaries direct to the various pagan courts. The Irish and Roman techniques for making proselytes were symptomatic of their different brands of Christianity; the former visited the folk as teachers; while the latter first converted the ruler with the comforting assurance that his subjects would follow his example. Their interests finally clashed in Northumbria and, although the famous Synod of Whitby was arranged in 664 ostensibly to discuss differences of ritual, the main issue involved isolation versus conformity, and the Roman party was probably successful precisely because of the political connections it had formed.

The first monuments marked with the cross-emblem have been found in Galloway, Wales and Cornwall. They are roughly-dressed slabs, narrow in relation to height, engraved either with a cross within a circle or the Chi-Rho monogram, with laconic Latin inscriptions. Similar to monuments in Gaul of the fourth and fifth centuries, they effect a compromise between continental Christian customs and native megalithic survivals in Britain.[2] Monastic liaison between Britain and Ireland explains the occurrence of similar examples in the latter country of about this time (fifth and sixth centuries), where the cross accumulated a pattern of Celtic spirals, and was given a variety of exotic forms derived both from continental and Eastern imagery, engraved on boulders or rough stone slabs.[3]

The worship of stones may have followed as a natural consequence of man's first use of them for commemoration, which involved the belief that they became the spiritual residences or counterparts of the dead. In Western Europe at least, those countries visited by the megalith builders show ample signs of this veneration in their folk-lore. Apart from tombs, characteristic menhirs with female attributes found throughout this area give evidence of the cult of a fertility goddess whose secret worship persisted until recent times.[4] In these early days of Christianity there certainly existed a nature worship focused on trees, springs and stones, which the new order did its best to suppress by various orders in council, made on several occasions from the fifth to eleventh centuries, that only show by dint of repetition how abortive must have been their results.

In practice the primitive mana of these stone "idols", in particular, menhirs, were converted to orthodoxy by having the sign of the cross engraved upon them. This simple device had a three-fold result: it drove out or exorcised pagan spirits; it showed the superiority of the new faith; and it reinvested the old haunt with new power, thus promoting a continuity of worship. The same spirit of compromise was implicit in Pope Gregory's letter to Mellitus in 601, when he advised him not to destroy the temples but turn them into churches; to keep the old festivals and allow the people to sacrifice their oxen, but to dedicate the feast instead in memory of some saint.

Although it can by no means be established as a general practice, evidence suggests that in some cases both churches and Christian burial-grounds either replaced or were attached to existing pagan sites.[5] The reasons for this may have been either simple convenience (such as the pillage of building materials, in the case of those erected near to Roman villas or camps); or the fact that such areas were still inhabited made them obvious centres; or there may have been a psychological reason, such as a desire to reaffirm that Christianity was the spiritual heir of the Roman empire.

In any case, we have no precise knowledge as to the genesis of the English churchyard and can only suggest certain precedents derived from Roman and Celtic Christian usage, which contributed to its establishment.

In Rome the practice of catacomb burial was supplanted early in the fifth century by nearby surface cemeteries, often with funerary chapels which eventually developed into basilican churches. Owing to the Barbarian plunder of both catacombs and cemeteries in the next century, and the consequent depopulation of the city, the ancient laws forbidding intra-mural interment were relaxed. The remains of martyrs were transferred to the city churches, and the customary desire of the faithful to be buried near such sacred relics led to the entrance court or atrium of the basilica being provided for burials. It should be realized that the Roman custom of first erecting churches over the tombs of martyrs led to the rule of making any altar a receptacle for some holy relic;[6] so that when burial within the church became customary the most coveted places of sepulture were those nearest the holy table. At first the privilege was limited to ecclesiastics and those of royal birth,[7] later to church founders and benefactors, until gradually the only criterion became that of wealth, as is somewhat cynically expressed in an epitaph at Kingsbridge (Devon) to Robert Philip, parish grave-digger, 1795:

> Here lie I at the chapel door,
> Here lie I because I'm poor
> The farther in the more you'll pay,
> Here lie I as warm as they,

and also at Corsham (Wilts.), "In this Church porch lyeth ye body of William Tasker Gent. who choose rather to be a doore-keeper to the house of his God than to dwell in the tent of wickedness", 1684.

It has also been suggested that the churchyard derived from either the architectural arrangement of early monasteries, or the preaching stations set up by missionaries during the time of the second conversion. Early Irish hermitages, whose occupants emulated in their sea-girt islands the desolation of the Thebaid, show the spartan components of enclosing wall, individual cells, garden-plots and well, church, cross and burial-ground, sufficient for the support of men united in life and death by worship in these "cities of God". Such a minute cemetery of cross-slabs starred with blossoms of sea-pinks, as that set on the dizzy crags of Skellig Michael above its wilderness of ocean, represents the beginning of the large garths that were to grow up about the architectural complex of the later abbeys. Other Irish monasteries such as Duvillaun and Kilmore-Erris consist of an external bank or wall, with the enclosed area divided unequally into two parts, the smaller containing an oratory, near which is a cross-slab commemorating the founder-saint. The whole enclosure may have been used as an open-air church, the septum-wall dividing the congregation from the sanctuary, within which the cell served both as sacristy and tabernacle, and where the wooden altar would be propped against the cross-slab.[8]

If we bear in mind the Celtic influence introduced into this country by Columba and the Iona evangelists, it would seem that these components of oratory, cross and graveyard within an enclosed area may have had some influence on the formation of our own garths.

On the other hand, missionaries seem to have established their preaching-stations by the provisional setting-up of a cross, probably the wooden staff-rood carried as their processional standard, or a stouter specimen hewn from a tree-trunk. They may have been buried near this cross, thus giving the spot a sanctity which encouraged the burial of their converts about them. The actual form of certain stone crosses, such as that at Gosforth which resembles a trunk chamfered to a square section, and other subsidiary details of carving, suggest that they may well be imitations of wooden prototypes.

As early as the sixth century a decree of Justinian specified that a cross should precede the building of a church, a practice indicated in a passage from the life of the eighth century English saint Willibald, which describes the custom of erecting a cross rather than a church on the estates of pious Saxon land-owners for the convenience of daily worship. Churchyard crosses continued to be made throughout the medieval period, and the numbers of them which are still extant in spite of later iconoclasm show how the sacred ensign was deemed to be an essential item in the burial ground and used as a focus for preaching and community meetings. The most famous of these preaching crosses was Old St Paul's, which until its destruction in the early years of the Civil War stood at the north-east corner of the churchyard. It consisted of a small octagonal building surmounted by a cupola with cross as finial, galleries for members of the Court and other dignitaries being placed against the walls of the choir.

Literary evidence is meagre, but from the evidence afforded by the various edicts of synods it becomes obvious that burial in churches was gradually condoned. Attempts were first made to limit the privilege to ecclesiastics, but the repetitive prohibitions against burial of the laity made from the sixth to ninth centuries prove by implication that it was fast becoming the rule rather than the exception.

As for churchyards, Gregory the Great recommended them for burial in preference to cemeteries so that worshippers walking by the graves before entering church could remember the dead in their prayers.[9] Gregory of Tours (sixth century) first mentions the consecration of a churchyard, and their establishment in England would seem to be confirmed in 752, when Cuthbert, Archbishop of Canterbury, obtained papal permission for their establishment within cities, and Egbert, his contemporary colleague at York, described a churchyard as a garden or atrium placed near the church. During the process of consecration by the diocesan bishop the extent of the churchyard was marked by four small wooden crosses, set at the cardinal points. Durandus, whose *Rationale* must be regarded as an idealistic encyclopaedia on church ritual and symbolism, rather than a manual of working practice, mentions divergent opinions that either a space of some thirty feet around the church or the ground defined during the bishop's processional circuit should be sufficient for burial. The more precise area of one acre, with the church at its centre, was prescribed in 943 by the Welsh King, Howel Dha; this provides a link with the Teutonic name of Gottes-acker (God's Acre). Even as late as the end of the fourteenth century, however, churchyards still had no legal recognition.

The right of sanctuary was early vested in the church and churchyard area; village property seems to have been kept there for safety on occasion; and all through the Middle Ages this privilege accorded to fugitives from justice was jealously preserved and, although severely limited by Henry VIII, remained in force until the year 1621. Though the act of consecration implied some means of defining the hallowed ground, the practice of setting up a boundary could have been by no means general. One of the Constitutions of William de Bleys, Bishop of Worcester, in 1229, specified that the churchyard should be properly enclosed by a wall, hedge or ditch, and no portion of it was to be built upon, and another bishop in 1267, after stating the necessity for enclosure, ordained that grazing animals should be prohibited. However, a later canon of 1603 makes it clear that it was the churchwarden's duty to ensure that the churchyard "be well and sufficiently repaired, fenced, and maintained with walls, rails or pales". It became customary to make local landowners responsible for such fencing; and several Sussex churchyards in particular furnish precise records as to the allotment of such responsibility, according to the size of the farmer's holding. For instance, at Cowfold, 1636, the fence was maintained by eighty-one individuals whose initials were cut on their particular rails; and at Chiddingley, 1772, there were fifty-six subscribers, their length of fencing varying from 3 to 45 feet. At Areley Kings (Worcs.) which has a record of church marks for the year 1753, a local squire, Sir Harry Consby (d. 1701) killed two birds with one stone by making his part of the churchyard into a personal monument.[10] Parish priests, who were so often smallholders through necessity, frequently grazed their livestock in the garth. During 1550, in the county of Essex alone, one vicar was fined for folding sheep within the church; another for grazing his horse in the churchyard, while a parish near Colchester was notorious for pigs rooting up graves and for cattle lying in the porch. Peter Kalm, that shrewd observer, noted in 1748 that churchyard grazing in Essex and the Rochester and Gravesend district in Kent was common practice; while in the same county, in 1603, the vicar of Lydden built himself a stable in the churchyard. In fact, after the Reformation the parson regarded churchyard grazing as a legitimate perquisite, and parishioners accordingly planted their graves with willow or pegged them with lengths of bramble to prevent spoliation from cattle.[11]

The various secular uses to which the church fabric was formerly put were due, not to irreverence, but to the fact that it was community property in which both the interests of God and man were invested. The chancel was God's house for which the priest was responsible; the nave belonged to the parishioners, who used it, along with the porch, for business and social purposes when the need arose. Towers were on occasion used as strong-rooms, and beacons were placed upon their battlements; bells were for alarm and curfew no less than summons to prayer; manorial courts and vestries were held both in church and churchyard, and the official notices still posted in porches today represent the fag-end of the custom. The porch, wherever it existed, became the usual resort for parish business; and baptism and part of the marriage service were performed there. It was also used as a school-room, a library or a store for parish arms.[12]

Unless it is remembered that, before the advent of village greens, recreation-grounds or parish-halls, the churchyard was the only convenient public meeting place, the various social activities which took place there might well scandalize the purist. The majority of these has some religious connection, and in certain cases pagan origins, but, human nature being what it is, they relapsed on occasion into rustic saturnalia, which brought down ecclesiastical censure but died hard nevertheless. As such customs have been often described by writers on church folk-lore, they need only a brief mention here.

In the past church funds were augmented by the running of local Church-Ales, for which liquor was brewed and sold (our contemporary bazaars and village teas being the pallid equivalent). Although their intention was good, these junketings were often the cause for censure. Village fairs, usually held on the dedication festival of the church, similarly invited clerical allusion to "cleansing the temple" as stalls were often set up in the church itself; Old St Paul's was a notorious example. Cattle were sold, labourers hired, while pedlars, jugglers and mummers offered their wares and entertainment. Although the holding of fairs and markets in churchyards was forbidden by the Statute of Winchester 1285, the custom died hard and in such a conveniently large churchyard as Laughton-en-le-Morthen (Yorks.) survived until modern times.

The various sacred dramas and miracle-plays, in which the clergy participated, were at first performed in churches, but about the twelfth century they were transferred to the churchyard which gave more space. They were taken over by the Trade Guilds and gradually lost their liturgical character, relapsing finally into rustic melodramas presented by strolling-players and "barn-stormers". Ritual dancing, related to pagan fertility cults, was performed in both church and churchyard by morris dancers and, although no English counterparts remain comparable to the extraordinary Whitsun dancing at Echternach, Aubrey mentioned Christmas Church-dances in Yorkshire during the 17th century, and the Abbotts Bromley horn-dance, a preliminary to parish perambulation, is still performed.[13]

Various sports were also enjoyed, including wrestling, ball-games, quoits and archery, which persisted throughout the Middle Ages and indeed were advocated as "lawful recreation" after Divine Service by James I in his *Book of Sports*. The game of fives was particularly popular in Wales, where some churchwarden accounts of the seventeenth and eighteenth centuries specify the setting-up of booths or arbours for spectators.[14]

Archery practice was encouraged in medieval times from boyhood, and the butts seem to have been placed in the churchyard or its vicinity in certain cases. This seems an appropriate place to scotch the legend that churchyard yews supplied the bulk of material for our native bowyers; indeed English wood was considered unsuitable and staves were imported from abroad in vessels engaged in the wine-trade. Its branches, however, were probably used as evergreens, and along with willow, as substitute for palm during the celebrations of Easter.

These various gatherings took place for the most part in the northern part of the churchyard. Widespread prejudice existed against burial in this area, rooted apparently in folk-beliefs which regarded the cold north as a source of evil, the "wrong side"—hence the scarcity of graves.[15] This superstition is clearly expressed on a headstone at Epworth (Lincs.) in 1807, with its implication of the crowded graves in the South which were the result.

> And that I might longer undisturb'd abide,
> I choos'd to be laid on this northern side.

If graves were originally grouped about the churchyard cross, or near to the church approach (as has been previously suggested), their invariable southern position in relation to the church may account for the preference to be buried in this sunny area. From the seventeenth to nineteenth centuries at least, it remained a vulgar belief that the northern part of the garth was more suited for the burial of strangers, paupers, unbaptized infants, those who had died a violent death and, in particular, suicides.[16]

The widespread practice of burying the corpse on its back facing the east on an east–west alignment, which became established as the custo-mary mode of Christian burial, had its origins in primitive sun worship. The importance attached to performing ceremonies involving move-ment clockwise or sunwise is shown by numerous instances in Celtic Christianity—where, for instance, Patrick consecrated a former pagan site for his cathedral at Armagh by a three-fold deiseal or circuit. In former times the funeral procession took such a course, and at Brilley (Herefs.), to quote a typical example, the coffin was carried three times round the funeral stone which stood outside the churchyard. In Devon, where the coffin was similarly carried round the churchyard cross, one parson took the drastic stop of breaking-up the monument to put an end to the custom.

Both in Scotland and Ireland during the nineteenth century, when the corpse was being carried to the distant burial-ground, it was usual to set up either cairns or small wooden crosses wherever the bearers paused to rest. There was some precedent for this, as William of Malm-esbury refers to stone crosses being set up every seven miles in one funeral procession of St Aldhelm in 710, while the crosses built wherever the corpse of Eleanor of Castille rested en route from Lincoln to London remain as magnificent vestiges of the custom. In 1447 the rector of Creed (Cornwall) left a bequest that stone crosses be put up in the county "where dead bodies are rested on their way to burial, that prayers may be made, and the bearers take some rest". The precise reason for the objection seems obscure, but two sharply-worded injunctions of 1571 and 1585 forbade this practice, as well as the making of "Wooden crosses ... set upon the cross in the churchyard or upon or about the grave". Many English churchyards are entered by the gabled lichgate (literally corpse-gate), built so that the bearers could rest with the corpse while awaiting the priest's arrival to recite the introductory sentences of the burial service. Some are provided with stone seats for the bearers and a slab for the resting of the coffin, such as St Levan (Cornwall) which has also a grid to keep out cattle.

The folk-lore and superstitions associated with burial custom are extensive, and we cannot deal with them here, apart from pointing out that their ambivalent character so often shows how the latent pagan background was reconciled to the demands of the Christian faith through a deliberate policy of compromise, initiated by Augustine and pursued by the established Church ever since. Broadly speaking, this primitive nature-worship (in particular the veneration of stones which most affects our subject) persisted longest in those districts where agrarian economy was least disturbed by industrial progress, most noticeably in the so-called Celtic areas of Great Britain.

Not only is it difficult to be precise about the origins of the church-yard, but also to determine to what extent monuments were erected within them before the end of the seventeenth century, when the number of existing memorials *in situ* and their general distribution throughout the country make it apparent that commemoration was customary. The monuments of various dates which make up the aggregate for the best part of this preceding thousand years is indeed small, due to circumstances that were little favourable to survival. These can be discussed under four headings:

(a) *Social conditions.* In the first place it should be recognized that earlier churchyard commemoration at least, rather than being a general custom, may have been exceptional, restricted by special circumstances, or limited to certain districts or particular periods of time. Apart from this, social prestige as well as wealth affected not only the formal character of monuments but their potential numbers. The cross-inscribed coffin-slab or ledger, bearing some representative emblem of the deceased's profession or occupation, which is the most numerous class of internal medieval memorials, shows that the majority were to clerics, soldiers, and merchants; a comparison of burials recorded in parish registers checked with existing eighteenth century gravestones reveals them as confined even in country districts to the wealthier members of its community, the farmers and craftsmen; and on the whole it was not until the growth of canals and railways reduced both the cost and transport of stone that monuments came within the purchasing power of the lower classes.[17]

(b) *Perishable materials.* Commonsense no less than evidence suggests that many early memorials were of wood and in consequence had a limited term of existence. It has already been noted that high crosses were likely to have developed from timber prototypes, and both the form and detail of many later stones show a technical imitation of wooden originals. With forest areas more extensive in the past than they are today, it was convenient to use the material at hand, hence the carpenter would be in more demand than the mason. John Coote, of Bury St Edmunds, for instance, in his will of 1502, asked for wooden crosses to be set up at the head and foot of his grave; while Aubrey noted in 1673 that in Surrey "they use no tombstones in the church-yards but rayles of wood over the grave on which are printed or engraved the inscription". Such grave-rails, deadboards, bed-heads, or leaping-boards (as they were indifferently called), consisting of posts supporting a board for the requisite text, are still a feature of the Home Counties, but they become rarer each year, as they fall rotten and are burnt by the sexton.

(c) *Neglect.* Any memorial, once set up in the ground and left undisturbed, has a natural life expectancy before sinking beneath the turf and being lost to sight and memory. An increased depth of soil produced by generations of interments within the confined area of the garth is apparent in many churchyards, raising them above the ground level, which can be detected from the trench cut round the base of the church wall for drainage. No general rate can be established for the absorption of stones into the earth, for size, weight, and type of soil differ widely. In individual churchyards, however, observation will give clues as to how long the process is likely to take, while an examination of contemporary prints and sketches will show what monuments formerly existed.

The incidental relics dug up by the spades of the sexton and restorer make it clear that churchyard sites have often been in frequent use for centuries, if not for worship, at least for burial. In most cases any scientific investigation today is ruled out by legal and pietistic objections but, in the cases of closed churchyards or isolated burial grounds where the church fabric is beyond restoration, such digging could offend no susceptibilities and, without doubt, would yield interesting data on many points relating to parochial history and custom of which we are at present ignorant.[18]

(d) *Destruction.* Sepulchral monuments have at all times been easy prey for re-use as building material, and there are comparatively few older churches in which they are not to be found, whole or in fragments, irrecoverably lost in the fabric or imbedded in the wall surface. Restoration occasionally brings them to light, and to this we owe the fortunate recovery of the largest single group of early medieval monuments, at Bakewell(Derbys.). Even during the medieval period it seems possible that stones were periodically removed, even voluntarily sacrificed, by parishioners to save expense when some addition to their church was made, as in some cases they must have been put to building use within a fairly short time after their manufacture. At Helpston (Northants.)[19] for instance, a restoration of the fourteenth century church tower revealed numerous coffin-lids only a century old; and in this vicinity alone many medieval fragments can be discovered at Bainton and Maxey (Northants.), and Liddington and Elston (Rutland).

The break with the Papal power and the setting-up of commissioners in every county during the sixteenth century with authority to destroy graven images and objects of idolatry and superstition led iconoclastic zeal into much senseless destruction of sepulchral monuments. This pillage had reached such a pitch that Queen Elizabeth in 1560 issued a proclamation "against breaking or defacing of monuments of Antiquitie, being set up in Churches, or other public places, for memory, and not for superstition", and ordered ecclesiastical authorities to restore or repair any damaged memorials; this obviously had little practical success, for it was followed by a sterner edict twelve years later.[20] About this time (to quote Weever) "there sprang up a contagious broode of Scismatickes" who rejoiced under the fantastic names of "Brownists, Barowists, Martinists, Prophesyers, Solsidians, Famelists, Rigid Precisians, Disciplinarians, and Judaical Thraskists", whose object was not only to rob the churches but to level them with the ground.

The Puritans also contributed their iconoclasm, giving to us men such as Dowsing of Suffolk to become bywords for misguided zeal, and their abolition of the Burial Service did nothing to encourage the erection of memorials. Gough gives many examples of wanton and wholesale destruction in his *Sepulchral Monuments of Great Britain*, and one can imagine, when reading of the sale of complete church fabrics, that bigotry must occasionally have offered excuse for peculation. In brief, putting together the effects of climate, of time, of being used for building material, or maliciously pounded into rubble, it is a matter for wonder that we have been left with so many surviving gravestones of this period.[21]

While simplicity and a folk-art element which occasionally becomes barbaric in feeling are typical of the Stuart period, Georgian work shows a sophistication of taste and virtuosity in execution which, although obviously inspired by church monumental carving and architectural ornament, is seldom directly imitative. The memorials of individual families are usually grouped in the garth, and tablets and large memorials built into the exterior fabric, but, apart from an obvious burial in rows, there was no planned uniformity of design and indeed, in respect to symbolism and epitaphs, presumably little clerical interference.[22]

The charnel devices which were an essential part of the interior tombs of the seventeenth century reflect the climate of opinion at this time, "haunted by the spectres of devouring time and change, the brevity, misery and vanity of life, the littleness of man in the cosmic panorama" (D. Bush, *English Literature in the Early Seventeenth Century*, p. 278). Its pessimism was epitomized in Burton's *Anatomy of Melancholy*—its Christian reconciliation in Browne's *Hydriotaphia*. But the Gothic mood which established itself in literature a century later gave "a sort of delight, ... alternately mixed with sorrow in the contemplation of death" (Steele, *Spectator*, 1711). This became the recipe for The Tale of Terror, while romantic titillations of the senses, in which men of taste indulged themselves through the dialectic of mock ruins and fake hermits set amid pagan grottoes and temples, expressed the doctrine of the Sublime and Picturesque. The literary stock-properties of the time occur in this description of a churchyard from William Mallet's *Excursion* of 1726:

> Behind me rises huge an aweful Pile
> Sole on this Blasted Heath, a Place of Tombs,
> Waste, desolate, where Ruin dreary dwells,
> Brooding o'er sightless Skulls, and crumbling Bones.
> Ghastful He sits, and eyes with stedfast Glare
> The Column grey with Moss, the falling Bust,
> The Time-shook Arch, the monumental Stone,
> Impair'd, effac'd, and hastening into Dust,
> Unfaithful to their charge of flattering Fame.
> All is dread silence here, and undisturb'd,
> Save what the Wind sighs, and the wailing Owl
> Screams solitary to the mournful Moon
> Glimmering her Western Ray through yonder Isle,
> Where the sad Spirit walks with shadowy Foot
> His wonted Round, or lingers o'er his Grave.

From 1742 to 1745 were published *Night-Thoughts* and *The Grave*, by Edward Young and David Blair, both serious and significant works of this class of literature. A few years later Gray finished his *Elegy written in a Country Churchyard*, reputedly the best-known poem in English, which made Stoke Poges, the scene of his meditation, the most visited of any churchyard. The same ingredients are present both in *The Excursion* and the *Elegy*; owl-call, ivy-clad stones, crumbling age, suggest the transitory nature of earthly grandeur, but the latter's quality of compassion "shows the awakening interest of the times in the lives of the humble and labouring classes, and in their social improvement through education".[23] At any rate, such literary emphasis on ruin and unkempt graves, even reckoning with poetic licence, reveals little regard for neatness or upkeep, apart from what care the piety of relatives bestowed on individual grave-plots.[24]

The first fantasies of the Gothick mood afforded an amusement for men of taste, but a serious interest in the sources of the Gothic style in building (due mainly to the Whartons and Gray)[25] was later taken up by an army of amateur antiquarians who skirmished regularly in the pages of *The Gentleman's Magazine* during the latter years of the eighteenth century. Their interminable arguments, a hotch-potch of aesthetics, antiquarianism and moral values, were further confused at the beginning of the Victorian era when the Oxford Movement tossed in religion. For the debility of the Anglican Church the Tractarians advocated a transfusion of ritual, adopting the Middle Ages as an exemplar. In 1839 the Camden Society was formed in the rival university by undergraduate fervour, publishing the first issue of its periodical *The Ecclesiologist* two years later, through which it became the official exponent of the "correctness" of church symbolism, based on a new translation of Durandus. Soon after its formation it had to face accusations of a leaning toward Rome. Typical of such onslaughts is the following extract from *Weale's Quarterly*, July, 1844: "An eleventh commandment seems to have issued from heaven itself, declaring, 'Thou shalt not worship the grandeur of Egypt, nor the beauty of Greece, nor the grandeur of Rome, nor the plastic varieties of Italy—but thou shalt worship only GOTHICISM!' ... Impotent incipiency of a bastard superstition! Hopeless tyranny of English church parsondom, seeking, under the banners of architecture to revive not the power of the Pope—

but the power of Popery in its own body! Sad acknowledgement of a want of vitality in Church of Englandism,—of utter despair in its originative influence on the noble art of architecture!" Nevertheless, the Camden Society weathered such storms, changed its name to the Ecclesiological Society, and resumed its self-appointed authority. In 1854 the editor of *The Ecclesiologist* dared to assert: "Church architecture is no longer tentative. It approaches to something of an exact science. It is admitted to be the subject not so much of taste as of facts." By a process of self-hypnosis which passed for logic the Society settled on the Decorated Style as the correct model for church design and ornament. As one of its principal aims was restoration, it is no matter for wonder that this became so often remodelling, and that much of Victorian quasi-Gothic wears fourteenth century fancy dress.[26]

So much for the reasons of this revolution. How did it effect sepulchral monuments? Although the medieval tradition, in the strict sense, never died, and debased forms of Gothic tracery and ornament can be found both in building and tombstone detail during the seventeenth century, and Gothic rococo in the Georgian period, to all intents and purposes the full-blown Revival in Victoria's reign presented the monumental mason with a crisis which affected not only his tradition of design, but of working practice, the most important being that of clerical supervision.

The Camden Society formed the pattern for other diocesan architectural societies, whose membership was largely made up of clergymen. Many of these enthusiasts for ecclesiology were ardent contributors to their various journals, in which they showed the typical bigotry of proselytes; developing the theory that good art could only be produced by good men, which they put into practice by attempting to suppress swearing among masons and bricklayers. A few published small treatises dealing with sepulchral monuments; one of the earlier being a *Tract upon Tombstones*, 1843, written by the Rev. F. E. Paget, a voluminous writer on church matters, and a member of the Lichfield Society for the Encouragement of Ecclesiastical Architecture. This pamphlet of twenty-five pages with seven line-drawings was imitated by several others and, as they are somewhat rare and inaccessible for general reference, it is necessary to quote them at some length, in order to show the changes that took place both in design and in the personal relation-

1. *Morley (West Riding), Henry and Martha Greetheed, 1718, 1722: upper and lower parts of ledger, 72 in. long, 28 in. wide. The churchyards of Morley and nearby Lightcliffe contain the best collection of eighteenth-century ledgers in Yorkshire, the majority of which have floral borders, and central panels with characteristic palmette patterns and florid lettering.*

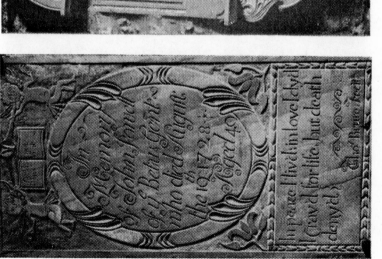

2 (left). Llantilio Pentholey (Mon.), John Powell, 1728; (centre) Llanbedr (Merions.), Thomas Brute, 1724: interior tablets by members of the Brute family, who made a speciality of colouring their sepulchral monuments (photographs by Miss M. Wight); (right) Medbourne (Leics.), John Goodman, 1768: tablet by James Hill of Great Easton. Gravestones signed by him and his father William are common in the Rutland–North Leicestershire border churchyards.

ships between stone-masons and clergy. Paget's *Tract* was intended to show how the erection of a tombstone could be made "a Christian act and one that shall benefit the living".

His first concern was for epitaphs, and he deplored the fulsome, bombastic and hypocritical sort of which admittedly the eighteenth century was all too fond, as well as pointing out the need to avoid errors in doctrine. His main reason for the latter criticism was the effect it might have on those "to whom the tombstones in the churchyard, are, as it were, a book, from whence they draw their reflections on man's mortality, and in which, every new inscription, is a fresh page. Who, that attends a village church, has failed to observe groups or individuals, Sunday after Sunday, conning over the epitaphs,—epitaphs known long ago, perhaps, by heart, but which from melancholy associations, probably, have an interest which even by the lapse of years is not lost, or worn out?"

The proper type of epitaph "should be characterized by Christian humility, kindness, and by a disposition to say *too little* rather than *too much*." The mourners' difficulties in composing an epitaph are such "that they frequently leave the whole matter to the taste and discretion of the stone-mason in the next market-town, and the result is just what might be expected. The preparation of gravestones being but one branch of this tradesman's business, it is not likely that he should feel any absorbing interest on the subject, or care to go out of his way to make improvements, while his customers continue satisfied with the present fashion. If they ask him for a durable material, he points to his pile of slate slabs, and declares (alas! too truly,) that nothing can surpass their durability; yet as a material, they are even more ugly than durable. If the applicants require a handsome inscription, with letters of white or gold (and it is hard to say which is the most mean in appearance), he will point with satisfaction to headstones which are in preparation in his yard and in which every variety of text,

𝕰𝖓𝖌𝖑𝖎𝖘𝖍,

ROMAN, *ITALIC*,

𝕮𝕷𝕭𝕬𝕽𝕬,

is to be seen in each successive line of the inscription; and every conceivable variety of letter,—whether

THICK, THIN,

or, in that odious sort of type, in which the usual thick and thin parts of the letters are reversed, and so are almost

ILLEGIBLE,

or in which they are reeling on their backs like

DRUNKEN MEN,

"With the same satisfaction he will point out the skill which his journeymen exhibit in flourishes, and perhaps will shew some cherub with a full-bottomed wig, or some dove with wings expanded, like those which are sometimes found in school-boys' cyphering books, and of which, I believe, the cleverness consists in their being executed in one unbroken line, without lifting the pen from the paper,—a process, which, it is unnecessary to say, cannot be so executed in stone." Following this mis-statement, he continues with a diatribe against Georgian imagery. To him its skulls, bones, scythes and hour-glasses, its doves, urns and torches, are all offensive. His comment on cherubs is incidentally of value, as it proves that in his day gravestones painted in full colour were by no means uncommon. "I suppose there are persons who admire these conventional forms of ugliness, with puffy faces of pink and white, black (often squinting) eyes, gilt hair and wings, which are intended as representations of one order of the Holy Angels. Certainly if tawdriness of colour can attract, these things look *smart* enough when they come out of the stone-mason's yard,—but let a few months pass, and what a change has taken place! The summer's sun has faded the red of the cheeks, and the damps of autumn have covered, perhaps, one half of the face with a mouldy green, so that the remains of its former brilliancy only make this ugly representation still more hideous". Mr Paget is most censorious about urns . . . "memorials of the abominable usage which the heathens, in their ignorance, inflicted on the bodies of the dead". He will have the "*one* emblem, perfectly unobjectionable, perfectly appropriate, full of consolation"—the Cross. "True, you will

34

say, but then the Cross is Popish." It was this anti-Papist feeling that explains the scarcity of the emblem on Georgian monuments; and it was a touchy point with the Tractarians, which they side-stepped by discriminating between cross and crucifix. Paget's recommendations for a memorial to the departed urges the mourner to spend his money on something for the Church. "Is there a new Prayer Book wanted for the reading-desk? a dish to collect the alms in at the Holy Communion? a new Altar Cloth? or is there a window which would be handsomer for the insertion of some painted glass? Why should you not consecrate your service to God, and at the same time make an enduring memorial of your deceased friend, by purchasing these things, and letting it appear upon them by some suitable inscription, that they were given in commemoration of the departed." But if a sepulchral monument was preferred, he suggested "that you make your monument of free-stone instead of slate, that it be neither high, nor wide (both being very unsightly) and that instead of going to the stone-mason and getting his opinion, you consult the Clergyman of the parish (without whose leave no monument can be legally erected) and request him to advise you in the preparation of your intended inscription." As an improvement on the "present fashion of huge, ill-proportioned, misshapen headstones", he advocates the use of either coped stones, or stone and wooden crosses—seven drawings of which conclude his little book.

Remarks on Christian Gravestones was published by the Rev. Eccles Carter, Canon of Bristol, in 1847, with assistance afforded by the Rev. John Armstrong. It is more moderate in tone than Paget, except for the astonishing suggestion that existing "heathen symbols, and blasphemous inscriptions" should be re-cut or erased—a scheme which, if carried out, would at least have prevented unemployment among stone masons. To introduce his eighteen illustrations (ten of which are headstone designs borrowed mainly from Armstrong's own tract, the remainder being medieval), he addresses "statuaries, sculptors, masons and others" pointing out that "much of the evil which has arisen in respect of gravestones with improper ornaments and inscriptions being placed in Churchyards, is owing to the thoughtless manner in which Stonecutters receive and execute orders, without first consulting the Clergyman in whose Churchyard the gravestone is to be erected. The proper punishment for such conduct would be for the Clergyman to refuse positively

35

to admit any stone, of which the design and inscription was not previously submitted to him, and so leave the Stonecutter and his employers to settle the matter together ... if Stonecutters would be content with a reasonable profit, such as they get for all other work, they may rely on it they would get much more employment than at present in this particular department."

In 1858 the Rev. Edward Trollope, Secretary to the Society of Antiquaries of Lincoln, published at Sleaford his *Manual of Sepulchral Memorials* which was a larger book containing eighteen plates of medieval monuments and examples of the contemporary Gothic Revival. The latter included two designs by Charles Kirk, a Sleaford architect, related to the Kirk family of stone-masons; and the booklet ended with forty-four pages of epitaphs chosen from the Scriptures and poetry.

He reviews the types of external and internal monuments and includes some acid comment on mural tablets, which shows clearly how the protagonists of the Gothic Revival detested Georgian monuments and thought no words too bad for them. "... unfortunately by far the most numerous class of Monuments, is that of Mural Slabs, ranging from ambitious specimens, loaded commonly with very indifferent sculpture, to those plain black and white tablets scattered here, and there, and everywhere, upon the walls of our Churches, without the slightest regard to the very injurious effect they have upon those parts of the fabric to which they cling, or any attempt at consonance with the style of its architecture.

"If we enter almost any town Church, we find the figure of a lady embracing a heathen urn, partly covered by an unmeaning cloth—the whole in white marble, surrounded in most cases by a glaringly black rim, with an attempt at some classical details and accessories; and this affixed to the wall by the mean expedient of cramps! ... If, however, hoping to discover something better, of a somewhat older date, we pursue our search, we shall find some coarsely foliated, or befruited production surmounted by an urn or sort of butter-boat, from which gilt flames are seen to issue; or else by an hour-glass, and one or more not very felicitous attempts to exhibit some repulsive relics of mortality— the whole sometimes protruding over a window, or even fixed to some beautiful clustered column, from which, perhaps, a portion has been ruthlessly chopped away, in order to attach such unseemly excrescence to one of the main features of the fabric.

"But far the most numerous class of mural monuments, we shall find, consists of White Slabs, more or less deeply surrounded by black borders perhaps simply washed in. There they are, in full array!—Greek tablets, Roman tablets, perhaps Egyptian tablets—but all in one garb of black and white, and almost all destitute of any Christian character, or artistic feeling; whilst the general repose of the sacred edifice is utterly destroyed ... by this medley of sepulchral placards."[27]

Trollope's remedy for reducing this chaos of mural tablets was to build arcades along the walls in which tablets could be placed with some uniformity or, failing this, to unite them with a framing of Minton tiles. Like Paget he pleads with the more wealthy mourner to make some contribution to the church fabric, as being the most enduring form of memorial. For the contemporary churchyard there is little praise. It may contain a few medieval monuments (naturally of irrefutable excellence!)—"But these are almost hid, in too many cases, by an exuberance of vast slabs, placed either upright, or horizontally, and by groups of nearly indescribable masses of stone of a box form, enclosed occasionally by a solid hedge of iron javelins, and indicative of no connection with Christianity. The turban marks the Mahometan's grave—the cross that of the Greek, and other Christian nations; but what is there in the form of a vast slab (now usually selected to stand at the head of British graves) to proclaim the faith of our dead?"

In his introduction to the illustrations he urges that monuments should have "their form and character improved, because these are usually not only very ugly, but very unchristianlike. A perfect forest of erect slabs towering ambitiously one above another clothes our Metropolitan cemeteries, diversified by a few would-be Egyptian obelisks, heathen broken columns, cinerary urns, and other most inappropriate devices, whilst Country Churchyards are filled with hideous slate slabs covered with a profusion of gold letters and flourishes, or else with the ordinary white stones abounding in such absurd or repulsive devices as make boys laugh, and Christian men sad when they look upon such an exhibition of folly, ignorance, and vanity ..."

Few would disagree with his rules for designers of gravestones which have a contemporary ring:

37

(a) These should be unmistakably Christian.

(b) They should be of enduring material.

(c) They should be of good quality rather than a large size.

(d) They should be of correct proportions; an appropriate, durable, well wrought and well designed stone, of very small dimensions, being infinitely preferable to a larger one ...

Such extracts show clearly that the contempt for Georgian monuments felt by their writers extended also to stone-masons, whom they regarded as neither strictly honest nor competent, and therefore in need both of supervision and instruction. These sentiments may not have been universal, but they sowed the seeds of a mistrust between clergy and stone-masons which is still in evidence today. Ecclesiological influence on gravestone design was more marked in larger towns than in villages, where country masons continued to produce their old-fashioned "pagan" designs well into the century; but its opinions were made available both to public and craftsmen through various pattern-books published by minor architects and local firms who were working in collaboration with church authorities and had become full-time monumental sculptors. These albums show a range of current styles, the composite use of materials, with insets of brass, mosaic or tile: cast-iron surrounds and grilles,[28] stone kerbs, and the growing use of imported stone, such as granite and marble. Owing to being in constant use for workshop practice, these books are now rareties.

While the advocates of Ecclesiology were responsible for some discouragement of the indiscriminate use of intra-mural carving, which they tried to limit to sepulchral wall-tablets less obtrusive in size and setting than their heroic Georgian predecessors, it was because of the introduction of cemeteries and the coincidental use of imported white marble that ambitious tomb-sculpture found a new home in the open air.

In 1843, when Paget published his *Tract*, the Royal Commission on *The Health of Towns, and the Sanitary Conditions of the Labouring Classes* and its select committee "to consider the expediency of framing some Legislative Enactments (due respect being paid to the rights of the Clergy) to remedy the Precincts of Large Towns, or of Places densely populated" concluded their labours. The beginning of the agitation which led to the forming of this Committee and the final closing of the Metropolitan graveyards was due to the zeal of a Drury Lane surgeon, George Alfred Walker, who published his *Gatherings from Graveyards* in 1839.[29]

Walker visited a large number of the London graveyards and collected information from abroad, where the problem had long been acknowledged and dealt with—the city churchyards of Paris having been closed as long ago as 1765. He aroused public concern, founded the Society for the Abolition of Burial in Towns, and finally gave evidence before the Commission, although the Bill which was to become known as the Burials Act was not passed until 1852. It should be borne in mind that the population of London *c.* 1800 was under a million, and that little, if any building had taken place south of the Thames, where Surrey was still a county of pleasant villages, but in fifty years it had more than doubled, and the Great Wen was already apparent.

By the end of the eighteenth century the London churchyards and their additional parish burial-grounds had become so over-crowded that private speculators often bought up land and opened up private cemeteries. It was largely owing to their existence and abuse that public opinion was roused and the investigations leading to the Burials Act set into motion. To attract custom their burial fees were generally lower than those of the churchyards, and in many cases the funeral officiants were undertakers' assistants, not ministers of religion. The example of Enon's Chapel in Clements Lane, must suffice as a typical example of this revolting corpse-trade. "The space available for coffins was, at the highest computation, 59 feet by 29 feet, with a depth of 6 feet, and no less than 20,000 coffins were deposited there. In order to accomplish this herculean task it was the common practice to burn the older coffins in the minister's house ... Between the coffins and the floor of the chapel there was nothing but the boards. In time the effluvium in the chapel became intolerable, and none attended the services, but the vaults were still used for interments, so 'that more money was made from the dead than from the living'—a state of affairs which existed in many of the private burial-places of the metropolis" (Holme, *London Burial Grounds*, p. 194). It is no matter for wonder that the sextons engaged in this gruesome business had to be drunk in order to endure the work.

Under the Open Spaces Act the old graveyards were gradually made into public gardens. Seven of the disused London grounds had been converted by 1877; the forming of the Metropolitan Public Gardens Association in 1882 accelerated the practice. Considerable philanthropy was exercised in this clearance, the work providing a means for employment among the poor, and by the end of the century nearly a hundred burial-places had been turned into small oases amid the desert of bricks and mortar. The many hundreds of tombstones destroyed in the process involved little irreparable loss in this particular case, for even those remaining in the Metropolitan area are often little more than blackened shards owing to soot pollution.

The closing of churchyards and consequent opening of new cemeteries formed a common topic in the Press at this time and, even before the Burials Act had finally been passed, seven were opened in the London area at Kensal Green, Norwood, Highgate, Abney Park, Brompton, Nunhead and Mile End, between the years 1833 and 1841. Kensal Green, including its Catholic portion, opened in 1858, contains one hundred acres, in which are displayed the best and worst of "sepulcrimagery" during the last 130 years. The first of the Metropolitan cemeteries to be opened, it was eminently respectable (for two members of the Royal family were interred therein), and also fashionable, being the "leading cemetery for what is called art and intellect". The eclectic progress of monumental design is here epitomized, for there is hardly an art-style unrepresented. Greek, Egyptian, Celtic, Gothic are all present, set amid mysterious catacombs and an elegant Attic cloister, from whose platform can be seen something of the London sprawl behind gigantic municipal gas-holders that can be easily imagined as ominous monumental forms of our own apprehensive time.[30] The majority of monuments in this crowded necropolis are of white Italian marble, and there was such a preference for the use of this material in cemetery memorials that it has now become a fixed custom and is still a dry bone of contention today.

With London still expanding space for cemeteries had to be sought even beyond the Metropolitan bounds. In 1853 the London Necropolis Company was formed, which bought up a tract of two thousand acres at Woking and established its own private railway for the conveyance of funerals, monuments and mourners.[31] "Here will be the graves of countless generations yet unborn; here, amongst the peace and solemnity of nature, those who never knew what either was, will return to dust; here, from reeking courts, alleys and mean rooms, the insentient body will rest in the summer's sunshine, and have over it the heath of flowers; and here, as elsewhere, man will work out, though unknowingly, a mighty law. Here he will form a desert into a garden—a waste, into the most fruitful land, which, in ages yet distant, may be golden with prolific harvests ... But it may be, in the fullness of time, when the facilities of transit are enlarged, incorporations will carry out the dead of London to still more distant heaths and solitary lands; or it may be that, in a still more distant time, advanced chemical knowledge will step in and return, by some instantaneous process, the body to its primary elements, and thus make graves and their corruption things only of record" (*Chambers Journal*, 1855, pp. 297–300).

Other utilitarian methods for the disposal of the dead, such as the use of perishable coffins or wicker baskets for the more rapid return of the corpse to its original elements, or burial at sea, to increase the fish supply, were aspects of prevalent materialist thought derived from the new scientific discoveries in the field of bacteriology and hygiene, which led, by inevitable logic, to cremation.

The ritual burning of the corpse of his son on a Welsh hillside by the eccentric Dr William Price in 1884, and the test-case which established its legality, founded the dramatic return of cremation to this country after an interval of over eleven hundred years.[32] The first cremation proper, in an apparatus similar to that devised by Brunetti in Italy in 1869, took place at Woking on March 26, 1885, the deceased being a woman. As many of its advocates were Radicals or free-thinkers there was some inevitable opposition from churchmen, nevertheless the custom spread rapidly throughout European countries, although Roman Catholics still object to the custom on doctrinal grounds.

According to recent statistics there is now a greater proportion of cremation to burials in England than in any other professedly Christian country,[33] and presumably the rate will continue to rise. One of the arguments used by the opponents of inhumation was that land devoted to cemeteries could be put to more practical use for farming or housing; and the new London cemeteries which sprang up at the time of the Cemetery Clause Act 1847 were not opened without protest or petition.

They were accordingly set on the fringe of the urban sprawl, even absorbing some part of its common-lands; and now history is repeating itself, and the Green Belt is threatened with similar occupation. Any planning of cemeteries will have to reckon with a psychological prejudice against them which, at present, has an adverse effect on land-values and house-property in their vicinity. The main reason for such dislike is probably a subconscious shrinking from any visible reminder of death, intensified to a neurosis by a lack of any real faith in an after-life.[34]

In the past, for many city-dwellers, the duty of tending graves on the Sabbath could be united with a stroll amid the cemetery walks *en plein air*, combining piety with leisure. The large necropoli, with their tree-lined avenues, entrance lodges and elegant mortuary-chapels, at their first inception resembled ornamental grounds laid out with displays of statuary, and they were visited and admired in much the same way as a contemporary public enjoys the displays of open-air sculpture in Battersea Park. Now they are less visited for such a purpose, except by the curious and the ever-dwindling number of descendants who tend the graves.[35]

Inevitably the time arrives when neither ancestral piety, personal feelings, nor religious convictions provide links to bind the dead to the living, and monuments shed their former private status and become public property. Unless collective opinion then agrees to retain them as historical relics, curiosities of custom or works of art, vested interests, which find them of no practical use, will threaten their existence. Some evidence would seem to suggest that man's urge towards perpetuation is temporarily quiescent or, in the course of some evolutionary process, may even be on the wane; sepulchral monuments are, however, still being made and erected in public places, and we can only examine existing conditions, and devise improvements wherever they may seem necessary.

Comment has already been made on various crises of this sort which have previously affected churchyards and their monuments; now another is evident, relating to old and new memorials in both churchyard and cemetery; for in the former their number are diminishing through neglect or premeditated destruction, and in the latter case invidious legislation exercises a stranglehold on contemporary design and production. Let us first discuss the progress of cemeteries.[36]

The primary purpose of the burial legislation which began in the mid-nineteenth century was the safeguarding of public health; and the authors of such acts avoided any aesthetic problems relating to the architectural or landscape planning of cemeteries, and the nature and form of the monuments they were to house. Some seventy statutes relating directly or indirectly to cemetery burial have been made between the years 1808 and 1947; numbers of which "have been amended or extended, in part or in whole, by those that follow them ... Many of the authorities to which they refer or to which they give powers are no longer in existence. It is by no means possible to tell with certainty which unrepeated section is in fact still effective" (W. H. Dudley "Monumental Legislation", *Monumental Journal*, April, 1950, pp. 237–242).

Burial grounds prior to 1852 were controlled by Vestries; the Burial Act of that year empowered such bodies to appoint Burial Boards to be responsible for all matters relating to the control of the burial ground and its monuments. There are now over two thousand such Burial Boards working individually to devise their own particular codes from this mess of legislation in which monumental masonry has no rights in law.

Any local authority wishing to increase cemetery fees needs only to advertise its intention in the local press and, unless objection be made within the stipulated time, it can then pass its resolutions unimpeded. Many regulations dictate not only the area of grave-space, but the type of memorial, curtailing the size, and even the amount of text to a crippling degree, often without prior consultation with local masons, who accordingly are faced by a *fait accompli* which they can combat only with difficulty. From the trade point of view it has been suggested that "although little assistance can be expected from the Ministry of Health, every regulation revisal should be contested, even where it is anticipated that a refusal to interfere will be made. Constant protests to the Ministry will obviously draw attention to the general discontent brought about by these activities of local authorities" (*ibid.* May, 1950, p. 303).

In brief, the rules of such boards are devised mainly to satisfy motives of economy, aesthetic considerations being conspicuous by their absence. There is little evidence of any sincere attempts to improve the visual appearance of cemeteries by consultation or co-operation with existing societies, architects or landscape gardeners who could help to devise suitable schemes according to the particular needs of each locality. In fact, the sole contribution towards such "improvement" within recent years has been the so-called Lawn Cemetery, whose most conspicuous feature, as its name suggests, is an expanse of turf, with the minimum number of shrubs and flowers placed to relieve monotonous rows of uniform headstones or small tablets laid into the grass, which can thus be most conveniently and cheaply mown.

In view of our fine tradition of landscape gardening in the work of such men as Capability Brown and Humphrey Repton, our technical equipment which now makes the moving of mountains less than a dream, and the potentialities that some contemporary equivalent of the Sublime and Picturesque could offer for public enjoyment, the Lawn Cemetery would seem an abject product of the neurosis which substitutes tidiness and conformity for beauty.

A similar tendency is becoming evident in the treatment of churchyards, whose laws also are in many ways obscure and out-of-date, badly needing revision for the sake of clarity. Here the problem is complicated by a need to strike a balance between the traditional aspect of the churchyard, contemporary tendencies in design likely to affect its future, and the inveterate question of maintenance. The main points in present churchyard law are as follows:

(*a*) Parishioners' rights are limited to burial, while the erection of any monument remains a privilege. Strictly speaking, a faculty for the erection of any monument should be obtained from the Chancellor of the Diocese, but in practice, the parson's approval, as the owner of the church freehold, is considered sufficient. Should he, however, consider a monument unsuitable for any reason, on the score of size, material, design or inscription, he has a right to refer the matter to the Chancellor for his consideration.

(*b*) Any proposed alteration or addition to a churchyard requires a faculty.

(*c*) The duty of maintaining the churchyard, formerly the task of the churchwardens, has been since 1921 vested in the parochial church council.

(*d*) When however a churchyard becomes full, the Minister of Health, if satisfied that no further burials should be permitted, may close it by order. The local authority then becomes responsible for the cost of its maintenance, although its control still remains in the hands of the incumbent and parish church council.

The Report of the Maintenance of Churchyards Commission, 1955, made various recommendations. For instance, to avoid as much as possible expense in obtaining new land for churchyards it condoned the ancient practice of a systematic re-use of ground for burials. It deprecated the granting of a right to the permanent and exclusive use of a grave-space, which encouraged the assumption that any monument thereon was private property, suggesting that this be limited to the term of a hundred years. With regard to large churchyards which may be full, but not officially closed, and which are inevitably a drain on parish funds, it suggested as possible solutions:

(*a*) Diocesan assistance.
(*b*) Making it easier for local authorities to take over their maintenance.
(*c*) The sale of part or whole of the churchyard in which there were no burials, the money to be used for the upkeep of the remainder.

We must mention here an important pamphlet: *The Churchyards Handbook*, 1962, first published by the Central Council for the Care of Churches under the title of *The Care of Churchyards* in 1930, which, although intended primarily as a guide to incumbents and members of Parochial Church Councils, presents an excellent summary for the layman of the various problems under present discussion.[37] Its suggestions are mainly directed to two objectives:

(*a*) Conserving the character of the traditional graveyard, ensuring the retention of all monuments of antiquarian merit, and the accurate recording of gravestone inscriptions for the purposes of genealogy.
(*b*) The improvement in design of contemporary memorials, which it is suggested, should be made of native materials.

In a recent memorandum, issued subsequently to the fourth edition of this handbook, 1952, the Central Council made more specific proposals relating to the growing tendency towards drastic clearance and replanning of closed churchyards, drawn up after consultation with several learned societies interested in the preservation of antiquities. While agreeing that a case for removal was legitimate for illegible or broken monuments, or those whose huddled condition endangered the safety of the church fabric, it suggested that in all cases where legible gravestones were removed, or alterations made in a churchyard of architectural, historical or general scenic value, the following tasks should be made a condition of granting the necessary faculty:

(a) That arrangements should be made with the County Archivist through the Society of Genealogists for recording inscriptions, and that copies be deposited in the County Record office and with the Society itself.

(b) That arrangements be made with the National Buildings Record for a photographic survey, and prints to be deposited in the Record's archives.

Such basic churchyard regulations and proposed additional safeguards can now be discussed in the light of practice.

The incumbent's decision upon any design for a monument submitted for his approval puts him on the horns of a dilemma; and many parsons, rather than reject an unsuitable memorial and possibly antagonise the mourner and virtually the parish, are apt to condone it as the lesser of two evils. However, during the last thirty years, *The Care of Churchyards* and other publications of similar nature have provided some principles for guidance and given a backing of authority sufficient to induce a stand being made on such an issue.[38] More recently the growing antagonism within the Church of England towards the use of white marble for churchyard memorials has crystallized into a veto on its use; the reason for such objection being its colour conflict with the church fabric and gravestones made of the mellower English stones, which it is suggested, should be habitually used for monuments.[39] In addition, stone kerbs, grave-plots covered with granite or marble chips, iron railings, and excessively large and ostentatious memorials such as crosses and angels have received sharp criticism. An increasing number of parish church councils are now forming model churchyard regulations based on these directives and removing the onus of individual decision from the parson. Owing to both labour scarcity and higher wages since the war, keeping down grass and weeds has certainly become both difficult and expensive, and a greater burden on the churchyard than cemetery, owing to its more limited funds. Yet considering what a variety of solutions are readily available, the problem has become so exaggerated out of all proportion to the difficulty, that the general removal of monuments is becoming established as the popular remedy. Much of the labour involved in mowing grass is admittedly due to the traditional grave-mounds (possibly the descendants of prehistoric tumuli) and, although these are still remarkably cherished in some areas, their general sacrifice, apart from retaining a few to serve as bygones, would be preferable to the wholesale removal of monuments. It should be borne in mind that chemical sprays and apparatus for retarding the growth of grass are now available, which although initially expensive, are definitely cheaper to use than the cost involved in the uprooting and refixing of memorials.

Unfortunately these proposed safeguards depend to a large extent upon goodwill, for it is virtually impossible to ensure authoritative supervision during all stages of an alteration or clearance, so that in practice these objectives can be defeated through carelessness or indifference. In some cases suitable protest has been made, and the matter righted,—but these are exceptional, for once a clearance has been made, restoration is seldom feasible because of the litigation, bad feeling and expense involved. If it is decided after most careful thought that removal of monuments is imperative, some tighter degree of control or inspection is necessary, and here a liaison between diocesan officials and a specially appointed sub-committee of the local archaeological society might be effective as a check. The urgent need for co-operation between the varied interests and organizations concerned is a point on which we can conclude this analysis of churchyard and cemetery development. These are the essential problems involved:

(a) The outmoded and conflicting rules governing the organization of churchyard and cemetery and their monuments.

(*b*) The need for planning to bring the cemetery into relationship with the urban and rustic environment.

(*c*) An agreement between the interests of cremation and inhumation in relation both to planning and monumental design.

(*d*) The issues and responsibilities involved in the maintenance of churchyards and cemeteries.

(*c*) The consideration due to older monuments in their artistic, antiquarian and genealogical aspects.

(*f*) The need for a fresh approach to monumental design compatible with contemporary thought and feeling.

3. *Linton (Herefs.).* (left) *Stephen Pimble, 1726;* (right) *Margaret Edwards, 1764: headstones by members of the Webb family of Linton, showing the change in style from rustic folk-art to rococo that occurred within less than fifty years.*

4 (left). *Whatton (Notts.), John Oliver, 1723;* (right) *Denton (Lincs.), Robert Wing, 1770, by Christopher Staveley of Melton Mowbray: headstones in Swithland slate, showing the same change from austere to exuberant design. With regard to lettering, spontaneity was replaced by planned symmetry.*

Notes

1. See also brooches in the shape of a Fish (symbolic of Christ through the Greek pun on His name) from Rotherley and Silchester and the Sator-Arepo word-square from Cirencester, another vestige of the early secret society stage of the faith. The painted chapel found in the Romano-British villa at Lullingstone (Kent), *c.* 350, as well as six figures standing beneath an arcade, contains three representations of the Chi-Rho, where it is enclosed by a circular wreath tied with ribands on which are perched birds pecking at fallen seeds. The significance of this device can be related to that of the Sacred Tree flanked by birds, found upon a nail-cleaner from Rivenhall (Essex), and a buckle at Stanwick (Yorks.) of the fifth century. *Antiq. Journal*, vol. XI, pp. 123–128.

2. Their numbers and distribution are: Galloway 5; Wales 2; Cornwall 6. While in Ireland it is possible to trace a logical evolution from cross-inscribed menhirs to later high-crosses, there is no apparent connection between such British slabs and the Anglian crosses of the seventh and eighth centuries, whose advent seemed spontaneous.

3. The quartered or quadrate cross (an ancient sun-wheel) had magic connotations, particularly with St Columba, being known as the Circle of Columcille. For Irish-Coptic parallels of cross-form, see *Journal Roy. Soc. Antiq. Ireland*, 1890, vol. I, p.346. The Copt adapted the ancient Egyptian life-sign or ankh to cross-form on his tomb-stones; and to him, Christ was the Scarabeus of God, inasmuch as the Christian Celt could affirm Him to be his Arch-Druid. The ankh is to be found among the Irish graffiti mentioned above, and a slab from Arundel Castle, having a cross with tri-angular loop, remains a unique and inexplicable English example (*Sussex Arch. Soc. Trans.*, vol. 47, p. 149).

4. Statues-menhirs are to be found throughout the Mediterranean area, being fairly numerous in France (Octoban, *Statues Menhirs*, 1931). In Guernsey one is called, from its site, the "Grandmother of the Churchyard" and was given offerings of fruit and flowers until recent times. Stones carved with characteristic spirals and circles from a dolmen in Alderney and from Great Hucklow (Derbys.) now in Sheffield Museum, are emblems of the Mother Goddess less popularly known than the chalk drums with owl-heads found in a round barrow at Folkton Wold (Yorks.).

5. Hadrian Allcroft's *Earthworks of England*, 1908, and *The Circle and the Cross*, 1927, include numerous examples in the attempt to prove that churches invariably occupied pagan sites. See also W. Johnson, *Byways in British Archaeology*, 1912, pp. 1–100. This book and its author's earlier volume, *Folk-Memory*, 1908, are brave attempts to bridge the gap between folk-lore and archaeology. The great Wessex tomb-complex surrounding Avebury and Stonehenge is still the most impressive example of burials over a long period of time being associated with sacred sites. Also remarkable are the

isolated church at Knowlton (Dorset) which stands within an earthwork or henge, probably built to consecrate this primitive monument, and the great 25 foot high menhir which stands amidst the modern gravestones in the churchyard of Rudstone (Yorks.). The churchyard of St Martin's, Leicester, rests on the site of a Roman building, and fragments of pillars still stand among the graves. Excavations at St Ninian's Isle in Shetland in 1955 revealed a small church built over an Iron Age site which had been in use as a burial ground for two thousand years.

6. Owing to the dearth of sacred relics for inclusion within altars, the Council of Chelsea, 816, introduced particles of the Host as substitute, a custom which persisted in England until the mid-fifteenth century (R. W. Muncey, *History of the Consecration of Churches and Churchyards*, 1930, p. 42).

7. The Emperor Constantine was the first to be accorded such privilege, which in spite of many successive edicts, beginning with that made by his successor Theodosius at the end of the fourth century, has persisted ever since. At first the characteristic large sarcophagi (such as those at Ravenna) were ranged against the entrance wall or about the atrium and provided an embellishment to the fabric. The final phase can be seen in any European cathedral, noticeably in the cluttered walls of our own Westminster Abbey.

Intra-mural burial was occasionally deprecated. Evelyn, for instance, writing of his father-in-law's death in his Diary in 1682, noted that his will enjoined churchyard burial, he "being much offended by the novel custom of burying everyone within the body of the church", being a favour previously granted to martyrs and great persons, as well as turning churches into charnels detrimental to health. The necessary payment for such privilege was lucrative enough. Thomas Bank's widow in 1805 paid £80 for the space in Westminster Abbey occupied by the modest tablet to the famous sculptor (C. F. Bell, ed., *Annals of Thomas Banks*, 1938, p. 60).

In 1521 at Banwell (Somerset) Robert Cabull and Robert Blundon buried their wives: the first in the porch for a fee of 3s. 4d., the latter in the church at double this sum (Churchwarden Accounts.).

8. F. Henry, *Irish Art*, p. 25. Circular and oval churchyards occur in certain Welsh districts and a few English examples. (Elias Owen, *Old Stone Crosses in the Vale of Clwydd*, 1886). The Welsh churchyards are usually encompassed or divided by a road, for which there seems no obvious public requirement and "may represent ancient ramparts, which separate the churchyard from common ground" (W. Johnson, *Byways in British Archaeology*, p. 98). Small cross-slabs exist in great numbers in Ireland, the most famous necropolis being at Clonmacnoise, with another also in Co. Offaly, at Gallen. At Inishcaltra (Co. Clare) the small monastic graveyard has remained undisturbed.

9. "The superstitious notion that souls were detained in purgatory for a longer or shorter period, according to the number of masses offered for them, naturally excited a strong desire to be buried where an interest in those services was most likely to be

effectually secured. Burial in the church was therefore first in request, as placing the tomb of the deceased immediately and constantly before the officiating priests. As a church became filled with tombs, or the fees for burial in it exorbitant, the adjacent ground was next sought in the hope of gaining the attention of the priests and worshippers as they assembled for public devotion" (W. H. Kelke, *The Church-yard Manual*, 1851). Anglican opinion at this time was no subscriber to the spiritual fire-insurance for which the chantry chapels and priests of the Middle Ages were dedicated.

10. Today, when the unfortunate practice of levelling graveyards is on the increase, headstones after eradication are sometimes set up along the boundary walls—an unattractive procedure, but at least an alternative to destruction. In Swithland churchyard (Leics.) is a fine box-tomb to Sir Joseph Danvers, built transversely into the churchyard wall. This unusual position is credited to the squire's request that his favourite hound be buried with him: putting part of the tomb in unconsecrated ground satisfied the clerical conscience over the presence of this spiritual watchdog. Fine iron gates and railings sometimes surround the churchyard: e.g. St George's, Manchester, Malpas (Cheshire), Melbourne (Derbys.).

11. At Braughing (Herts.), Matthew Wall in his will of 1696, asked that his grave be yearly "brambled", a custom still kept up (*Country Life*; January 9, 1937, p. 355). Gay mentions the practice in his *Dirge*:

> With wicker rods we fenc'd her Tomb around,
> To ward from Man and Beast the hallow'd ground:
> Lest her new Grave the Parson's Cattle raze,
> For both his Horse and Cow the church Yard graze.

A picture by the pre-Raphaelite, Arthur Hughes, "Home from the Sea", painted in 1857, shows a country churchyard with grazing sheep and a grave-mound pegged with withies; and ironically enough in a catalogue of gravestone-designs issued by Theophilus Smith of Sheffield, *c.* 1864 (which was also a puff for his cast-iron surrounds to grave-plots) the mounds having been carefully withied by his draughtsman. Even as late as 1895 Prideaux's *Churchwarden's Guide* accepted the fact that the parson could "turn a horse or a few sheep into the churchyard to pasture", but deserved censure only if loose animals profaned the graves, or if he turned the church porch into a stable! The scarcity of cheap labour to keep down churchyard grass has been so acute in recent years that in 1932 Dr Percy Dearmer in *The Parsons' Handbook* allowed there to be "no objection to the pleasant grazing of sheep", which the Maintenance of Churchyards Commission re-iterated in their 1962 report and added "other creatures, such as goats and geese" as a further possibility (p. 16).

12. John Evelyn, referring to the year 1624, mentions being taught in the porch at Wootton (Surrey). At Berkeley (Glos.) and Malmesbury (Wilts.) porches were places for teaching up to the last quarter of the nineteenth century. School was held in the south aisle of Hornsea (East Yorks.) up to *c.* 1850.

13. Malkin, in *Scenery and Antiquities and Biography of South Wales*, 1804, noted that "dancing in the churchyard at their feasts and revels is universal in Radnorshire, and very common in other parts of the Principality." The ceremony of "Clipping the Church", in which village or charity children joined hands to encircle the building was performed at several churches in the Midlands down to the mid-nineteenth century and is still practised at Painswick (Oxon.). Clipping may have followed the principle of beating the parish bounds by emphasising the area of consecrated ground. The elaborate ceremonial circuits which took place in North and South Uist in the early nineteenth century had a more obvious relationship to the old fertility pageants of the Dying Year.

14. Fives was played before Sunday matins at Clocaenog in the early years of the nineteenth century. The game was usually played against the north wall, and its windows were sometimes protected by shutters for this reason. Hammer-throwing, prisoner's base and ninepins were also favourite sports (Elias Owen, *Old Stone Crosses in the Vale of Clwydd*, p. 37). Parson Woodforde, in his diary entry of June 22, 1794, mentions losing an evening game in Babcary churchyard. At Buckland Denham, near Frome, parish records of 1756, 1761 and 1803 refer to digging up the Fives Place, presumably in attempts to stop the game; this the churchwardens at Midsomer Norton accomplished in 1780. The remains of hinges for shutters are to be found at Wrington, while other village fives-courts (not in churchyards, however) remain at Combwich, Bishops Lydeard and North Cheverton, all in Somerset (various correspondence in *Country Life*, May–July, 1961).

Less innocuous pastimes were not unknown. There is evidence of a cockfight which took place on Shrove Tuesday, 1637, in the chancel of Knotting (Beds.). Cockpits existed in the churchyard of Pennant Melangell and Llanfechan (Montgoms.) and Alsop-le-Dale (Derbys.). The practice was made illegal in 1849, but it is by no means extinct.

Games of marbles used to take place in Essex and Sussex during Lent—the sole survivor of these being played at Tinsley Green in the latter county at this time of year. See Roger's *Pleasures of Memory:*

> On yon grey stone that fronts the chancel-door
> Worn smooth by busy feet, now seen no more,
> Each eve we shot the Marble through the ring.

The game of merelles, or nine men's morris (the predecessor of noughts and crosses) occasionally relieved the tedium of church services, for merril-boards have been found cut on stone benches in the cloisters of Westminster Abbey and Wells Cathedral, on sedilia in All Saints, Maidstone, at Finchingfield (Essex) and on a medieval gravestone at Compton Abdale (Glos.).

15. The superstitious fear of being the first burial may also relate to the ancient custom of foundation or dedicatory sacrifice; such as the infant with cleft skull found at Woodhenge, and the youth buried at the foot of one of the menhirs of the Sanctuary

at Avebury. The curious story of Odhran or Oran, described in *The Life of St Columba*, suggests his burial as a living sacrifice for the foundation of the monastery at Iona (O'Donnell's *Life of Columcille*, 1918, pp. 201–3). Elizabeth Robert, 1672, was buried at Llanychan (Denbighs.) "under the first stone in this holy ground".

16. In the graveyard scene from Hamlet, the sexton's direction to set Ophelia's grave "straight" suggests a practice (once said to be traditional in the south-east counties), whereby a suicide was admitted into sanctified ground but distinguished by being set north to south rather than in the usual oriented manner. In Scotland suicides were placed outside but near to the churchyard wall, a plan afterwards "modified to the extent of allowing the body to come technically within the yard, but to be placed actually beneath the wall so that no one might walk over the grave" (W. Johnson, *Byways in British Archaeology*, p. 359).
Later in the graveyard scene the priest retorts to Laertes:

> But that great command o'er sways the order,
> She should in ground unsanctified have lodg'd
> Till the last trumpet; for charitable prayers,
> Shards, flints, and pebbles, should be thrown on her.

17. Owing to poverty it is not uncommon to find older monuments doing double duty, with an added inscription for a more recent interment: e.g. Gainford (Durham), a fine twelfth century slab used by Lawrence Brockett, 1784; Eccleston (Lancs.), a medieval slab for John Rigby, 1696; or Sockburn (Durham) where a piece of medieval moulded ashlar served as a 1697 headstone. Rough stones or boulders, plain, or inscribed merely with initials and dates are to be found, for instance, in villages in the vicinity of Walesby (see note 18), presumably home-made products by parishioners unable to afford stonemason's work. Sarsens were also used; at Chadwell St Mary (Essex), a block is inscribed "N.G. 1691" (the tombstone of Nathaniel Glascock, churchwarden). As for snob value, a family vault was advertised for sale in *The Times*, November 6, 1914 "in the *best part* of Highgate Cemetery".

18. Medieval monuments excavated by the author and his former colleague, Mr Birkin Haward, were found at Grantham and Walesby (Lincs.), Stansted Abbots (Essex), and Salthouse (Norfolk), some of which had served as secondary commemorations (illustrated and described: *Monumental Journal*, March, 1948, 135; October, 1942, 267.) Some dozen headstones of seventeenth century date were dug up at Ripple (Worcs.) and preserved through the enterprise of Mr Edward Gray, a local resident. They lay two to three feet below ground level (*ibid.* August, 1956, pp. 489–496).

19. Matthew Bloxam, in his *Companion ... to Gothic Ecclesiastical Architecture*, 1866, when describing this find, asked the pertinent question ... "how came these numerous sepulchral slabs and headstones to be worked up in the walls of the tower within a century of their execution? Was the churchyard thus early despoiled of its monuments all of the thirteenth century, for materials to be used in the re-building of the church

only a century later?" He suggests that as Helpston was only three miles from Barnack quarries, they may have been part of "an undisposed stock-in-trade of some adventurous stonemason in the locality, the fashion of such articles having changed" (p. 337).

20. There is little doubt that the main purpose of this proclamation was to ensure the safety of family monuments of the rich and great, and the fact that the remaining bulk of medieval sculpture consists of effigies shows that in spite of our several periods of iconoclasm there was "hardly ever a time when the nobility and gentry lost the ability to protect the memorials of their ancestors" (Lawrence Stone, *Sculpture in Britain*, 1955, p. 2).

21. Darley: the tombs and gravestones with metal in them, and roof of church, aisles, etc., sold for £20.

Dale: iron, glass, gravestones, etc., sold for £18.

At Letheringham (Suffolk) the church and monuments were sold to a builder; some of the fragments being rescued by the Vicar of Brandeston and made into a pyramid in his garden, inscribed "Indignant Reader! these monumental remains are not, as thou mayest suppose, the Ruins of Time. But were destroyed by an Irruption of the Goths so late in the Christian era as 1789. Credite Posteri". It was destroyed a few years ago. A farmer near Bath filled his farmyard with gravestones and tablets removed from the Abbey Church during restoration, being told he might use them for stone dykes, if he would cart them away at his own expense (*Notes and Queries*, vol. 3, 1857, pp. 366, 453). In disused Northumberland graveyards local "muggers" used to break up gravestones for sale as sandstones for cleaning hearths (*Arch. Aeliana*, vol. 13, 1887, p. 65).

22. Such *laissez faire* was in some degree due to absenteeism—rife in the eighteenth century. Even in 1813 it was reckoned that out of 10,800 livings, 6,311 were without resident clergy, and in the earlier years of the century the proportion of absentees was still higher (W. Addison, *English Country Parson*, p. 132). The parish clerk in the past therefore exercised considerable influence; and in some cases he was also a gravestone-maker, such as Robert Waddington of Clipston (Northants.), 1717–91, whose engraved slates show him to have been an accomplished penman.

23. J. H. Harder, *Observations on some tendencies of Sentiment and Ethics chiefly in Minor Poetry and Essay in the eighteenth century*, Amsterdam, 1933, p. 88. K. Clark, *The Gothic Revival*, 1928, gives a summary of the literary origins and architectural development of this style, and its links with archaeology and romanticism.

24. The practice of planting flowers and shrubs on the graves, and their regular dressing with flowers at Easter and Whitsuntide, even for as long as twenty years after a death, was common in South Wales during the early nineteenth century.

Where grazing rights were enforced, some parishioners became Dissenters "for the singularly uncommon reason that they may bury their Friends in Dissenting Burying-grounds, plant their Graves with Flowers, and keep them clean and neat, without any danger of their being cropt" (Malkin, *Scenery and Antiquities and Biography of South Wales*, p. 606). Strictness in Sabbath observance, with which Sunday became identified, was an obvious feature of Puritan life and, although relaxed after the Restoration, was again encouraged by Nonconformity. In the nineteenth century the type of Sabbath encouraged by the "shopocracy", by depriving the lower orders of most forms of recreation, gave to the tending of graves something of the nature of "a day out".

25. *The Beauties of England*, and *Architectural and Cathedral Antiquities*, issued as a series by John Britton during the early nineteenth century, helped to popularize Gothic. Richard Gough's *Sepulchral Monuments of Great Britain*, 1794, and Charles Stothard's *Monumental Effigies of Great Britain*, 1812, were magnificent works enlarging the scope of John Weever's *Ancient Funerall Monuments*, 1631. See H. M. Colvin, "Gothic Survival and Gothick Revival", *Architectural Review*, March, 1948.

26. The adoption of the Decorated style was announced in *A Few Words to Church Builders*, 1844. Out of the 214 churches built as a result of the Church Building Act 1818–33, at a cost of £6 million, 174 were in Gothic, which seems to have been decided on largely for motives of economy in this case, classical buildings requiring more stonework, whereas brick and cast-iron could be used for the rival style.

27. Apart from the black-bordered variety, nineteenth century undertakers supplied mourners with embossed memorial cards, intended to be fitted in mounts fretted with Gothic tracery, angels, urns, etc. These were often framed and glazed, and hung up in the parlour, as described by Richard Heath, *The English Peasant*, 1872. For illustrations see B. S. Puckle, *Funeral Customs*, 1926, pp. 30, 244.

28. There may be a certain amount of truth in the popular notion that iron grilles or palings surrounding tombs were intended as a deterrent to the stealing of corpses for anatomical research. The first indictment for such a desecration, which took place in St George the Martyr ground near the Foundling Hospital, was in 1777. St Pancras and its vicinity was notorious for such operations, which were checked by setting night-watchmen on guard in small buildings or watch-boxes set in the churchyard. Examples occur at Wanstead (Essex) and Warblington (Hants.) which has two small flint huts set at each end of the churchyard. It was owing to difficulty in obtaining cadavers that the infamous Resurrection-Men, Burke and Hare, committed their sixteen murders in Edinburgh during the early years of the nineteenth century. Patent coffins of iron, or *mort-safes* were used in Belfast and Scotland for the protection of corpses; and societies were formed which paid small contributions for the use of such contraptions, one Scottish club being in operation as late as 1860. A correspondent in *The Quarterly Review* (vol. 23, 1820, p. 558) thus described a mort-safe: "The iron

cage or safe is a Scotch invention which we have lately seen at Glasgow, where it has been in use between two and three years. A framework of iron rods is fixed in the grave, the rods being as long as the grave is deep. Within the frame the coffin is let down and buried. An iron cover is then placed over the grave and fitted on the top of the rods and securely locked. At the expiration of a month, when no further precaution is needful, the cover is unlocked and the frame drawn out. The price paid for this apparatus is a shilling a day." At Pannal (Yorks.) is the so-called Resurrection Stone, weighing over a ton, which used to be hired out at a guinea for two weeks to prevent corpse-stealing (*Country Life*, no. 5, 1943, p. 825). At Sutton (Surrey) the grave of Mary Gibson, d. 1773, is still annually inspected in accordance with a bequest to see that it has not been disturbed.

29. The dangers to health of intra-mural and crowded churchyard burials had been pointed out in the early eighteenth century by the Rev. T. Lewis in his pamphlets *Seasonable Considerations on the Indecent and Dangerous Custom of Burying in Churches and Churchyards*, 1721, and *Churches no Charnel-Houses, being an Enquiry into the Profanesses, Indecency, and Pernicious Consequences to the Living, of Burying the Dead in Churches and Churchyards*, 1726.

30. Thomas Willson exhibited at the Royal Academy in 1824 a design for a "pyramid Cemetery for the Metropolis", the base intended to cover 18 acres, "which being multiplied by the several stages to be erected over above the other will generate nearly one thousand acres, self-created out of the void space overhead as the building progresses above the earth".

31. An enterprise reminiscent of American memorial parks and gardens of rest, which were first satirized by Charles Dickens in *All the Year Round*, November 30, 1861, pp. 226–228. "The cemetery has quite superseded the churchyard in America. That wonderful striped building, the great church, generally known to the too irreverent rowdies as 'The Holy Zebra' has no real churchyard, at least no enclosure, I think, devoted to burials. The cemetery, conducted by a joint-stock company, is a truly business-like affair. The body can be forwarded by car, or train, or steamer, at a stated hour, with safety and with dispatch. The distracted mourner knows just when he has to pay, and the ground he buys is inalienable. You get away from the noise of the city—the smoke in New York is immaterial—and you leave Mr Elijah Specklebury quietly asleep among sun-flowers and Virginia creepers, in a snug little railed-in garden, or in an Egyptian vaulted tomb. You go and take your family to see the place now and then on a Sunday, and if you like, you can have a key to the garden railing if you wish to plant everlasting flowers or other sentimentalities." Mr Evelyn Waugh's *The Loved One* satirizes the contemporary American funerary industry and memorial parks, which in spite of their brash ostentation, are serious attempts to use monuments in conjunction with landscape gardening. Forest Lawn, California, is perhaps the best-known of these cemeteries, and Europe is scoured for statuary with which to embellish it.

32. Until recently, cremation was thought to have been introduced during the Bronze Age, "but it is now known to be of much greater antiquity, and its origin must be sought either in indigenous invention in these islands, in some way connected with the Ronaldsway cemetery, or elsewhere" (J. F. Stone, *Wessex*, p. 58). This late Neolithic cemetery from the Isle of Man can also be compared with Wessex communal cremation burials of the "Dorchester Culture", arranged in flat cemeteries accompanied by rings of holes or pits of a ritual nature; with earthen long barrows in Yorkshire where bodies were partially cremated over trenches lined with wood pyres; and a recently excavated long barrow at West Rudham (Norfolk) where the burning had apparently been carried out on a gravel platform and accompanied by libation ceremonies (R. Rainbird Clarke, *East Anglia*, pp. 56, 57).

It is interesting to consider the civilized religious implications of inhumation and cremation, representing the belief in Resurrection of the Body and Immortality of the Soul.

33. In England, during 1961, there were 224,464 cremations, 36·45 per cent of deaths. Cremation relative to death percentages for 1959 were Australia 30, New Zealand 29, Denmark 29, Sweden 25, Norway 19, West Germany 10, Holland 4, France, Italy, Belgium about 0·2 .

34. See "Planning the Cemetery of the Future", *Monumental Journal*, April, 1953, pp. 237–40; May, 1953, pp. 301–304. It has been reckoned that out of the total land area of England and Wales, 37,133,000 acres, cemeteries occupy about 25,000 acres, roughly one acre out of every 1,500 being used for burial purposes. The increase of cremation and restrictive practices of both church and cemetery authorities have been considered by some monumental stonemasons as designed to eventually suppress the craft. During 1955–57 the Joint Committee of the British Monumental Industry conducted a public relations campaign designed to combat such restrictions (*ibid.*, March, 1959, p. 63).

35. In Tottenham's 40 acre cemetery (known locally as The Jungle), in 1955 out of 40,000 graves the superintendent stated that only 1,000 were regularly tended by relatives.

36. A list of contemporary cemetery buildings and their architects include:
1827 A. C. Pugin associated with Brunel in the layout of Kensal Green cemetery, exhibiting a design for one of its gateways at the Royal Academy in 1827.
1829 Liverpool, St James's Cemetery chapel, etc., by John Foster.
1835 Leeds Cemetery chapels and lodges by John Clark.
1836 Sheffield General Cemetery entrance and Doric chapel by Samuel Worth. Nottingham General Cemetery entrance gate flanked by twelve "hospitals" for aged folk, and Ionic chapel by S. Rawlinson.

1839 Highgate Cemetery: Egyptian Avenue and Gothic catacombs by Stephen Geary, architect to London Cemetery Company, who designed cemeteries at Nunhead, Peckham, Westminster, Gravesend and Brighton.

1840 West London Cemetery, Brompton, by Benjamin Baud.

1843 Reading Cemetery; entrance gates and chapels by William Brown.

1844 Bath, Lyncombe cemetery chapel (Norman style) by George Manners.

1845 Lewes, Warenne Cemetery (in collaboration with Benjamin Ferry) built by John Latter Parsons from the remains of the old Priory for £413 3s. 7d.

1848 Osemey, Holywell and Holy Sepulchre Cemetery chapels by H. J. Underwood.

1852 Leamington Cemetery chapel and lodges by David Squirehill, built by local builder and gravestone maker William Ballard.

1855 Hartlepool Cemetery chapel by John Dobson.

37. It takes its place in churchyard history as one of the successors to the Ecclesiological pamphlets of a century before, such as those by Paget, Carter, and Kelke's *Churchyard Manual*, 1851; agreeing with them on several points of principle, but showing an amusing change of taste in advocating a return to the Georgian models which they abhorred, as an inspiration to modern design. Slate was the bug-bear of the Camdenians, white marble of the neo-Georgians; both unite in trouncing the stonemason.

38. In 1925 a joint Committee of the British Institute of Industrial Art and the National Association of Monumental Master Masons held a conference at the Victoria and Albert Museum and as a result published a report *Graveyard Memorials in Stone and Wood* (reissued in 1934), which gave a list of British stones suitable for monuments. While attacking white marble monuments, it also advocated an improvement in standards of design. Anglican inspired, and with the assistance of such sculptors as Eric Gill and Gilbert Ledward, Sculptured Memorials was founded in 1934, a private group of craftsmen who have produced work in native stone with admirable lettering and carving inspired by Georgian originals. The Guild of Memorial Craftsmen (founded 1945) and the Guild of Lettering Craftsmen have upheld similar views, based on the work of Gill and Edward Johnson, in particular the use of Roman lettering which is usually eschewed by the trade element. The oldest established societies are the College of Masons (founded 1892) and the National Association of Master Monumental Masons (founded 1907) "to uphold the status of the craft, to safeguard the interests of members, and to combat restrictive practices and to give help and advice." In 1951 the author organized for the Arts Council "English Churchyard Carving", the first exhibition of its kind, which visited various provincial towns during the next two years.

39. Foreign marbles have been imported for use on interior tombs since the Conquest; and our own export trade in alabaster during the Middle Ages enjoyed a European reputation. Churchyard monuments in composite stones, both native and

foreign, are occasionally found in the eighteenth century, the marble often weathering to the texture of fine Portland. Much of the eye-blinding quality of marble cemetery memorials is due to a regimentation without greenery. Kensal Green best shows the use of the material over the last 130 years, and its capacity for weathering; and, although unkempt, the monuments can be seen in their most kindly environment when patterned by the light and shade of evergreen trees. As early as 1820, the Carrara Marble Works had been established by the dull and prolific firm of Gaffin. Italian marble imports ceased during World War II, but the trade has since been resumed.

2

Types of Monument: Historical Analysis

ALTHOUGH man buried his dead at an early stage of his history, with a degree of ritual that could argue some form of magical or religious belief in an after-life, many millennia elapsed before he first set up some form of visible token or marker over the grave and thus instituted commemoration.

Any discussion of burial rites is beyond the scope of the present work, and for its starting-point it is sufficient to notice that the various forms which commemoration has taken since its inception seem to fall into two main categories which, in spite of regional and historic interchanges and combinations, have preserved their essential identities.[1]

Prototype of the first is the menhir, whose precise significance is still unknown despite archaeological research, but which probably had a phallic or fertility origin, an assertion of man's abounding vitality, which to primitive minds resided in the stone, investing it with personality, and giving it the character of an anthropomorph.

The second group depends upon conceptions of the tomb as a substitute for the cave or shelter which was for so long man's early dwelling, for the houses and fanes he later built for comfort and worship, or even as a stone replica of a spiritual womb from which he anticipated re-birth.

Primitive beliefs that stones could become the residences of spiritual forces or assume human traits or personalities were also associated with memorials to the dead, and the original megalithic structures devised for this commemorative purpose seem to have persisted as prototypes by virtue of this ancient respect. While it is rash to claim any continuity of tradition between the monuments of prehistory and civilization there often exists a basis of folk-lore and structural resemblances enough to justify comparisons at least.[2]

In this way the menhir, first as a natural boulder, or with the minimum of artifice, became in civilized times an upright slab or stela, used first in Egypt and attaining a remarkable elegance in classical times. During this period it also took on the form of pagan altar or cippus, the pillar, obelisk and pyramid. At a later date it was consecrated by the missionary with the Christian emblem and changed its form to that of a high cross, finally reverting to the headstone, most ubiquitous of monuments.

In similar fashion, following the bare interment of the corpse in a hole or grave, it was next protected from scavengers by enclosure within a cist or coffin, in the form of a wooden shell or stone chest. In historic times the body was hermetically sealed in coffins of different materials, and buried either beneath a tomb, or placed directly within a sarcophagus above ground. As an alternative, the coffin was interred, leaving its cover flush with the surface. This slab also assumed the rough shape of a body (coffin-slab); or became a simple rectangle (ledger); or was made three-dimensional, in the form of a roof or gable (coped stone). From the coffin-slab carved with a simulacrum of the deceased developed the recumbent effigy, which combined with the architectural structure of contemporary shrines to grow into that flower of the Gothic tomb-maker's art, the canopied tomb. This consisted of three parts: an effigy, the rectilinear plinth on which it reposed, which was given the appearance of a house-body by panelled arcades or niches, and a roof of intricate tabernacle-work suspended above; the complete edifice expressing the conception of the house of the dead with the illusion that its roof had been raised, to reveal the deceased as occupant. This formal scheme persisted after the Renaissance, although the canopy during the sixteenth and seventeenth centuries was made like a bed-tester to convey the notion of the grave as a bed of rest;[3] in turn, as the posture of the effigy changed from recumbent or kneeling humility to a heroic stance, it became a military tent or field pavilion.

Apart from ideological significance, monumental design has also been affected by social and economic conditions, and the problems involved in differences of technique and material. It was naturally influenced by the current aesthetic, and particularly by the prevalent mode in architectural design. An obvious case is the classic bias initiated after the Reformation, and the absorption into its repertoire of foreign forms such as the pyramid, obelisk, pillar and mausoleum; others are the antiquarian reversion to Gothic in the nineteenth century, and later in Victoria's reign the indiscriminate borrowing of ornament from numerous sources.

As the use of monuments spread to the middle classes towards the end of the Middle Ages, their value as symbols of social status led craftsmen to devise substitutes for the more expensive tombs, thus satisfying both the pride and purse-strings of their humbler patrons. In this way, those unable to afford a marble effigy could have one carved in wood or freestone or, more simply, engraved on a brass plate or stone slab; or in lieu of the luxury of a canopy tomb be content with the stone chest which formed the simplest part of its structure.

The prerogative of burial and erection of tombs within churches, which eventually became a common practice, led to an inevitable congestion of space. Although in some cases the local squire or patron continued the medieval precedent of building a private chapel or separate mausoleum for family monuments, the problem in general was solved by statuaries designing their memorials as part of the fabric; the most elaborate were sculpture, grouped within niches, or placed against pyramidal backgrounds in bas-relief, the simplest cartouches or tablets, whose design was often adapted for use on gravestones.

The form of monuments was also affected by imitation of material, whereby wood or metal motifs which originally had some ritual significance were at first literally copied in stone but gradually came to terms with the demands of the new material. Such a process can be seen in the stone imitations of the wooden deadboards that were once indigenous in wooded districts; or the evolution of the headstone from the high cross that superseded the missionary's preaching-staff; and the various guises of the house-tomb—either as a classical temple, a wattled hut, a metal reliquary, a bed-tent or pavilion.

The individual qualities of local stones, and their problems of transport, were also factors which to some extent determined regional differences in form and design. In stoneless districts such as East Anglia brasses were widely distributed during the Middle Ages, as being cheaper and more readily available than tombs in alabaster, while later churchyard stones in this area are often unenterprising in design due in part to the initial costs of raw material. On the other hand, in the Midland zone stretching from the Severn to the Wash, where quarries were numerous and carriage-costs negligible, churchyard carving was experimental in form and ambitious in size. The available bulk of raw material as dug from the quarry-beds, and its capacity for being sawn or cleft, as well as its relative hardness and texture, which offered the extremes of bold relief or delicate incision, should also be taken into account.

Above all other stones, the beauty of marble led to a wide demand for its use in tomb-sculpture. When the veins of our native marbles such as Purbeck and alabaster gave out, supplies were obtained in increasing bulk from abroad. The competitive prices of marble monuments ousted those in native stone and, being at first largely shop-made by Italian workmen in a debased style which can best be described as wedding-cake baroque, introduced a vulgar streak into our tradition of design which is still in evidence today.

Although the basic types of external monuments were comparatively few, considerable variations, both local and regional, were made upon their themes. Such differences were presumably the results either of individual invention; the collective style founded by workers settled in the vicinity of a quarry, or established in temporary headquarters near some major building-project; or the expression of a communal idiom or local folk-art. As the majority of gravestone-makers and their patrons were rustics, in whom the well of folk-memory ran deep, such eccentricities of design or reversions to archaic forms that occur may well be freshets from this latent source.

(Before analysing in detail the historical development of the various types of sepulchral monument, some explanation of the terms used to define them is necessary. Unfortunately, as in architecture, names have become attached by custom to certain memorials that in the light of more recent knowledge appear mis-nomers. In some cases these have accordingly been changed, although the author, forced to invent others for monuments previously ignored, is put in the same quandary. For the sake of clarity each historical section is headed with its appropriate list of memorials, which are defined in the glossary of terms and illustrated in Figure 1. A brief list of books for consultation is given at the end of each section.)

FIG. I. Development of headstone: I. *Menhir.* 2. *Roman stela.* 3. *Anglian high cross.* 4. *Cornish cross.* 5. *Medieval discoid.* 6. *Georgian headstone.* 7. *Victorian broken column.* 8. *Marble angel.* Development of head and footstones: 9 & 10. *Deadboards.* II. *Head, foot and bodystone.* 12. *Head, foot and coffin-stone.* 13. *Victorian rustic cross and scroll.* 14. *Marble headstone with curb and immortelles.* Development of the house-tomb: 15. *Prehistoric cist or stone coffin.* 16. *Roman sarcophagus.* II. *Romanesque shrine-tomb.* 18. *Hogback.* 19. *Medieval coffin.* 20. *Medieval canopy, tomb-chest and effigy.*

21. *Midland gabled chest-tomb.* 22. *Chest-tomb.* 23. *Table-tomb.* 24. *Bale-tomb.*
25. *Cotswold chest-tomb.* 26. *Greek Revival house-tomb.* 27. *Greek Revival chest-tomb or arca.* 28. *Georgian wall-tomb.* 29. *Pedestal-tomb with urn.* 30 & 31. *Obelisks on base.* 32. *Gothic Revival shrine-tomb.*

PREHISTORIC MONUMENTS (2500 B.C. – A.D. 1)

Menhir; chambered tomb; covered gallery, or long cist tomb; cursus; henge; barrow; coffin and cist; cairn.

Our earliest and most impressive stone monuments belong to the Neolithic period, *c.* 2500–2000 B.C. Built of megalithic masonry or roughly hewn blocks, they can be numbered in hundreds from Lands End to the Orkneys; and their distribution around the west coasts and near to inland waterways within easy access of the sea shows the east–west wave of immigration followed by their makers. These men were a maritime people interested in metallurgy, who probably originated from the Mediterranean area, imitating in these large-scale monuments the subterranean rock-tomb of their homeland.

The immensity of such "temples" as Stonehenge and Avebury have tantalized both learned and popular imagination; and in view of the comparatively small population of our islands during the period it has been suggested that the religious impulse responsible for such giant undertakings was a cult of such magical power as to be regarded with awe by the native population who volunteered the necessary labour for the collection and transport of the immense masses of stone involved in their construction. This indigenous population (known as the Windmill-Hill Folk), who themselves had migrated from southern France, built large earthen barrows or cairns of stone, sometimes 200 to 300 feet long, to cover their communal burials. Their burial-rites may have involved a two-stage process, the corpses of the family or tribe being first collected into temporary mortuary huts, which at a later date were enclosed within a mound. This practice of house-burial, where in certain cases the actual dwelling became the tomb, lingered into the Iron Age, where children's bodies have been found buried in huts or storage-pits.[4]

Menhir. An early sepulchral use of a menhir was found in a Windmill Hill barrow at Warminster, which contained a five foot high standing stone, while a smaller example, associated with a mid-Bronze cremation burial was excavated in 1926 at Kilpaigon Burrow barrow, Pembroke. Apart from these, many of the burials associated with menhirs may have been dedicatory, such as those found in the "Aubrey

66

Holes" of Stonehenge, or at the foot of sarsens in the Kennet Avenue at Avebury.

The majority of megalithic monuments consist of a series of chambers made of stone slabs which, although covered with mounds, were intended to be reopened for successive burials when need arose, in the same way as the family vaults or mortuary-chapels of historic times. They belong to two main types, with several variations, due probably to lack of labour and materials, or local differences of ritual.

Chambered Tomb, or Passage-Grave. These consisted of a corridor with side chambers or transepts. The finest group is concentrated in Cotswold and round the Severn, where along its steep scarp they are set on headlands overlooking the valley prospect. The number of these ante-chambers, in which the interments were placed, may vary from a pair as at Nympsfield (Glos.) to three pairs at Nempnett Thrubwell and Stoney Littleton (Somerset.). The finest of these monuments is the great tomb at New Grange, near Drogheda (280 feet in diameter with the grave of 80 feet), walls and threshold are inscribed with repetitive magical patterns, which are similar to other Irish rock-scribings. The designs of the chalk drums found in a barrow at Folkton Wold (Yorks.), would appear to be symbolic of a fertility goddess cult, expressed on statues-menhirs and cult-objects in all districts visited by the megalithic builders.

Covered Gallery, or Long Cist Tomb. These tombs were set up by men from the Pyrenees and southern France, who sailed up the Irish Sea and western coasts to settle in south-west Scotland, Ulster and Man; they consist of a passage having no transepts, but which is divided throughout its length into compartments by septal slabs, usually with low roofs, having none of the spacious quality of those set up by what could be called the rival sect of tomb-builders. The best of them is Cashtel yn Ard (I. of Man); here the passage is divided into five compartments, opening on to a paved forecourt defined by a façade of upright stones. It was formerly covered with an oval cairn which projected at each side of the entrance in flanking horns. The majority of megalithic tombs were covered with long barrows having the broad and higher end shaped in this way into a forecourt, which it has been supposed had a ritual purpose, perhaps as a place for offerings or sacred dances. Eventually the original megalithic structure was omitted, and chambers were inserted into the sides of the barrow, which still retained its horned forecourt, but with a dummy portal or false door, which has been compared with a similar device found in Egyptian mastabas.

A small group of megaliths, separate from such Mediterranean influence, exists in the Medway valley, probably the memorials of immigrants from the Low Countries and north-west Germany, who imitated structures similar to the "Hun's Beds" of Drenthe from their homeland. They were rectangular chambers covered with straight-sided long barrows enclosed by palings of upright stones; Coldrum is the most complete specimen, although "Kit's Coty House", probably by virtue of its name, the most familiar.

Cursus. With long barrows are to be associated immense elongated banked enclosures, such as the earthwork half a mile north of Stonehenge to which Stukely in 1727 gave the name of *cursus*, from its superficial resemblance to a racecourse. Although these banks are nearly two miles long, a cursus in Dorset has been traced for over a length of six miles, in which the immense tribal labour necessary for its construction involved the removal of over six million cubic feet of earth. It has been suggested that they were ritual processional ways, which later developed into such stone alignments as the sixty or so examples on Dartmoor, a number of which approach burial cairns.

Henge. Apparently inspired by large stone-circles and other ring-monuments such as Durrington Walls and Woodhenge in the Wiltshire complex of burials are a few monuments of the *henge* type which are confined to Great Britain, originated during late Neolithic times and attained some popularity during the Early Bronze age with the Beaker Folk. They consist of circular earthen banks with internal ditches and one or more causeway entrances, enclosing burials. A small specimen at Fargo Plantation (three-quarters of a mile north-west of Stonehenge) and just over 20 feet in diameter, showed signs of a deep hole inside the south entrance which may have held some form of totem or grave-post.

Barrow. The characteristic monument of the Bronze Age is the Round Barrow, one of the commonest of our field antiquities on down and moorland, where its characteristic shape can be seen silhouetted against the skyline. Varying greatly in size from about 12 to 180 feet in diameter, they were made of stones, turf covered with boulders or bare earth, according to the nature of the available material, the invariable ditch or magic circle about their perimeters being sometimes emphasized by rings of posts or upright stones.

Coffin and Cist. In contrast to the megalithic family vaults of the Long Barrows, these later tumuli invariably cover a single interment, cremated or inhumed, placed at the centre of the mound, very often in a small stone receptacle or cist made of slabs.[5] Other coffins made from hollowed tree-trunks, sometimes in boat-form, were used for interments by the Northern Food-Vessel Folk, similar to contemporary developments in Scandinavia, where this tradition of boat-graves reached its flower in historic times, being re-introduced into England during the Anglo-Saxon invasions. As these men of the Food-Vessel Culture were middlemen traders, transporting the goods of the Highland zone metal workers to British and foreign customers in their dugout canoes, such funerary boats may have had the significance of a last voyage to the Other World.

Cairn. Upon upland regions with scanty soil, the tumulus was formed from a heap of stones. In the great cairn at Loose Howe in Rosedale (Yorks.) a merchant sailor was inhumed in such a dug-out, with another placed above as cover, and a smaller one, dinghy-fashion by its side. In Cardiganshire two dugouts were placed within a ring of standing stones at the centre of a round barrow, while in Dorset, Wiltshire and Sussex remains have been found buried in wooden coffins or on floors of plank.

The custom of burying beneath tumuli or barrows remained in almost continuous use for over three thousand years, from Neolithic times until the seventh century pagan Anglo-Saxon period, of which the finest most recently excavated interment is the great ship-burial at Sutton Hoo (Suffolk), the treasures from which can be seen in the British Museum. The first long barrows left their vestiges in the form of the small mounds heaped over the dead in many of our churchyards. Similarly, in the communal grouping or clustering of prehistoric burials about sacred sites, which is so noticeable in the great Wiltshire necropolis, the beginnings of the same impulse which led eventually to cemeteries and churchyards can be seen.

FURTHER READING

R. J. C. Atkinson, *Stonehenge*, 1956; J. G. D. Clark, *Prehistoric England*, 1940; G. W. Daniel, *The Megalith Builders of Western Europe*, 1958; Sir C. Fox, *Pattern and Purpose—a Survey of Celtic Art in Britain*, 1958; L. V. Grinsell, *The Ancient Burial-Mounds of England*, 1953, 2nd edition; J. & C. Hawkes, *Prehistoric Britain*, 1948; E. T. Leeds, *Celtic Ornament*, 1933; S. Piggott, *The Neolithic Cultures of the British Isles*, 1954.

ROMANO-BRITISH MONUMENTS (A.D. 1 - 450)

Stela; sarcophagus; coffin; cist; barrow; mausoleum; cippus.

The first stone monuments with dedicatory inscriptions and funerary symbolism were introduced into Britain during the time of the Roman occupation. The sepulchral art of our remote island was modest compared with the richness and variety of the more intensely Romanized provinces such as Gaul; we possess few elaborate monuments such as abound in the present museums of Italy, and no remaining streets of tombs like those at Rome or Pompeii.[6] Nevertheless, a characteristic insularity of expression is shown in some works where the imposed Mediterranean tradition has been modified by native Celtic influence to give a certain barbarity and vigour that has more appeal to our contemporary aesthetic sense than stock-types in the classical idiom. Other carvings show a serenity and grace anticipating the Romanesque style, in contrast to the frigidity of Roman sepulchral portraiture, which was based on a sculptural use of the wax death-masks which wealthier families kept in their wooden shrine in the house-atrium. Such monuments can be studied in the Lansdowne and Ince Blundell private collections,[7] but in the native treatment of this type of funeral monument the portraits are hieratic puppets rather than individual effigies.

The bulk of Roman monuments in Britain consist of inscribed tablets, stelae and coffins of lead and stone; more elaborate and imposing memorials are rare. Paradoxically enough, the anglicized versions of these pyramids, mausolea and sepulchral cippi can only be studied when classical fashion and local wealth helped them into existence during the post-Reformation period.

Stela. The average stela or grave-slab was narrow in proportion to its height, which may vary from 2 to 7 feet. The tops may be squared or have a single or triple gable, treated either in flat silhouette or carved in relief as a rudimentary façade which is sometimes supported by pilasters, in derivation from the Greek architectural frontispiece with its pediment and flanking acroteria (Fig. 2). Single figures or symbolic groups were usually set within a niche, whose spandrils above have simple ornament or, in more splendid examples, such as that commemorating Regina, wife of Baratres (South Shields Museum), may be enriched with a hood mould and pilasters, imitating in relief an exedra, or vestibule to the dwelling house. Apart from the

FIG. 2. *Roman stela (Carlisle Museum), 48 in. high, 27 in. wide.*

plainest stelae which bear merely text, the majority have a letter-panel defined by a moulded border or recess in the centre of the slab, except for those with figure carving, in which case it is usually placed on the lower part (Figs. 3 and 4).

Sarcophagus. The fragments of a sarcophagus built into the old city wall near the present Trinity House Square, London, were discovered in 1852, with the addition of its lower part in 1935. A final restoration of this monument, unique in Britain, was made in 1959 by the authorities of the British Museum, where it is preserved. Said to commemorate Julius Classicianus, procurator of Britain A.D. 61–65, soon after the Boudicca rebellion, it consists of a large moulded plinth with moulded top on which are the characteristic unrolled pallet-ends or bolsters, a variation on the prototype of all such monuments, the sarcophagus to Scipio Barbatus (third century B.C.) in the Vatican Museum, of which several admirable replicas can be seen in Kensal Green cemetery. The procurator was probably a member of the Gaulish Treveri, and the precise form of the tomb resembles a type found in the Moselle valley, the home of this tribe.

Coffin. Monolithic stone coffins are usually wedge-shaped, or rounded at one end, having lids that may be flat, coped or curved in section. The simpler, roughly-dressed ones were apparently buried—others more highly finished were fixed above ground within the walls of the family burying-ground or mausoleum. The example discovered in 1853 in Haydon Lane, London (also in the British Museum), has a gabled top ornamented with acanthus leaves, the front bearing a central

FIG. 3. *Roman stela (Colchester Museum), 72 in. high, 28 in. wide.*

FIG. 4. *Roman stela (New-castle-upon-Tyne Museum).*

tondo with portrait, flanked by strigillations, the sides carved with baskets of loaves and funerary offerings. It contained a lead coffin ornamented with strips of bead-and-reel moulding together with scallop shells. A coped stone coffin in York Museum has an inscribed tablet on the front face, flanked by the conventional shield or pelta device. Tapered or rectangular lead coffins are numerous and were often enclosed in wooden chests, stone coffins, or cists made of flag-stones or tiles (Figs. 5 and 6). Liquid plaster-of-paris was sometimes poured over the corpse, to fill the coffin. From the seven examples of the second to third centuries in York Museum, it has been possible to reconstruct details of features and clothing from such moulds as have survived, which show that corpses were buried both in shrouds and full costume. A plaster-burial at Keston (Kent) found in 1938, and a similar example at Dartford, showed the remains of shrouds, made of linen in the Dartford case, where it was accompanied by ritual ears of corn.

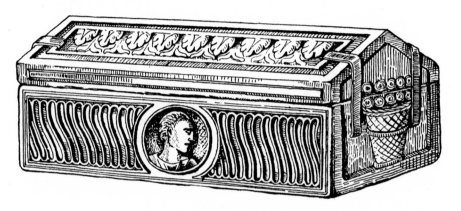

FIG. 5. *Roman sarcophagus containing (Fig. 6 below) a stamped leaden coffin (British Museum), 60 in. long, 24 in. high.*

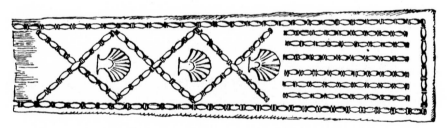

Cist. As well as rectangular examples made from slabs, both cylindrical and cubical cists of stone have been unearthed. A specimen from Harpenden, now in the British Museum, consisted of a thick drum sandwiched between two slabs 5 feet in length and 1 foot thick; while a cylindrical cist from Cirencester had a solid drum as its coverlid. Following a Greek precedent (in fourth century B.C. burials near Troy bodies were disposed beneath a penthouse of tiles) similar gabled or box-like cists provided cheap memorials at St Albans (Herts.), Higham (Kent), and at York and Colchester, where they were made in the garrison's tile-factory. Before inhumation began to oust burning in the third century, ashes were deposited in pottery urns (sometimes a wine-jar with broken-off neck in the cheaper sort), glass bottles or, more rarely, leaden canisters, and enclosed by a cist of tiles, wood or stone.

Barrow: Mausoleum. Roman tumuli are not infrequent, and can be distinguished by their conical shape, perhaps the best known group being the original seven barrows near Ashdon (Essex) known as the Bartlow Hills, one of which is nearly 150 feet in diameter and almost 50 feet high.[8] The fashion may have been adapted by the Romanized aristocracy from native examples, which inspired recollections of Etruscan prototypes in Italy. Such tombs, which were themselves masonry imitations of earlier tumuli, developed into such grandiose mausolea as those of the Emperors Augustus and Hadrian in Rome, in which the older tradition of the earthen mound was combined with an edifice of wrought stone. From their remains, aided by contemporary accounts, it can be conjectured that they consisted of colossal stone drums set upon a podium or base, topped with a terraced tumulus, planted with trees bearing a statuary group at its apex. At Pulborough (Sussex) the remains were discovered of a circular tomb, consisting of a wall 60 feet in diameter and nearly 12 feet in thickness which was presumably covered with a conical tumulus; another was found at West Mersea (Essex), resembling a cartwheel in plan, which may have had a similar mound topped with a statue.

Cemetery sites are particularly numerous in North Kent, and here at Springhead and Lockham were found the remains of private walled burial-grounds, which in the latter case included two tomb-houses, square and circular, with tiled roofs and brightly painted stucco. At Holwood Hill, near Keston, are the remains of a similar painted circular tomb, some 30 feet in diameter, supported by buttresses.

Cippus. The structure and ritual offerings of the primitive stone altar were later conventionalized and used for sepulchral purposes in the form known as the cippus. This usually consisted of a squared pedestal decorated with the heads or skulls of oxen and rams, sacrificial victims, looped with festoons of flowers or leaves about the moulded panel which enclosed the inscription. The top of the monument, in the form of two opposed S-scrolls was a conventionalized representation of the focus or hearth, with its faggots for burning the offerings. Some foreign monuments have been found where the funerary cippus had a drain connected by a pipe to the coffin below, with the object of permitting the customary libations to benefit the *manes* of the corpse. Two of these curious burials have been discovered in England, at Caerleon and Colchester, but in neither case was an altar discovered.[9]

FURTHER READING:

R. G. Collingwood, *The Archaeology of Roman Britain*, 1930; I. A. Richmond, *Roman Britain*, 1956; E. Strong, *Art in Ancient Rome*, 1929; J. M. C. Toynbee, *Art in Roman Britain*, 1962; *Royal Commission on Historic Monuments, Roman London, Roman York*; *British Museum Guide to Antiquities, Roman Britain*, 1958.

ANGLO-SAXON AND DANISH MONUMENTS (450 – 1066)

High cross; cross-slab; headstone; pillow-stone; house-tomb; coped stone; hogback.

After the withdrawal of the Imperial forces from Britain in the mid-fifth century, successive inroads of Teutonic and Scandinavian tribes, and their eventual settlement, drove part of the indigenous Celtic population, including many Christians, to seek refuge in Wales, Cornwall and Strathclyde. In some areas, however, Britons and Saxons existed in mutual toleration, for Elmet, near Leeds, was maintained as a British state up to the early seventh century. In such western refuges have been found a handful of Christian stelae belonging to the fifth and sixth centuries, engraved with a sacred monogram or cross, and bearing laconic inscriptions. They are of local stone, narrow in width, varying from 5 to 7 feet in height, and of interest mainly as being our first Christian memorials. The example to Carausius at Penmachno (Caerns.) has an unusual text recording its placing upon a cairn.

The invading tribes eventually established their particular territories, which, broadly speaking, led to the dominance of Northumbria in the seventh century, Mercia in the next, and Wessex during the ensuing two hundred years.

Northumbria was important not only politically, but by virtue of missionary influence, which if not already effectual from Iona (founded

563) was certainly evident after the foundation of Lindisfarne in 635. The two strains of Roman and Celtic were present in its culture, transmitted to its own bloodstock in Mercia after the appropriate death in battle of the obdurately pagan Penda in 656 had enabled this kingdom tardily to accept the new faith. During the course of the ninth century Scandinavian invasion imposed its dual control, so that by its close, most of England north of a line drawn from Chester to London was Danish, whereas the Norse established colonies in the Outer Islands, the east coast of Ireland, Man and the English north-west.

While Wessex under Alfred's leadership led a resistance policy, its enlightened king, one-sixth of whose revenue is said to have been devoted to the support of artist-craftsmen, maintained diplomatic and trade relations abroad, in particular with the Frankish court, from whence came scholars and artificers to preside over schools and monasteries and train native craftsmen. Lindisfarne and other strongholds of Anglo-Saxon monasteries never fully recovered from Scandinavian pillage;[10] and the next Benedictine phase flourished in the south inspired by such clerics as Oswald, Aethelwold and the versatile Dunstan, full of "holy guile".

Some 2,500 fragments of Anglo-Saxon carving alone still remain in England and southern Scotland and, apart from those which were architectural features, the bulk are crosses and sepulchral monuments of different types. The majority of the High Crosses presumably marked the site of preaching-stations or meeting-places, the smaller free-standing crosses being tombstones.

It is remarkable that so many have survived iconoclasm, although in a mutilated condition. The Ruthwell Cross, for instance, was shattered by Scots fanatics in the seventeenth century, but its fragments were buried and later re-assembled. *The Dream of the Rood* inscribed upon it, in which the cross speaks as if invested with personality, suggests that such monuments may have acquired the supernatural character of totems.

In Ireland, Scotland and Wales both free-standing crosses and elaborate grave-slabs are numerous. The type of cross-head used is that known as Celtic, having squared arms linked with a hoop or rim, the result of Irish-Scandinavian influence, which originated either in Ireland or Man, where both slabs and crosses appear to follow a common

evolution. In Irish and Scottish stones a derivation from metal-work is notable in the
figure-panels of the former and the spirals
and bosses of the latter, which follow manuscript traditions in their use of interlacing,
but are unique for their use of enigmatic
"Pictish" symbols. Welsh slabs and crosses
alike show Irish and Merovingian borrowings,[11] but the figure-work is small both
in amount and vitality, and the use of interlace, although often ornate, shows little
sense of structure. Cornish crosses, linked
with the Celtic element in their use of the
wheel-head, follow a separate tradition in
their austerity, which invites comparison
with work in South Wales and, more particularly, Brittany.

High Cross. Less than a century after ac-
cepting Christianity Northumbria had become a centre of learning and artistic activity,
with such notable clerics as Benedict Biscop
and Wilfrid importing glaziers and masons
from Rome and Gaul for the building of
their new churches, and collecting art treasures from abroad for their enrichment, and
with Bede at Jarrow and Eadfirth preparing the great Gospels in the Lindisfarne
scriptorium.

The form and decoration of the earliest
Northumbrian high crosses provide one of
the mysteries of English art. While the development of those in Ireland can be traced
typologically from the incised menhir
through successive stages of relief into three-
dimensional splendour, no transitional forms

FIG. 7. *High Cross (Irton, Lancs.) 10 ft. 4 in. high.*

fill the gap between post-Roman stelae and the sudden appearance of
this cross-type in Northumbria. The ornament used has affinities not so

77

much with continental Byzantine motifs, as with their more remote Syrian and Alexandrian sources. From the influence of Coptic monasteries in Ireland, and consequent Celtic links with our northern province, it has been argued that its crosses were made by craftsmen, who, if not actually oriental, were at least trained under such influence.

The finest, and reputedly the earliest of these monuments are those of Ruthwell, Bewcastle, Hexham, Easby and Otley, all with slender tapering shafts, decorated, except for Hexham, with figure-subjects and ornament in framed panels. From the weathered Runic inscription on the Bewcastle cross,[12] it has been interpreted as a memorial either to King Alcfrith, or as celebrating the conquest of Cumbria c. 670. Hexham, supposedly a monument to Bishop Acca (Wilfrid's successor) who died in 740, is unique for its delicate pattern of naturalistic vine-scrolls. None of the original cross-heads remain in position except that at Irton (Lancs.), the only complete specimen of the Northumbrian pre-Danish group, where it has the heraldic form of a cross-paty, possibly derived from the small jewelled pectoral crosses worn by ecclesiastics at this time.[13]

The more elaborate of the Mercian crosses are to be found in the north-west Midlands, such as the brace of richly carved shafts at Sandbach (Cheshire), and especially those of Derbyshire from a production centre at Bakewell, with some sixty-five remaining examples. In the dumpier types of Mercia, the arms were squared into the familiar Celtic shape, which with the addition of a connecting hoop, became the wheel-head. The tenuous proportions of this feature as depicted in Scotland and Ireland, particularly on the earliest of the high crosses at Ahenny,[14] has suggested a derivation either from metal originals or wooden processional staves, where the quadrants of the wheel were added for strength, and which may themselves have been metal-plated.

A latter group, found mainly in North Mercia, which was largely colonized by Norse settlers from Ireland or Man, has cylindrical shafts trimmed to a square section above to support the wheel-head, a feature reminiscent of a wood-carving technique, which has related their origin to the staff-rood.[15] The most characteristic is at Gosforth (Cumb.) some 14 feet high, whose figure subjects show a mixture of Norse and Christian mythology. Others mainly from the North Riding, bear ornament upon the cross-shaft, not necessarily round, in linear imitation of this chamfer, such as the one at Whalley (Lancs.).

While it is debatable whether the wheel-head was an Irish importation or the invention of the Manx carver, Gaut Bjarnson, who claimed on the Kirkmichael cross that he made it "and all in Man", its occurrence down the western fringes of Britain from Cumberland to Cornwall seems to bear out the suggestion that the island was a production centre.

What becomes apparent from an examination of the many variations of cross are the sculptural expedients by which masons strove to reconcile original metal or wooden prototypes with the technical demands of stone-cutting. Whereas in Ireland there was a logical evolution from the inscribed slab to free-standing cross, in England, by an inverse process, the wheel-head became transformed into that early medieval variety of headstone for which the term discoid is appropriate; the wheel or rim was moved to the circumference, to form a circle or disc, on which the cross could be displayed either by relief or incision. Ambiguous forms of cross-head were devised during this transition, whereby the cross was suggested by emphasizing the interstices between rim and arms, reducing them to a quadruple pattern of pellets or bosses—or by bites taken out, as it were, from the edges of the circle, producing a cross-effect by illusion rather than construction. At this period such variations were most evident on the crosses of Cornwall, made chiefly of granite, which discouraged easy detail, where the stock-type became a circular head blending with the straight or tapered shaft to form a key-hole silhouette (Figs. 9 and 10). Cornwall was more closely connected with South Wales and

FIG. 8. *High Cross (Gosforth, Cumb.), 14 ft. high.*

79

FIG. 9. *Cross (Llantwit, Glam.), 6 ft. high.*

Brittany than with Ireland, and in both British areas, in addition to this form, there emerged another with a diminutive shaft and dominant head, like a tab or marker in appearance: Margam (Glam.), St Columb Major and St Levan (Cornwall).

Cross-Slab. While in Ireland, Scotland, Man, and to some extent in Wales, both high crosses and slabs had a mutual development in design, in England they followed separate traditions. The majority of our native slabs are rectangular or have slightly curved sides, varying from 3 to 6 feet in length, bearing long-shafted crosses with plain or plaitwork backgrounds. They may have been intended for use either as ledgers or coffin-slabs and for the most part are works of no exceptional merit. One of the few complete stone coffins[16] with its original

5 (left). Long Sutton (Lincs.), Katherine Bowker, 1763, by William Cross; (right) William Wallis, 1826, by Samuel Andrews of Wisbech, 56 in. high, 36 in. wide: contrast of rococo and neo-classic design. Long Sutton is among the finest of the Fenland churchyards, which are crammed with magnificent headstones cut from the Midland oolites.

6. *South Littleton (Worcs.), Mary Gibbs, 1804: headstone, 60 in. high, 43 in. wide by Francis Ballard of Littleton. Owing to the recent deterioration of the stone from which these monuments were made, all traces of their sumptuous carving will probably have vanished within the next fifty years.*

cover-lid exists in Dinsdale churchyard (Durham), where the massive slab is slightly convex in section, ovoidal in shape, and decorated with a simple square-armed cross with long shaft. More impressive is the example at Monkwearmouth bearing a cross with block-terminations and well-cut Latin capitals commemorating Heribericht, or a more ornate specimen with similar cross and plant-scroll background at Kirkdale (Yorks.). Others have no cross, but a continuous spread of interlace, such as Miningsby (Lincs.), Barningham (found in 1816 but since lost) or a fragment at Sinnington (Yorks.). Here also is part of a "dragon-slab", with its sprawling Jellinge-style beast (so called from the decorated royal graves at this Danish site), a Scandinavian motif seen to better advantage at Levisham (Yorks.).

Primitive in design and execution are fragments from Aspatria (Cumb.) and Glenluce and Craignarget (Scotland), which from the combined presence of the cross and swastika incised upon them may

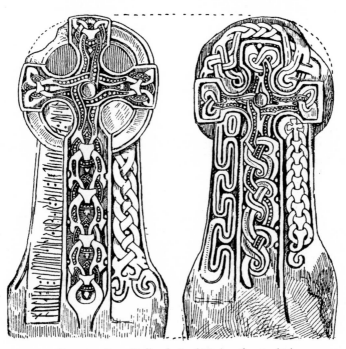

FIG. 10. *Cross (Ballaugh, I. of Man), 4 ft. 7 in. high.*

FIG. 11. *Headstone (Hanley Castle, Worcs.), 20 in. high, 12 in. wide,*
9 in. thick.

be memorials to Danish converts, who still entertained some superstitious reverence for their pagan symbolism.

Headstones. Apart from the smaller crosses whose purpose seems ambiguous, there exist two monuments which from their size and decoration are undoubtedly headstones. Both have rounded tops and are carved back and front. The first, known as the Lechmere stone, at Hanley Castle (Worcs.) is 20 inches high, 12 in breadth and 9 inches thick. On one face is a standing figure of Christ with triangular pleated drapery, holding a book; on the reverse, a circular-headed cross set on a baluster staff and flanked with a fruit-bearing scroll of Byzantine type, the edge decorated with a cable moulding. That at Whitchurch (Hants.) is rather larger, 24 inches high, 21 in breadth and 7 inches thick, and in bolder relief, with a bust of Christ on one face set in an arched recess, an incised wiry scroll on the back, and an inscription in Latin capitals on the edge commemorating Frithburga, the deceased.

In contrast to these stones with their Mediterranean affinities are some admirable Viking monuments with ornamental devices in the Ringerike style, developed in Scandinavia and its dependencies, but owing inspiration to the spread of Scythian motifs transmitted from the East. They differ in shape, being either rectangular or trapezoidal, and were presumably fitted into sockets to stand upright. The finest of these is a slab of oolite, cut in low relief, found in St Paul's churchyard and now in Guildhall Museum, which shows a magnificent Great Beast characteristically involved in plait-work derived from its own anatomy. Fragments of similar type found in the same vicinity, and now in the British Museum, include an inscription to Tuki, one of Canute's ministers, who died c. 1035. Of similar date, but rougher workmanship, are two headstones in the possession of the Society of Antiquaries,[17] one carved with beast-motifs front and back, the other similarly showing a cross and dragon (Fig. 12), an appropriate mingling of emblems of old and new faiths. Less vigorous in design, but more markedly in the developed Ringerike manner, is the gravestone from Bibury (Glos.), with scroll-work sprouting into lion-heads. The trapezoidal shape is peculiar to these Danish headstones and left no descendants, for the rounded or circular silhouette was adopted during the last stages of the

FIG. 12. *Headstone (collection of Society of Antiquaries, London), 18½ in. high, 13 in. wide, 2¼ in. thick.*

FIG. 13. *Headstone (Guildhall Museum, London), 24 in. wide.*

Romanesque period, while the rectilinear slab did not become common until after the Reformation.

Pillow-Stones. This dubious term was coined to describe a number of small tablets averaging 8 inches by 6 in size, belonging to the early Northumbrian period and found mainly in remains of conventual burial-grounds at Hartlepool and Lindisfarne. They were apparently placed over the face or breast of the corpses (whose heads reposed upon plain slabs) and all show crosses either incised or in very slight relief with central bosses. Those from Hartlepool are rectangular in shape, with block or semi-circular terminations to the cross-arms, while the Lindisfarne slabs have rounded tops and circular-ended crosses. They have been compared with the design of the cross-pages in contemporary Gospel-books, and also to the great collection of memorial slabs in Ireland at Clonmacnois and have thus been attributed to Irish influence. An alternative theory has suggested their origin in certain Germanic metal crosses with central lockets made to contain sacred relics. Rather larger tablets, which may have been deposited in similar fashion, have been found at Billingham and Birtley (Durham) and West Witton and Wensley (Yorks.), the latter bearing the name Donfrid below a cross with splayed arms and conventional bird and beast forms on the background.

House-Tomb; Coped Stone. According to Bede's description, the memorial of St Chad (d. 670) was made of wood in the shape of a gabled house.[18] Theories to account for the immediate derivation of such monuments include their possible origin from Roman tile-tombs or mortuary chapels, or else third century Italian tombs which imitated huts of wattle and daub. Our most important memorial of this kind is the "Hedda stone" in Peterborough Cathedral, with its file of six sacred personages standing beneath arcading, and gable ornamented with panels of entwined beasts and plait-work, obviously related to the shrines and caskets common throughout Europe at this time (Fig. 14). But the more usual treatment of the house-tomb gave it the proportions of a penthouse coffin,[19] such as Dewsbury (Yorks.), with tiled roof, baluster mouldings and walls of plant-scrolling, examples in the York Hospitium and Durham Cathedral library collections, or the solitary Cornish example at Llanivet, with rudimentary arched side-walls and key-patterned gable. Sculptural economy omitted the side-walls and reduced it to a rectangular prism or steeply-pitched roof (Bakewell,

FIG. 14. *The "Hedda stone", shrine-tomb (Peterborough Cathedral), 60 in. long.*

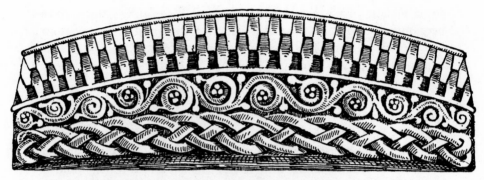

FIG. 15. *Hogback (York Hospitium), reconstruction from remaining fragment, 27½ in. long, 20 in. high.*

Derbys.). Further reduction of the gable gave the final form of coped slab, as at Wirksworth in the same county, similar to the top of a late antique sarcophagus, whose unusual iconography of figure-subjects suggests some borrowing from a continental source.[20] The stone from Bexhill (Sussex) is a unique example, being coffin-shaped in plan—a truncated pyramid in section with cable-moulded edges, and having panels of plait-work and serpents, the top arris decorated with two cross-heads and knot-work of Scottish type.

The design of long-armed cross and interlace background common to the coffin slabs was transferred to the coped stone, the pole-shaft being placed on the ridge crowned with a splay-armed cross-head, sometimes with transverse bars dividing the surface into panels. Such features are to be seen at Hickling (Notts.), together with a pattern of conventionalized bears, linking it with the Brompton hogbacks about to be discussed.

Hogback. This uncouth term was coined to describe a type of memorial with characteristic curved silhouette, a short-lived Scandinavian variant of the house-tomb, whose prototype was a cruck-built house in which the slope of wall and roof was continuous. Its preliminary form can be seen in those bauta-stones, or small segmental-arched boulders (such as an example from Harrogate), which had been set over burials as early as the Bronze Age and had become common in Viking times. The mature convention can be seen in a specimen built in as a door lintel at Crathorne (Yorks.), with its graceful outline, and

86

decoration of plait-work and running-spirals, similar to another in Durham Cathedral Library with a tegulated roof made separately from the base. The elegance of these memorials, together with one lesser-known at Sockburn (Durham) distinguishes them from the average clumsy carvings of this class. The serpent finials at Sockburn, similar to those at Cross Canonby (Cumb.), may be referred to the Norse mythological belief that the house of the dead was wattled with snakes. This motif occurs on two unusual stones in Durham Cathedral Library and Ramsbury (Wilts.), where the simulated gable is more smoothly rounded, rising to a slight ridge defined by the bodies of two snakes ending in bifurcations, the rest of the stone being decorated with interlacing and, in the latter case, also with beasts framed in circles. A similar memorial of domical shape at Ramsbury is covered with running spirals ending in arrow-headed leaves, which taken together with fragments of later design, suggest this place may have been a Wessex centre of monumental production.

These finials can be related to the ornamental figure-heads found on Scandinavian stave-churches, or on buildings depicted in contemporary manuscripts such as the Canterbury Psalter, where a stag's head hangs from a ridge-pole. This architectural device was adapted to unique monumental use by a group of masons centred on Brompton (Yorks.), where it assumed the form of a brace of muzzled bears clutching the roof-tree with their fore-paws. There were originally ten of these hogbacks at Brompton (five of which are now at Durham), and the majority, similar to others in nearby villages, show also the vertical

FIG. 16. *Hogback (Durham Cathedral Library), 52 in. long, 18 in. high.*

panels of plait-work which imitate early post and wattle huts (Fig. 16). Only two other bear memorials have been found outside this area, at Heysham (Lancs.) and Lowther (Westmd.). In the latter village are two hogbacks showing female heads, and a naval scene with warriors and a long-boat, along with others both in this county and Cumberland, where in Penrith churchyard are four large stones, practically of semi-circular shape, patterned with tiles and ornament in the Jellinge style.

FURTHER READING

J. Romilly Allen, *Early Christian Monuments of Scotland*, 1903; G. Baldwin Brown, *The Arts in early England*, vols. 5, 6, 1921, 1930; W. G. Collingwood, *Northumbrian Crosses of the pre-Norman Age*, 1927; Stewart Cruden, *Early Christian and Pictish Monuments of Scotland*, 1957; T. D. Kendrick, *Anglo-Saxon Art to 900*, 1938, *Late Saxon and Viking Art*, 1949; P. M. C. Kermode, *Manx Crosses*, 1907; A. J. Langdon, *Old Cornish Crosses*, 1896; V. E. Nash-Williams, *The Early Christian Monuments of Wales*, 1950; A. Kingsley Porter, *The Culture and Crosses of Ireland*, 1931.

ANGLO-NORMAN MONUMENTS (1066 – 1200)

High cross; cross-slab; headstone; house-tomb; coped stone.

In the field of politics the Norman Conquest cut England from her Scandinavian shoots and grafted her into a cross-channel empire, whose roots settled more tenaciously in the cultural soil of Rome and Byzantium. Much of Northern England was laid waste to effect this manoeuvre, and the many fragments of earlier carving put to building use in church walls testify to the ruthless energy of the new war-lords, who instantly began a great church building programme, establishing Norman ecclesiastics in such diocesan and monastic control that by the end of the eleventh century not a single English abbot is said to have remained in power. Nevertheless, as artistic changes lag behind those in thought or policy, it is understandable to find them in confusion during the half-century or so succeeding the Conquest.

Scandinavian influence died hard, and the barbaric sinuous coils of its last manifestation, the Urnes style, and even earlier Ringerike motifs persisted and indeed enjoyed a brief antiquarian revival and refurbishing. One of our oldest decorative designs, the interlace, and its fellow knot-patterns, being easy to execute and effective as ornament, persisted well into the twelfth century. In Northumbria itself the monumental work of this overlap period remained as a sort of sculptural amnesia in broken recollections of former decorative magnificence until fresh schools of design revived after the lapse of a century. In the early part of this period at least, the art of the decorative carver is found not in the greater fanes whose austerity of form was dictated by monastic idealism, but on smaller churches and their furnishings, where the inhibitions of Cistercian puritanism were presumably less dominant. Characteristic of this tendency are the number of richly-carved church doorways and fonts in Herefordshire, which suggest the existence in the mid-twelfth century of a group of masons, centred perhaps on Leominster, whose work shows cultural affinities with both Western France and Scandinavia. At Kilpeck the latter influence may have been transmitted via Irish metal work.

Gradually however, links with the Continent strengthened, so that along with the native invention of the chevron pattern and the tendency towards abstract ornament, insular art became infected with influence from France and even Northern Italy.

The richly endowed monastic scriptoria afforded pattern and other literary sources for the inspiration of the stone carver. Some of these themes, of pagan origin, held a universal rustic appeal, such as the signs of the Zodiac or Labours of the Months; others were moral or didactic, the *Psychomachia*, or battles between Vices and Virtues, or the pseudo-Aesop fables (such as can be seen in the borders of the Bayeux Tapestry). Towards the end of the Romanesque period, the Bestiary, an exciting hotch-potch of beast fact and fable, became the main primer for the eager pillage of the artist-craftsman during the whole of the medieval period.

Throughout Anglo-Norman carving there runs what has been aptly named a "haunted tanglewood",[21] a magic hunt, where ferocious combats of dragons and men take place amid sadistic vegetable coils, personifications maybe of the conflict of good and evil, or even images of pagan demons which it was thought prudent to propitiate. In similar fashion the Agnus Dei was used as a charm to avoid evil, and the various forms given to the Cross itself often show hints of older sun and cosmic symbols. The oriental theme of the Tree of Life flanked by bird or beast attendants is a familiar pattern on the ceremonial fabrics treasured in cathedral and monastic sacristies but, rather inexplicably, its use in carving is by no means rare. During the early years of the Gothic period its attendant genii disappear, and the more abstract forms of cross-symbol are patterns of vegetation combining the themes of Cross and Tree. Indeed most of these semi-magical items wane with the twelfth century, being replaced with a more orthodox imagery, due perhaps to the spread of Benedictine influence throughout the country.

The desire of the new ruling class to be vindicated in death as in life is shown by the growing custom of burial within churches, limited at first to ecclesiastics, but spreading, as their power grew, to the military caste and given visible expression as the monumental effigy. Series of such monuments to churchmen can be seen in various cathedrals, such as Peterborough, Salisbury, Exeter and Westminster Abbey, where recumbent figures in conventional poses are carved in a flat formal relief on grave-slabs principally of Tournai marble. Such memorials (like the fonts in the same material) may have been ordered by their princely bishops from foreign workshops. One of the three effigies at Salisbury (moved from Old Sarum when the new cathedral site was founded in 1226) is made of our native Purbeck marble, which being similarly capable of a high polish, and cheaper owing to ease of transport, replaced the foreign material in the thirteenth century.

The impact of style can be detected even in the simplest of memorials, and a group of slabs, mainly in Barnack stone, distributed principally in the area bounded by Peterborough, Norwich and Cambridge, suggest that native craftsmen were beginning to standardize designs produced in workshops near the quarries. Both in the design of this particular group, and in other more isolated examples which anticipate monumental devices matured in the thirteenth century, the carver can be seen using technical expedients to reduce the labour of cutting, and yet simulate the appearance of more ostentatious originals such as shrine-tombs and effigies. The beginnings of a similar process were being effected during the later stages of Anglo-Scandinavian influence, when the wheel-head cross changed insensibly into the discoid—the standard form of headstone during the early medieval period, and surviving in isolated cases even into the eighteenth century.

The fortunate discovery of sepulchral monuments *in situ* at monastic burial-grounds from Old Sarum (Wilts.) and Strata Florida (Cards.) proves that by the twelfth century external memorials such as ledgers and coped stones with both head and footstones attached had become customary, while the remains of an extensive parochial necropolis at Bakewell provide evidence that simpler stone monuments were coming into more general use. The Canon's cemetery at Old Sarum was excavated in 1914,[22] in the course of which some score of memorials of diverse types were revealed. Six monuments had coped or flat body-stones, three being linked by rectangular head and footstones, decorated with crosses, and three more with footstones only. There were also an oblong block with rounded top and ends cut with crosses, a coped slab in the form of a truncated pyramid, similar to the earlier Bexhill stone, but devoid of ornament, stone coffins, slabs and coped stones, and an unprecedented table-tomb consisting of a slab supported by six square pillars.

When the Cistercian Abbey of Strata Florida was excavated in 1847, on the east side of the south transept were uncovered the remains of some dozen graves, the majority consisting of diagonally tooled tapered slabs having headstones of various types, and in three cases both head and footstone, one of which had been broken and repaired with leaden cramps.

In 1841 the tower and transepts of Bakewell church were removed for restoration, when about three hundred monuments ranging from the pre-Conquest period up to the mid-thirteenth century were found built into the fabric. Some seventy of these were happily preserved by being built into the south porch, but the rest unfortunately suffered a repetition of their former fate without any record of their appearance being made. The remnants are mainly coffin slabs or headstones, the latter forming the largest single group of such a date yet to be discovered.

High Cross. In a few isolated instances carvers continued to make free-standing crosses with tapering shafts reminiscent of earlier models. Broken fragments exist in the Rotherham area, at Thrybergh, Barn-

FIG. 17.   *Coffin slab,*
Burstall (Yorks.).

brugh and Rawmarsh, and a restored example (of which only the shaft is original) at Castle Hedingham (Essex). These shafts are practically square in section, with chamfered corners punctuated at intervals by bosses. The surface decoration consists of acanthus scrolls; Barnbrugh shows the "Cimitile" pattern derived from Italian originals of the eighth century, while the Essex shaft bears the regular heart-shaped palmettes that were one of the stock patterns of the twelfth-century craftsman, and a particular favourite of the glass-painter for his window-borders. Presumably a product of the mason's yard at the Cathedral is the only figured cross of this period at Kelloe near Durham. Its Maltese cross-head is linked by a narrow band, with shaft divided into three panels meagrely framed with flat acanthus leaves representing scenes from the unusual theme of the Invention of the Cross.

Cross-Slab. Rectangular or tapered slabs, intended either for recumbent use as ledgers, or in some few instances as upright stelae, are the most numerous of Anglo-Norman gravestones. Work of the overlap period is usually roughly incised or in shallow relief, with designs that are degenerate forms of more vital originals. Some examples in Anglesey have crosses associated with rudely-scribed spirals; at Kirklaugh and Minnigaff in Galloway plait-work has been reduced to a mere crazy pavement design or rustication, while at Burstall (Yorks.) the entire surface is covered with an asymetric chequerwork, presumably an abstract version of a key-pattern (Fig. 17).

Both Sockburn (Durham) and Spennithorne (Yorks.) show late Scandinavian ornament combined with double-headed crosses, linked dumb-bell fashion by a cross bar, which anticipate the design of a group of some forty monuments, mainly in Barnack Stone, to be found in villages scattered in the Peterborough, Norwich, Cambridge areas.[23] The largest single collection of these double-crosses was discovered in 1811 beneath the ramparts of Cambridge Castle and must therefore pre-date its building *c.* 1070. In other cases the extremities are forked and the cross-shaft is strengthened with transverse bars, while all have background patterns of regular plait-work. Presumably they were intended to represent a coped stone reduced to flat pattern but, whatever the intention may have been, the result has considerable charm. An

A.

B.

FIG. 18. *Cross-slabs (A. Peterborough Cathedral; B. Cambridge Castle).*

individual group (where the interlace is omitted) occurs in Sussex at Chithurst, Stedham and Steyning (Fig. 19).[24] Creeton (Lincs.) has a variant with circles linked by cable moulding, and a chip-carved background; while at Crowland Abbey (Lincs.), Salthouse (Norfolk) and Stanstead Abbots (Essex) lozenge-shaped patterns straddle the ridge.

Other crosses show cable-twist stems and cross-paty or circular heads derived from the portable or processional type. At Newcastle Bridge

End (Glam.) the motif is accompanied with rectilinear plaits and knotwork, the sides decorated with rudimentary arcading, and Cross Canonby (Cumb.) has a scrawled zigzag background and diminutive figure. One of three coffin-slabs from Llanfihangel Abercowin (Carms.), all with head and footstones, bears such a cross with anthropomorphic head and forked foot. Latent Merovingian influence appears on slabs from Howell and Hackthorn (Lincs.), the former bearing three crosses, the latter, a Latin cross with cable-twist edging set amid flat knot-patterns and stylized eagles. In contrast, a broken stone at Heath old church (Derbys.) has its cross-shaft flanked by "marigolds",[25] with an enigmatic figure-group possibly representing the Betrayal and Resurrection, including a bird-headed personage derived from Irish sources.

FIG. 19. *Cross-slab* (*Steyning, Sussex*), *66 in. long.*

Other simple techniques, such as chip-carving, were used by Anglo-Norman gravestone makers. A tapered coped slab from Trowbridge (Wilts.) is decorated with pairs of semi-circular hoops cut in this way, together with a small diabolo device presumably intended for a chalice.[26] The custom of introducing emblems representing the deceased's profession began at this time, as simple cross-slabs showing long-shafted axes of the type familiar in the Bayeux Tapestry occur at Biddulph (Lancs.), while Ebberston (Yorks.) has a small carving of a Viking sword in its scabbard, a type of weapon that remained popular until the thirteenth century.

On small slabs at Bakewell ornament consists solely of a decorated rosette placed towards the top of the memorial; and in other examples such as the richly carved gravestone to Maurice de Londres at Ewenny (Glam.) *c.* 1150, the shaft bears no organic relation to the rose above. This new treatment of the cross-head as a pattern made up of interlaced rings is also found at Dewsbury (Yorks.), where the cross-shaft rises from steps, sprouts side-shoots and finally emits its blossom.[27] With its dracontine attendants it prefigures the Tree of Life theme adopted during the medieval period, linking it with representations of the Tree of Jesse, of which a much-worn coffin-slab in Lincoln Cathedral is the first sculptural treatment.

At Bishopstone (Sussex) a formal cross of processional type rises from steps, its cross-head occupying the centre of three circular panels defined by a fat cable, and containing an *Agnus Dei* and the oriental motif of birds sipping from a vase, which is found upon those large fonts imported from Tournai, of which Winchester is the best example. Apart from such fonts, and the effigies already mentioned, three memorial slabs in Tournai marble, which may well have been imported ready-made, occur at Ely Cathedral, Bridlington (Yorks.) and Lewes (Sussex). The first, and finest, shows a majestic winged figure of St Michael (whose cult was encouraged by the Normans), holding the soul of a bishop in a napkin, set beneath a lavish canopy depicting a cluster

FIG. 20. *Tournai marble slab* (*Ely Cathedral*).

of buildings supported by pilasters. Bridlington has freely distributed decorative motifs; and the well-preserved slab from Lewes Priory to the Conqueror's daughter Gundrada has an elegantly inscribed metaphorical epitaph dividing the surface into two panels, filled with formal swags disgorged from animal-masks enclosing acanthus palmettes. Such grotesque masks, ultimately derived from classical sources, were familiar elements in contemporary illumination from whence they were adapted to carving practice. They are to be found set amid knot-work on a gravestone at St Peter's, Northampton, *c.* 1150, a product of the mason's workshop during the time when the church was being built.

Headstone. The undisturbed grave-sites found at Old Sarum and Strata Florida show that by the twelfth century it was customary to use both head and footstones in association with coffin-slabs or ledgers. Existing examples show several basic shapes: rectangular (Old Sarum, Cambridge Castle), post-like (Lythe, Yorks.) with rounded tops (Adel, Yorks., Trowbridge, Wilts.), horseshoe shape (Bakewell, Temple Bruer, Cambs.) or discoidal (Crathorne, South Kilvington, Yorks.). Not unexpectedly, three specimens at Strata Florida show Celtic characteristics in their shape and interlacing, for the older patterns in these areas persisted undisturbed by European trends. The unusual stela at Mirfield (Yorks.), practically square in section, bears disorganized plaits on the sides, a rudimentary figure holding a cross on the front, with the top edge decorated by a degenerate form of bear's head, a link with the hogbacks.

House – Tomb; Coped Stone. The memorial in Winchester Cathedral popularly ascribed to William Rufus, but more likely that of Bishop Henry of Blois,

FIG. 21. *Tournai marble slab (Lewes Priory, Sussex).*

7. *Bretforton (Worcs.), Sarah Ford, 1797: headstone in Forest of Dean stone, by Samuel Hobday of Honeybourne. This lavish decoration of native fruits and flowers, classical "anticks" and Gothic monsters is characteristic of the work of the stonemasons Hobday, Ballard and Wheeler, neighbours and contemporaries.*

8. *Deene (Northants.), Isaac Webster, 1786: headstone in Ketton stone, 48 in. high, 30 in. wide. Such accomplished work is a commonplace in the village churchyards near the Midland quarries. This stone is similar in style to others at Great Casterton (Rutland) of 1791 and 1803, signed respectively by John Holmes and John Haines of Stamford.*

1171, simply consists of a plain hipped gable set upon a moulded base. In other cases (cp. Bakewell) the roof body may have been made separately and placed upon a plinth. Here a steeply-pitched monument had a cable-edging to panels of plait-work, which included the Tree of Life motif. A later compromise with the tapered coffin-slab is shown in two other cases from this necropolis: one decorated transversely with chevron pattern, the other as if in imitation of clinker-building. A few monuments such as that to Bishop Radulf in Chichester Cathedral, *c.* 1123, have the double chamfered form which has already been seen in the Bexhill stone, whose date may be anything between the ninth and eleventh centuries.

More roughly carved productions from Gainford (Durham) and St Alkmunds, Derby, have their sides covered with arcading; but the most important of this class, with carefully rendered architectural detail is in Fordwich (Kent), where a roof of fish-scale tiles is supported by a pillared arcade of intersecting arches, inviting obvious comparison with the conventional buildings shown in manuscripts, and the detail of Bosham chapel in the Bayeux Tapestry.

The most ornate of these coped stones (Fig. 23), at Conisborough (Yorks.), was probably made when its great castle was being built. The gable and front face only are carved,

FIG. 22. *Anglo-Norman headstones: A. Bakewell, 17½ in. high, 12 in. wide, 6 in. thick; B. Darley Dale, 17½ in. high, 5¾ in. thick; C. Adel, 33 in. high, 21 in. wide; D. Bakewell, 13 in. high, 10 in. wide; E. Lythe, 24 in. high, 11½ in. wide, 5 in. thick.*

showing that it was intended to be placed against a wall. The carvings would seem to be a decorative hotch-potch of popular imagery derived from pattern-book sources rather than any didactic scheme. The signs of the Zodiac are linked with the Temptation of Adam and Eve and a brace of armed cavaliers upon the gable; while the front bears a mask disgorging acanthus scrolls, a bishop standing by a font (?) and holding a pastoral staff, and a knight armed with broad-sword

FIG. 23. *Coped stone (Conisborough, Yorks), 70 in. long.*

and kite-shaped shield engaged in combat with a winged dragon or Hydra grasping a fallen adversary, its mouth emitting monstrous heads, and its tail writhing in convoluted tendrils.

Some isolated Welsh gravestones would seem in their design to anticipate the so-called half-effigy, a monumental makeshift which became popular during the thirteenth and fourteenth centuries. Llantwit (Glam.) has a coped stone with central ridge decorated with lozenges broken at the top by a quatrefoil recess enclosing a human head, the rest of the stone consisting of ring-interlacing and vegetable meander. A fragment from Cilcain (Flints.) shows a half-length figure in a cloak fastened by a ring-brooch with hands over the breast, the lower part apparently consisting of an inscription set on a vertical band flanked with late acanthus scrolls. Similarly, among the group of slabs with head and footstones (one of which shows a horse and figure) at Llanfi-hangel Abercowin (Carms.)[28] is a curious ideogram of a figure consisting of a head ending in two arms with a cross-tablet placed upon the breast, the lower part of the slab being covered with reticulation. Christ Church, Oxford, has a small mask at the head of the slab above a regular pattern of concentric semi-circles; and the same abstract decoration is cut in relief upon a coped slab at Trowbridge (Wilts.) accompanied by head and footstone.

FURTHER READING

T. S. R. Boase, *English Art 1100-1216*, 1953; D. T. Rice, *English Art 871-1100*, 1952; F. Saxl, *English Sculptures of the Twelfth Century*, 1954; G. Zarnecki, *English Romanesque Sculptures 1066-1140*, 1951, *Later English Romanesque Sculpture 1140-1210*, 1953.

MEDIEVAL MONUMENTS (1200 – 1550)

Coffin-slab; headstone; coped stone; chest-tomb; half-effigy.

Whereas in France social revolution led to the major destruction of larger tombs but left religious carving untouched, in England the reverse was largely the case, so that our knowledge of Gothic sculpture is, owing to insular iconoclasm, founded perforce upon the surviving bulk of monumental carving.

Because of the growing demand for tombs during this period, the range of patronage widened, so that at its close country gentlemen, priests and the professional classes could afford to pay for tombs that were often more ornate than the most lavish monuments of the Anglo-Normans. This was largely due to the development of local stone quarries, around which tomb-makers established workshops and thus evolved individual styles, as distinct from the peripatetic masons engaged on building work who congregated at architectural sites. The luxury trade in tombs was dominated by the use of two native marbles, Purbeck in the thirteenth century and alabaster during the next two hundred years, when in the early fifteenth century its products not only dictated the style of memorial sculpture in England but followed next to wool in importance as a national export.

During the course of the Middle Ages English art, although influenced at times by continental trends, established its own national style and, in architecture at least, made an entirely original contribution to the mechanics of Gothic form. The thirteenth century showed the growing change from formal to humanistic art; the darkness of the tanglewood broke into dawn, the doctrine of the Divine Mother's intercession for Man gave him new hope, and the change of heart is shown in this very image of the Mother and Child, which sheds the quality of a fetish and takes on humanity. The fresh approach to nature shown by scholars such as Albertus Magnus, or pantheists such as Francis of Assisi, was reflected through the artist's keener eye; later, this characteristically divided into two trends:

FIG. 24. *Tomb of Aylmer de Valence, West-minster Abbey, 1326.*

the artificial Paradise Garden associated with the Tournament and the Courts of Love, and the bucolic world of seed-time, harvest and hurly-burly of common life. A hectic reaction to the terrors of plague and social unrest induced a secular treatment of religious art, angels became ladies of fashion, and sacred personages swayed modishly in extravagant costume. Succeeding civil war and economic depression had small truck with chivalry, and the herald of growing unease was a morbid preoccupation with death. In tomb-sculpture it was given gruesome reality by setting a cadaver beneath the pomp of the effigy to point man's inexorable and common fate.[29] It became customary for the rich to spend a high proportion of their private fortunes upon tombs, charities and soul-masses, established in the chantry-chapels which became their private mausolea, epitomized in the apotheosis which Henry VII prepared in his chapel at Westminster. In this same century before the Dissolution, more was also being spent on church building, so that it became a time of high wages and full employment for the stone worker, whose status (never at any time high in the social order) rose under affluence to the ranks of the urban bourgeois. The years of iconoclasm, when churchwarden records were sadly full of accounts, not for the making but breaking of works of art, had little effect on tomb-sculpture, although probably those in a smaller way of business were ousted by the well-established monopoly men.

During the thirteenth century the development of the Purbeck marble quarries near Corfe (Dorset) supplanted the Anglo-Norman imports from Tournai, and their material, easily worked and capable of a high polish, became popular for architectural detail and effigies. The earliest of these are to ecclesiastics, and show the change in treatment from low to alto-relief; the majority, representing knights, and testaments to the growing power of the military caste, were largely made at Bristol; the latest monument of this sort, to Sir Robert de Keynes, 1315, is at Dodford (Northants.).

As well as effigies the workshops also produced shrine-tombs such as those to Archbishops Hubert Walter, 1205, in Canterbury Cathedral, and Gray at York, of 1255; in these the tomb-chest was shaded by a gabled roof upon a pillared arcade, forerunners of later canopies, fretted with soaring gablettes and pinnacles. The desire for polychrome, in which the effigy was picked out with gesso, gilt and colour, led to the eclipse of Purbeck and the use of wood and freestone. Early wooden effigies,[30] such as William de Valence, 1296, in Westminster Abbey, were also covered with metal and enamel plates, and the majority belong to 1280–1360, although they had a brief revival after the best alabaster veins for effigial sculpture grew sparse. The work of freestone carvers has been divided into schools: the North using Tadcaster limestone and Ancaster oolite;[31] the South-Western, Bristol and Doulting oolite, Beer stone, clunch and Chilmark limestone; the South, Midland sandstones, Barnack oolite, Petworth marble and Reigate sandstone—the nature of the material largely affecting the design and detail.

Apart from the larger free-standing tombs in cathedrals, recesses were made in the walls of parish churches to house effigies, usually with a gabled canopy above, but by the mid-fourteenth century, ogival arches topped with horizontal or battlemented cornices began to replace the earlier tabernacle work, and by the turn of the century wall-tombs were being spanned by four-centred arches surmounted by panelled tracery.

About this time the design of the tomb-base became standardized for the best part of the succeeding century. It was composed of three parts: the recumbent effigy, the base, divided into niches or housings containing the diminutive figures known as weepers,[32] and the plinth, usually a series of square traceried panels containing shields for heraldic display.

Alabaster had been used on the west door at Tutbury (Staffs.) c. 1160, and the earliest effigy in the material is at Hanbury c. 1300, in the same county; but it did not come into general use until the mid-fourteenth century, when its workshops rapidly set the fashion for tomb-design during the next two centuries. The effigies were invariably recumbent, having little of the variety of pose with which the freestone carvers had experimented. The man's head rests upon a helm, to hold which angels assist as pages, the woman's upon a cushion; their hands are folded in prayer or clasp each other's, their feet rest upon lions, the wife's sometimes upon her pet dogs.

The main centres of alabaster production were London, Chellaston and York, which had its own variety at nearby Buttercrambe, but about the mid-sixteenth century the trade centre moved from the Nottingham district to Burton-on-Trent, where a number of craftsmen continued to make effigies in a rather old-fashioned style for the Midland market, and finally a series of coarsely-executed incised effigial slabs.[33]

Substitutes for carved effigies were engraved metal plates of latten (an alloy of copper and tin), imported from Flanders and Cologne and popularly known as brasses.[34] For reasons of economy and imitation, these plates were cut into silhouettes representing figures and canopy-work, engraved, and set into stone slabs placed either on the floor, on the tomb-chest or, about the mid-fifteenth century, upon the walls of churches. First introduced into England in the latter part of the thirteenth century, a century later they had become the popular monuments for the lesser gentry and professional and merchant classes, with their main production centre in London.

Most existing brasses are to be found in the Midlands and Eastern counties, but immense numbers were destroyed during the Dissolution for the sake of their metal, and it has been estimated that the remnant is but one fortieth part of the total production, which even so is greater than the rest of Europe put together.

Their style was largely influenced by the work of the alabaster men, but by the mid-fifteenth century both their size and quality began to decline, probably in the effort to keep in competition with marble by reducing prices.[35] Apart from the figures placed under canopies which were imitations of effigial carving, the brass-engravers invented more modest memorial types. These included floriated crosses enclosing busts or demi-figures; bracket-brasses, where figures stand upon a corbel or support; chalices with inscribed tablets[36] (probably a Yorkshire invention c. 1430 which spread into Norfolk); hearts, accompanied by lettered scrolls and cadavers borrowed from the macabre effigies, both introduced at about this same period.

Owing to the great demand for carving on both architecture and tombs, there are signs even as early as the fourteenth century of a separation of function between master-masons, carvers and imagers. This process was also at work in the tomb-trade itself, for it would seem evident that the makers of churchyard monuments and the simpler intra-mural monuments for the lower grade of patron felt little of the conflict of trade interests that existed between the brass-makers and alabaster men.[37] On the other hand, there is evidence in the early years of the sixteenth century at least of firms developing the modern trend of contracting, and thus establishing a local monopoly. We find gravestone-makers borrowing from the themes of the tomb-carvers, inventing expedients of design such as the half-effigy and chest-tomb that were economical evocations of the canopied effigies, technical shifts by which the freestone masons emulated the richness of design possible in native marble. The bulk of their remaining products, however, consists of coffin-slabs and ledgers engraved with crosses and emblems representing the deceased's livelihood, mostly devoid of inscription. In brief, all that is shown in this corpus of memorials of the important evolution

FIG. 25. *Coffin slab (Llan-fair, Anglesey), thirteenth century.*

taking place in the arts is limited to the changes in ornamental and architectural detail.

Coffin-Slab. Slabs of stone, either coffin-shaped or later rect-angular, both flat or slightly coped, are the typical monu-ments of the medieval period. They were laid over coffins as lids, or placed on church floors and in the garth as ledgers, and usually bear a Latin cross incised or in relief, together with em-blems or tools which signify for the most part the profession or livelihood of the deceased.[38] Being usually devoid of inscrip-tion, they are often difficult to date, so that ornament and the various decorative changes in cross-treatment provide the main criterion for judging their age. During the thirteenth century, the rose or cross-head composed of links or an interlaced horse-shoe pattern, which occurred during the late Anglo-Norman period and may have had Mer-ovingian origins, is found in various parts of the country, but particularly in Herefordshire, where a series of superbly ornate slabs, in which the mis-named stiff-leaf foliage emulates the work of the smith, testifies to the presence of a local workshop.[39] In later work of this period, the formal acanthus is treated in a more robust manner, and the cross assumes the vegetative characteristics of the Tree of Life, such as Llanfair y Cwmwd (Anglesey) c. 1225; Raunds (Northants.); or at Great Milton (Oxon.) and Tickhill (Yorks.), both the latter including an *Agnus Dei*, the Northern example also showing the older motif of dragons gnawing the tree. This emblematic representation of the eternal combat between Good and Evil also occurs on a fine Purbeck slab at Brent Pelham (Herts.) together with a demi-angel holding the soul in a napkin surrounded by the four ideomorphs representing the Evangelists.

Another local style is evident in slabs distributed mainly in Cambridgeshire and Norfolk and in the central Midlands, with long-shafted crosses (some with double cross-heads) decorated with four curved appendages which it has been suggested were intended to represent the scarves or infulae attached to processional crosses. From the shape of this device the cumbrous name of "Omega-slabs" has been given them, and their area of distribution, which approximates to that of the Anglo-Norman slabs of the Cambridge style, suggests that they were products from the Midland quarries.

Simpler crosses of the thirteenth century (such as the latest specimens at Bakewell) show cross-endings in the heraldic cross-fleury form, which along with similar treatments derived from heraldry was to persist as the stock-form during the fourteenth and fifteenth centuries. An outstanding example of the continuity of design can be seen in a magnificent series of slabs in the Priory church of Brecon, dating from the thirteenth to late seventeenth centuries, all of which have cross-heads ending in fleurs-de-lis, the later examples following the style of medieval originals both in this ornament and their excellent border inscriptions.

Traces of naturalistic foliage are rare; Dereham (Cambs.) shows oak-leaves combined with an earlier formal rose; Hickling (Notts.) is based on the bryony; Laughton-en-le-Morthen (Yorks.) has an intricate involute vine, which at Hexham Abbey is reduced to a flatter spread of leaves, whose central stock forks from the mouths of masks (an antiquarian reminiscence of this Anglo-Norman device). The main change in vegetation is one of leaves, rather than scrolls, usually flat and five-lobed, with little of the febrile character taken on by the crockets and finials in contemporary tracery.[40]

FIG. 26. *Coffin-slab in Purbeck marble (Brent Pelham, Herts.)*

FIG. 27. *Coffin-slab (Hickling, Notts.), fourteenth century, 79 in. long, 25 in. at head, tapering to 19 in.*

Slabs of the fifteenth century tend to be rectangular, and the crosses they bear are given moulded shafts and bases, with their arms ending in fleurettes or finials. The majority, however, are less ornate, and symbols of occupation scarce. Christ's own heraldry, the emblems of the Passion, occur in a few rare cases. Kirklees (Yorks.) has the Five Wounds; Hulne Abbey (Northumb.) the Three Nails; Bere Ferrers (Devon) the Sacred Heart and IHS in glory; the latter device is also

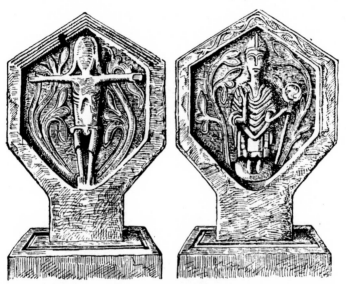

FIG. 28. *Headstone (Llanynys, Denbighs.), fourteenth century, 28 in. high, 27 in. wide, 7 in. thick.*

found at Lowther (Westmd.), Lanlivery (Cornwall) and Hinton (Kent). Abbey churches, even up to the eve of the Dissolution, contain fine grave-slabs to the heads of their houses, as at Jervaulx, Whalley, Tintern and Brecon (1569) where a cross is flanked with heraldic badges. One of the latest series of cross-slabs is to be found throughout Devon, of simple though unorthodox design, such as Drewsteighton, where three small crosses sprout from a central boss at the end of a shaft. After the Reformation, with rare exceptions, the cross was no longer used as an emblem until its re-introduction during the Gothic Revival in the mid-nineteenth century.

107

Headstone. A number of head and footstones belonging to the early period of the Middle Ages have been discovered, but later examples are rare—while some, recorded in such manuals of sepulchral monuments as those by Cutts and Boutell, have since disappeared. Complete or fragmentary discoids (apart from those of Bakewell) have been found at New Romney (Kent), Helpston, Brockhall (Northants.), Horley (Oxon.), Darley Dale (Derbys.), Kildale (Yorks.), Hanslope (Bucks.). East Bridgford (Notts.) has a tapered foot, suggesting that, unless there was also a bodystone with prepared sockets [as at Cotterstock (Northants.)], these markers were simply stuck into the turf.

FIG. 29. *Medieval headstone (Grantham, Lincs.).*

The most elaborate medieval headstone, at Llanynys (Denbighs.), in spite of its archaic design, was credited as fourteenth century in the Royal Commission's survey of the county's historic monuments. It has a hexagonal head, carved front and back with a figure of a bishop and a Christ with extended arms. Cambo (Northumb.) had formerly a headstone of cross-fleury silhouette; and, of others no longer visible, Tackley (Oxon.) was of penthouse shape and Handborough from the same county had a gabled top with engrailed cross, similar in form to the three-dimensional example recorded at Detling (Kent).

At Broadway (Worcs.) are three small stone markers, two of which are head and footstones, carved front and back with traceried trefoils and a rough shield device, to Ann Davis, 1516.[41]

Coped Stone. Although in the earlier thirteenth century shrine-tombs to ecclesiastics were being set up in cathedrals, and manuscripts of rather later date show similar monuments in the churchyard, actual specimens of coped stones remain rarities. A diminutive version of a house-tomb with tegulated roof pattern commemorating Roger de Fulthorp, 1337, at Grindon (Durham), and stones of truncated pyramidal shape (similar to the Bexhill stone) at Lanercost Abbey (Cumb.) and Monk Heselden (Durham) show the persistence of former prototypes. A new departure in design, however, resembling a model of a church with transepts, was made at Bredon (Worcs.), Hauxwell and Fingall (Yorks.), a form which was re-introduced in the nineteenth century.[42]

FIG. 30. *Chest-tomb (Loversal, Yorks.), fourteenth century.*

Chest-Tomb. These tombs were derived from the house-body or base, on which reposed the effigy in stone or brass. The earliest is at Loversal (Yorks.), fourteenth century, and is unique for the various patterns of window tracery carved upon its sides, which would seem to be taken from some master-mason's pattern-book. It was not until the fifteenth and sixteenth centuries, however, that this type of monument achieved its standard form of thick moulded ledger and base, with the surface of the tomb divided either into panelled tracery or a series of quatrefoils enclosing shields. There are at least some forty surviving examples of pre-Reformation date, mainly concentrated within a belt drawn from the Wash to the mouth of the Severn, with the greatest number in Somerset. Representative examples include Sutton Courtney (Berks.), Saxton (Yorks.), Teynham (Kent), Buckden (Hunts.) of 1551 with coped top, Mitchingley (Somerset), 1538, probably to Thomas

Yve, the last prior, St Nicholas, King's Lynn (Norfolk), both the latter monuments bearing metal plates for the inscription.

The chest-tomb preserved its medieval characteristics even when reduced to the simplest elements of moulded ledger and base joining a body of brick or ashlar, when it became widely distributed after the Reformation. In the Cotswolds some unknown carver of the seventeenth century borrowed features from the medieval effigy and originated the sumptuous bale-tomb as the last house of rich wool-merchants.

FIG. 31. *Chest-tomb (Buckden, Hunts.), sixteenth century, 84 in. long, 30 in. wide, 40 in. high.*

Half-Effigy. This type of monument, usually made for the church interior, was a sculptural device of the freestone-masons, intended to combine the appearance of the coffin-slab and effigy. While foreshadowed in Welsh examples of the Anglo-Norman period which have been already described, and showing its earliest mature treatment on the coffin-lid[43] at Baron Hill, Beaumaris (Anglesey) to Princess Joanna, *c.* 1240, it would seem to be related, if not derived, from slabs and brasses of the second half of the thirteenth century having busts or demi-figures placed above a floriated cross. It remained fashionable during the fourteenth century, the majority of examples being found within the central limestone belt, with the greatest area of concentration in the central Midlands.

At first the simple bust was carved in relief above a cross (Bitton, Glos., Monkton Farleigh, Wilts., which originally had a score of these monuments). It was then placed in a recess (Liddington, Rutland, Kedleston, Derbys.) which, after a similar aperture had been made for the feet (Gilling, Yorks.), completed the illusion of a coffin from which sections have been cut to reveal the effigy which it contained. The finest examples at this stage of its development are those to Sir William de Staunton (Staunton, Notts.); Sir John Daubygne (Norton Brize, Oxon.) in which a shield and helm are placed between the feet and head, and one at Kingerby (Lincs.), all of the first half of the fourteenth century. The carvers then introduced a gable over the central portion of the slab, while retaining the head and feet within recesses (Hambleton, Rutland); and finally made the complete torso in relief appear to emerge from the lower part of the coped or flat slab (St John's, Chester), thus returning in effect to the original Beaumaris design in which the demi-figure protrudes from a sheath of foliage.[44]

FIG. 32. *Half-effigy (Norton Brize, Oxon.), 1346.*

FURTHER READING

M. D. Anderson, *The Medieval Carver*, 1935; M. H. Bloxam, *Companion to Gothic Architecture*, 1866; C. Boutell, *Christian Monuments in England and Wales*, 1849; F. H. Crossley, *English Church Monuments 1150–1510*, 1921; E. L. Cutts, *Manual of Sepulchral Slabs and Crosses*, 1849; H. A. Haines, *Manual of Monumental Brasses*, 1861; J. Evans, *English Art, 1307–1461*, 1949; J. Harvey, *English Medieval Architects*, 1954; D. Knoop and G. P. Jones, *The Medieval Mason*, 1933; H. W. Macklin, *The Brasses of England*, 1907; E. S. Prior and A. Gardner, *An Account of Medieval Figure-Sculpture in England*, 1912; L. Stone, *Sculpture in Britain in the Middle Ages*, 1955.

POST-REFORMATION MONUMENTS (1550–1900)

Headstone; ledger; bodystone; coffin-stone; coped stone; chest-tomb; bale-tomb; pedestal-tomb; table-tomb; mausoleum.

During the reign of Queen Elizabeth, much wit was exercised at the expense of the Englishman who had visited the Continent and from France or Italy brought back with him all the novelties he could muster, absorbing culture with the same rapacity as has been credited in our own time to another stock figure, the American abroad. On the other hand, it was no zest for sights but the need for a mild climate of religious tolerance that led a stream of Flemish immigrants to settle in England. They included a high proportion of skilled workmen, whose effect on native labour caused inevitable resentment, given sharp expression by the apprentices' May Day revolt in 1517. Nevertheless these craftsmen settled in little colonies throughout the East Anglian towns to which they gravitated by a traditional affinity and carried on their various trades. From the Low Countries too, and in particular from the cultural and commercial centre of Antwerp, came a spate of pattern-books which introduced a gamut of ornament which could be plundered by all art-workers who wanted to be abreast of the new fashion. Flemish influence largely dominated the tomb-trade, as can be seen in the work of such adopted settlers as the Johnsons, Hollemans, Colt and Cure, who established the tradition of the sepulchral bed tester, its cresting replete with heraldic achievement, or the new

9 (above). *Wisbech (Cambs.), Elizabeth Brooks, 1767; (below) Bedford (St Paul's), Thomas Empy, 1807: showing the upper part of headstones with rococo and neo-classic ornament, the latter the work of Charles Drew of Bedford.*

10 (above). *Wilford (Notts.), Elizabeth and Rebekah Cumberland, 1758: upper part of headstone by Joseph Radcliff of Nottingham, whose only other known work is a tablet at Lockington (Leics.) of 1769; (below) Epsom (Surrey), Matthew Moy, 1817: upper part of headstone. The poppy symbolizes the sleep of Death, with the waking soul above flanked by guardian angels.*

allegorical figures sheltering the recumbent effigies tricked out in their best clothes and coloured as to the life. But this polychrome became outmoded and dismissed as City taste at a time when the next generation of English carvers such as Christmas, Evesham and, above all, Stone, cut their marble with more limpid understanding. To Charles II's French tastes, gained in the years of exile, was indirectly due the new fashion for putting statues into classical dress, in emulation of Louis XIV's garb as Caesar. To this time, when Wren was establishing our national masterpiece at St Paul's (which was to become the museum for the display of Royal Academy heroic sculpture inspired by its first President's admiration for the Ideal and Typical), belong a succession of tomb-makers whose merits are at last acknowledged, the Stantons and Pierce, Bird, Green and the enigmatic Bushnell, who contributed to design the great architectural frontispiece framing the standing effigies below. Again, when the star of the House of Hanover moved west, accompanied by another influx of such foreigners as Scheemakers, Rysbrack and Roubiliac, their fresh acquaintance with Italian Baroque reintroduced the ancient fashion of husband and wife reclining on the tomb, and the use of the great pyramidal background, before which allegorical figures played their part in marble histrionics, where Charity pinned up the medallion of the departed, and Time sprung aghast from Death. These dramas were succeeded by *tableaux vivants*, inspired by the study of Graeco-Roman provincial works from Herculaneum and Pompeii, which via Winckelmann became expressions of the Greek Revival, its sculptural exponents such men as Banks, Chantrey or the better-known Flaxman. Now the deceased no longer wore the toga, but the chiton or chlamys, architecture had frozen to Attic simplicity, and ornament was confined to the meander and elegant anthemion. The succeeding Battle of the Styles, at first a polite joust in which the Greek and Gothic factions took part with little rancour, became exacerbated by ecclesiologist insistence that art-style be identified with religious conviction, and ended in the latter's victory. Since this time comparatively few large tombs have been set up within churches; many of those that have been built have been designed by architects, showing successive mannerisms of style.

It should be borne in mind that these veerings of taste were not entirely an imposed aesthetic, but influenced also by the bias of patronage. During the seventeenth century a large clientele was drawn from the class of rich city merchants whose business interests encouraged a Dutch and Flemish trend; in the Georgian period the leisured land-owner who, by virtue of Italian travel, had acquired the status of con-noisseur set the mode; while the redistribution of wealth during Queen Victoria's reign led to a broader democratic custom whose untutored taste inclined it towards vulgarity and excess.

Turning to external monuments, we find their decoration to be affected by the same changes in style, although in more remote country districts these are often manifest later than in town areas which were more immediately sensitive to the whims of fashion. By the middle of the eighteenth century the repertoire of monumental types was wide, showing a good deal of ingenious regional variation, particularly in such a new memorial as the pedestal tomb which had some pretensions to being minor architecture, consisting of one or more decorative plinths, supporting a pyramidion, sarcophagus or urn. The growing popularity of churchyard monuments, ranging from the humblest headstone to such edifices as this (often erected to minor gentry or retired city tradesmen), encouraged a wide employment of craftsmen both in villages and towns, the latter including men of some local im-portance, who were statuaries and master masons engaged in building, often supporting more than one workshop.

This individually organized craft, along with the integrity of design that was its conspicuous feature, gradually disintegrated in the course of the next century, a victim of the complex changes in social condi-tions that are conventionally described as the Industrial Revolution. For instance, the effects of land enclosure crippled the class of yeoman farmer, for generations the mainstay of the country gravestone maker's employment, and the old cottage industries which had established some degree of craft fellowship within the villages were killed by factory competition, and this also led to shifts in population disturbing the family heritage of skill handed down from one generation to the next.

In the less tangible realm of social relationships, the natural accept-ance of an aristocracy of birth, intellect and taste, which to a large extent had ensured a permeation of culture throughout the different ranks of society, was beginning to dissolve into envy, doubt and unrest. In this respect the understanding between the aristocrat and the master mason, based on a tacit respect for each other's interdependent abilities, was disturbed by the intervention of the professional architect, which in effect deprived the dilettante of his role as artistic arbiter and the craftsman of his function as a decorative designer. Tractarian concern for church ritual also led to clerical interference in architecture, dictating not only conventions of style to the architect, but a code of behaviour for builders and stone-masons which was fondly believed to be modelled on medieval lines and, by some species of sympathetic magic, to improve their workmanship. This new dominance by both architects and clergy not only reduced the independent status of the mason but, it is reasonable to assume, did much to undermine in him that confidence which is inseparable from pride in work.

By the middle of the nineteenth century the altered structure of village economy could no longer support the same numbers of independent craftsmen, many of whom were either forced to become wandering journeymen or to seek employment in the towns, where monopoly firms were becoming established similar to those of building contractors today. The individual ownership of local quarries which had formerly enabled the mason to operate in self-supporting independence began to be replaced by company investment. With the opening of cemeteries, vested interest in foreign marble grew to such proportions as to make these imports competitive and eventually to cripple the native stone industry.

The Victorian etiquette of piety, which encouraged commemoration as a social obligation, filling the green tracts of cemeteries with a multitude of monuments, not only led many town businesses to engage solely in memorial production, but large firms to standardize designs which could be ordered through the medium of the illustrated catalogue, and imported ready-made from abroad. Admittedly this system of prefabrication for stock was nothing new; it had been customary in the past for masons to cut blanks during the winter months when weather prohibited building or repairs. In this case, however, both design and inscription were under the deliberate control of one man and possessed the integrity of personal expression, whereas in subdividing the activities of carver and letterer the possibility of the final product's becoming a work of art was diminished.

It is difficult for us critically to assess these monuments of the last

115

century in an impartial spirit. Our own age is in reaction against the ethical and moral standards they represent, permitting us to see in them little else but bathos and sentimentality. Their indiscriminate use of derivative imagery, along with an inveterate technical facility and mania for pattern, have perhaps something in common with the incoherent work of the Jacobean period when its carvers were learning the grammar of the Renaissance. Late Victorian art in a similar predicament was attempting to cope with the confusing dialects of European art-history.

Within recent years the progressive elements in the monumental industry have effected a return to a more obviously native idiom, the model chosen being the Georgian period. While many stones of great dignity and beauty have been cut by the sculptors concerned with this latest antiquarian revival, they have little in common with the creative experiments being made in church decoration today where the traditional fabric of Christian ritual has been designed in contemporary terms.[45]

Headstone. Headstones of the early part of this period show some affinities with medieval work, as well as technical characteristics that seem based upon vanished work in wood. They were at first small, thick, and boldly cut, sometimes both back and front; but during the course of the eighteenth century they developed into slabs invariably decorated upon one face only, often of considerable size, with the head of the stone cut out in various silhouettes to correspond with the ornamental scrollwork that accompanied the symbolic imagery. By the mid-nineteenth century, under the dual impact of the Greek and Gothic Revivals, the slab assumed the shape and proportions of the Attic stela and finally, with the acceptance of the latter style, was often replaced by various forms of free-standing cross, given a discoidal, pierced or fretted form, with three-dimensional characteristics. This tendency was further developed in cemetery monuments of white marble, often consisting of statuary, in which both the forms of monument and their ornament drew inspiration from almost every European art-style of the past known during the Victorian period.

Remaining headstones of the sixteenth and early seventeenth centuries are such rarities as to suggest that many were either of wood, and have consequently perished, or the monumental type had fallen into

disuse, due to the inhibiting factors of iconoclasm and the lapse of burial-rites and
distaste for monuments during the Common-
wealth. The majority date from the Restoration and, with their variety of silhouette and
partitions of the surface made to accommodate
text and ornament, certainly give the impression that the carvers were experimenting
afresh with what had virtually become an un-
familiar monument.[46]

Georgian topographical engravings of
churchyards often show monuments of wood,
resembling a rail between two uprights, which
at first sight seem part of a broken fence.[47] In
Surrey at least, during the seventeenth century,
these were the sole means of commemoration,
and it is evident that throughout the Weald,
and in other wooded areas of the Home Counties, where the heavy clay-lands made transport of stone difficult, wooden memorials
were once numerous, for in spite of their
vulnerable nature, many still exist, albeit
decrepit and illegible.

In the churchyard at High Easter (Essex)
two oak headposts of eighteenth century date
still retain distinct vestiges of mortality emblems, together with a more ornate, but
weathered specimen at nearby Little Easton;
while Rendlesham (Suffolk) has a square post
with moulded top, decorated with a death's-

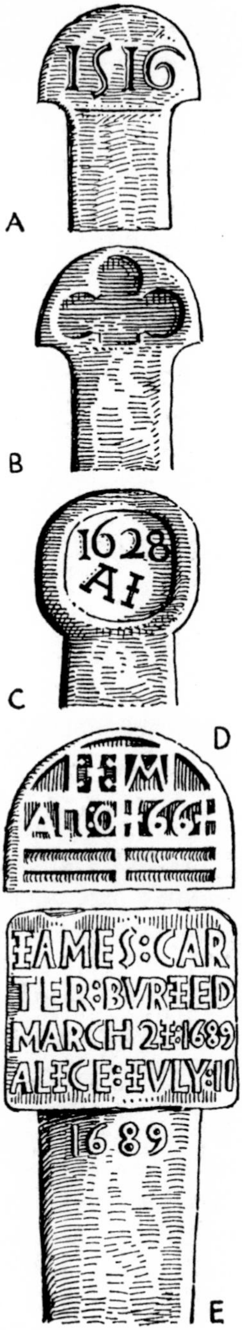

FIG. 33. *Headstones: A, B. Broadway, Worcs., 17 in. high,
12 in. wide, 4¾ in. thick; C. Lower Swell, Glos., 16½ in.
high, 13 in. wide, 5 in. thick; D. Over Silton, Yorks., 12 in.
high, 18½ in. wide, 6 in. thick; E. Woodplumpton, Lancs.,
39 in. high, 18 in. wide, 8 in. thick.*

head and darts, credited to William Simonds who died in 1753. Probably the oldest wooden grave-rail yet discovered is a square wooden beam, lettered in relief on two faces to Thomas Greenwood, 1658, at Sidlesham (Sussex), similar to a later counterpart preserved in Seaford church of 1781. These monuments were presumably supported either on simple crucks, or by posts at either end. At a later date they were imitated in stone, at first by fixing a strut of wood or metal between the head and footstones, as suggested by sockets found on stones at Wrentham (Suffolk) 1689, East Grinstead, 1703, and Billingshurst (Sussex) 1734. A more decorative translation of the wooden prototype can be seen in the churchyards of Ardingly, Balcombe, Horsted Keynes, Maresfield, Westfield, etc. (Sussex) in which the posts have been replaced by massive stone uprights topped with polyhedral heads, joined either by flat or rounded bodystones or vertical moulded slabs, dating between the seventeenth and nineteenth centuries. Three examples in East Grinstead of the eighteenth century show the connecting slab brought down to ground level and given a gabled or segmental silhouette, and this literal translation in stone of the plank of the grave-boards which succeeded the grave-rail remained stabilized as a Sussex type well into the nineteenth century, even being imitated in cast-iron, as the dozen grave-boards in that material with pricket tops, 1828-87 in St Anne's, Lewes. Eastbourne, as well as this Sussex type, contains a variation which was developed in the Home Counties, and particularly in Essex and Hertfordshire, whereby the bodystone was given either an anthropomorphic shape, or else became a high brick or stone coffin flanked by head and footstones.

Throughout the rest of England seventeenth century headstones are generally found of small size, seldom protruding more than 2 to 3 feet above ground, tending to be blocks rather than slabs, often with wide moulded edges, and occasionally, in the Northern counties in particular, being worked both front and back.[48] Towards the close of the century a common decorative feature was a simple hood-mould, either of opposed S-scrolls reminiscent of a Roman cippus or, in a Norfolk variety, made up of C-scrolls flanking a skull or hour-glass. On the Kent-Surrey border these hood-moulds became yoke-like patterns supported by simple pilasters, but the characteristic headstones of Kent and Sussex have silhouettes resembling the section of a mid-Gothic pier combined with supporting consoles or brackets, reminiscent of those fixed to the grave-boards.[49]

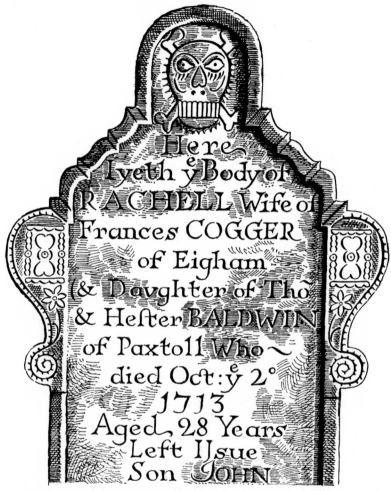

FIG. 34. *Headstone (Ightham, Kent), 1713.*

These headstones are often of some thickness, with prominent cham-fered edges and, when seen collected together in a churchyard, give a curious anthropomorphic impression of being a series of cloaked per-sonages, an illusion further increased by the small masks placed beneath the hoodmould, which itself has often the precise shape of the head-recess in a medieval coffin. In both Yorkshire and Durham, squared blocks or posts of stone, lettered also on the top face so that the inscription would retain its legibility to sinking-point, are common, as well as certain varieties of discoid and semi-circular stones, lettered merely with initials and dates of death in bold relief.[50]

Towards the closing years of the seventeenth century Midland masons, particularly those who worked in Hornton stone, probably in the vicinity of the quarries, began to stabilize the arrangement of text and ornament, producing a great many small boldly-cut stones of compact design, which can be divided into two categories.

(a) An architectural arrangement (similar to contemporary door-cases) in which a hood-mould or entablature, supported either by pilasters, columns or by flanking scrolls, encloses a letter-tablet with moulded rectangular frame.

(b) An ornamental arrangement (similar to interior wall-tablets) in which the text is cut upon a cartouche, shield, oval, circle or heart, surrounded by scroll-work, curtain-swags and fruit and flowers spilling from vegetable sheaths or cornucopias.

Both these devices were used separately or in combination by masons working in Ketton stone (Fig. 35), whose astonishing products are to be found throughout Rutland and the adjacent counties, where along with their fellows using Swithland slate or Ancaster free-stone they developed the cartouche memorial type into a rich extravagance of rococo design through the virtuosity of its prominent exponents, the Staveleys of Melton Mowbray and the Hibbins of Ketton.[51]

In the Vale of Evesham the Laughtons of Cleeve were producing, with more restraint, delicate renderings in low relief of such architectural surrounds, while in Cornwall Robert Oliver of St Minver in the early years of the nineteenth century, borrowing an older device, was setting a semi-circular arch between his pseudo-Corinthian pilasters.

In the majority of these examples text was completely enclosed by ornament but in those less ornate it was displayed on a spread of curtain, or the open pages of a book (a device carried to later and lamentable excess on many a white marble ornament in the modern cemetery). Instead of pilasters side borders of draped festoons or formal ornament were also used.

FIG. 35. *Headstone (Loddington, Leics.), 50 in. high, 36 in. wide.*

On a series of slate headstones found mainly in the Vale of Belvoir, and probably the products of a workshop at Hickling (Notts.), a triple division of the surface was made—with a band of ornament at the head and text and epitaph below—an arrangement defined by mouldings or pattern in the case of freestones elsewhere in the Midlands. In the Home Counties during the eighteenth century headstones were of such uniformity as to suggest some degree of shop-work, the ornament being confined to the upper part, whose silhouette was defined by bracket-scrolls. Double commemorations to husband and wife were shown by dividing the surface into two parts by a pilaster or band of ornament, or by twin oval panels; a family headstone more rarely included several tablets which could be lettered as occasion arose (Plates 10, 11).[52]

This two-dimensional treatment of the surface tended to be replaced towards the end of the eighteenth century by imitations of the architectural frontispieces used on mural tablets,[53] such as sarcophagi and pyramidions set up on plinths, from which the letter-tablets were often suspended, the various architectural units being broken up into tondi, lunettes, segmental or diamond shapes, or the shape of an urn supplying the textual field.[54] During this same period the Greek revival was beginning to supersede the rococo style of the Great Stone Belt, with the urn as its inveterate symbol, accompanied by delicate arabesques, and medallions or paterae suspended from drapes or ribands, in its later stage adopting austere anthemion scrolls and borders of key or guilloche pattern. Stones took on the appearance of Attic stelae, rectangular or tapered, the heads either imitating the classical altar by a low gable flanked by volutes, or else an architectural façade with pediment and acroteria. Although in some areas, such as the environs of London, or in watering-places such as Bath and Brighton which attracted architects and builders, sepulchral stonemasons were quick to adopt current fashion, the majority used the new motifs with caution, mingling them with older well-tried patterns. An excellent instance of this versatility can be found in Stoke Poges, most visited of churchyards, which contains three headstones made by John Merryman of Windsor, to himself, his wife and father-in-law. All include neo-classic motifs, but the latest, 1800, has skulls and an antique fleur-de-lis on the base; the second, 1779, has bracket-scrolls flanking an urn; while the oldest, 1776, bears anthemion volutes. In similar fashion (to pick an example at random)

James Coles of Thrapston used such patterns on his headstones but, on an interior tablet at Ringstead (Northants.), was content with outmoded acanthus scrolls current a century before.

Men whose lives bridged the gap of changing fashion had perforce to follow its whims. A well-documented instance is that of James Sparrow, born in 1716 at Radcliff-on-Trent, one of the finest of the Nottingham slate-engravers; his early work shows an apprenticeship in the calligraphic style, his middle period rococo with Gothic piquance, and his latest products, cut in his seventies, a graceful acceptance of the Adam style, which his son, George Sparrow of Grantham and Stamford, practised with gusto (Plate 30). Other men, like him, who flourished when style was temporarily static, showed this consistency in their work. Charles Drew of Bedford, a freestone worker in territory farther south, was an orthodox exemplar of the Adam style; while a village mason such as James Colecom of Merstham (Surrey), whose finest youthful work was a pyramidion to Baron Masseres, 1825, at Reigate, later evolved his own headstone pattern in Attic mode and remained unaffected by any Gothic tendencies. Of unknown workmanship, but showing signs of mass-production, are a series of Sussex monuments also in Portland stone—figures of mourning widows enclosed by niches hung with swags, which well deserve the customary epithets allotted to the Greek Revival of being "chaste, neat, and elegant". In the essentially conservative North it is surprising to find in remote churchyards such as Upleatham and Yarm (Yorks.), monuments of the 1780s with key patterns and Doric columns; yet on the other hand, at Narborough (Leics.), there can be seen a whole batch of bold slates with urns, drapes and pedimental tablets, worked by the prolific Leicester statuary Samuel Hull as late as the 1850s. Indeed, when the Greek revival became tardily adopted into the northern artists' repertoire, its ornament was often treated with Spartan brutality. Vigour, rather than frippery, is also characteristic of work in the Fenland churchyards, magnificent repositories of carving which are ample reward for the dreary traverse of its landscape. Such decorative motifs as fan-patterns, spindle balusters and roseate festoons were grouped arbitrarily but with superb decorative effect on headstones of Barnack and Ketton oolite by the carvers Samuel Andrews and William Charlton of Wisbech; farther south, at Bury St Edmunds, John and Benjamin de Carle, whose extensive building practice included work at nearby Ickworth House, were responsible for many of the interior tablets and gravestones throughout West Suffolk during the first half of the nineteenth century (Plate 5).

While in ornament the gravestone-cutters were able to effect a truce in the Battle of the Styles, by putting quatrefoils, tracery and pinnacles cheek by jowl with pilasters, triglyphs and urns, the majority found themselves unable to cope with the new directives imposed by those ardent Camdenians among the clergy who required a complete break with the Augustan elegance they now branded pagan. This practical dilemma was solved, not by the medieval copies published in the slim tracts of Paget, Armstrong or Trollope, and hardly through any know-ledge of the ideals of Pugin or Ruskin (although reprints of the latter's chapter on Gothic from *The Stones of Venice* were sold to working-men for 6d. apiece in 1852), but with the aid of pattern-books produced by a few minor architects and statuaries. The most prominent of these men, to whom a great deal of what passes for Gothic Revival tomb-carving is due, were John Gibbs, of Oxford, D. A. Clarkson, and Theophilus Smith of Sheffield.[55] Gibbs's first *Series of Design for Gothic Monuments ...* published when he was living at Wigan in 1852, was succeeded in 1864 by *Designs for Christian Memorials* (Plate 12), which ran through eight editions, the last being intended for the American market. Their style, although influenced by Ruskin's early advocacy of Italian Gothic, is highly individual and ranges from the simplest of headstones to large gabled erections, supported by columns of marble with busts in tondi and pierced crossheads and inset drapes, together with obelisks and pyramidions reconverted by Gothic pattern. This new style had nothing in common with the Gothic rococo familiar to the Midland masons, and one can see the beginnings of the separating functions of designing apart from stone-cutting in Ketton churchyard itself, where amid the virtuosity of his forebears in the craft Robert Hibbins is commemor-ated by a large headstone adapted from Gibbs, no longer cut from the local stone, but made of composite materials (Plate 12). D. A. Clarkson published *Monuments in the Grecian, Italian and Gothic styles* in 1852, basing his Gothic upon the Decorated period and showing large pin-nacled monuments on buttressed plinths, and free-standing crosses enscrolled and cusped set upon bases of quatrefoil. W. T. Vincent, whose book *In Search of Gravestones Old and Curious* (1896) was the first to attempt some adequate description of Georgian monuments, describes cemetery carving of his day as being "founded in great

FIG. 36. *Medieval coped stone (Bredon, Worcs.), after Cutts; a type of memorial imitated in the nineteenth century, as in this design by Charles Kirk of Sleaford from Trollope's* Manual.

measure upon the artistic drawings of Mr D. A. Clarkson, whose manifold suggestions, published in 1852, are still held in the highest admiration" (p. 61).

Theophilus Smith, "sculptor and ornamentalist", of Sheffield, produced his *Original Designs for Christian Memorials* in 1864 (Plate 13), issuing it in monthly parts, which included some 150 designs for headstones, incised slabs, coped stones, altar-tombs, churchyard crosses, samples of alphabets and epitaphs, together with an essay on the use of heraldic and symbolic devices. A second series was issued later, and the essay on heraldry as a separate pamphlet in 1877. These designs, mainly in the Decorated style which the ecclesiologists accepted as orthodox, and obviously intended for execution in freestone, albeit derivative by their terms of reference, show considerable invention, especially in those for coped stones, used both separately and with head-stones. The plates are well drawn, some in colour showing the use of polychrome tile insets, rubricated and painted lettering, and interesting details such as the custom of brambling graves, as well as the emphasis of the grave-plot as a piece of property by railings in cast-iron. In fact the Smith firm was in a large way of business, producing not only memorials for the Sheffield area, but chimney-pieces, decorative church carvings, gates and railings in wrought and cast iron, and interior metal work. The printed designs of these tomb-grilles show clearly that much of the existing Victorian iron-work of this sort came from these York-shire workshops.[56]

These monuments of the Gothic Revival, although no less derivative than their Georgian predecessors, had the redeeming feature of being cut in native stones, whose idiosyncrasies of colour and texture brought them into tonal harmony with the church and English scene. The rise of cemeteries, however, offered in the cold-blooded business sense new markets and led to a trade in white marble monuments, often shipped ready-carved from their main source at the Italian quarries of Carrara.

Although headstones in white marble continued to be made in almost every historic style then known, the virtuosity of the foreign workman led them towards asymmetry and three-dimensional expres-sion in preference to bas-relief. By a lamentable mimicry headstones were made to ape rustic work, as if made of logs or boughs entwined with ivy, or as faithful simulacra of anchors with heavy cable, open books or obese scrolls. The popular memorial was some form of cross, often combined with a statuary angel, either a cherub in a scanty vest, a replica of the little ornamental bambini hawked by itinerant Neopoli-tans, or a pudescent maiden in nightshift-cum-chiton, clinging to the Cross in Topladian style, or standing before it with welcoming arms, as well as crucifixes or statues of Christ in the role of Good Shepherd or Comforter.

In due course the large firms specializing in white marble employed English designers who, although committed in many cases to perpetuating designs which by their original imposition on a public with little cultivated taste had established a tradition, nevertheless attempted to free memorial carving of its derivative nature and evolve new expedients. In the case of headstones these often took the form of reducing the surface into simple units, linked together by abstract blocks or buttresses, reminiscent of the new functional elements in architecture, and combining them with the stone kerbs initiated by Victorian practice, which were often punctuated by stone posts or urns.

FIG. 37. *White marble cemetery memorial.*

After World War I, and the spate of memorial production due to its hiatus, rising costs enforced a reduction in the size of monuments, which under the influence of the small official tablets to war dead became dwarfs seldom more than 3 feet in height, with an inevitable decrease in text and ornament. This trend towards small and uniform monuments has persisted and is a notable feature of many cemetery regulations being currently enforced.

On the other hand, during the last forty years churchyard authorities have been reacting strongly against the use of white marble and its foreign design idiom; and a certain body of enlightened opinion has led to the advocacy of British stone, and the Georgian monument as exemplar, thus encouraging, in headstones at least, a return to the slab or stela in bas-relief (Plate 32).

Cognate revivals abroad, notably in German memorial art which is largely inspired by the work of Edward Johnston and Eric Gill, have been more successful than the English in producing a contemporary style, and within recent years have correlated monumental forms with abstract elements. In our country it seems that economic factors and antiquarian prejudices rather than aesthetic or religious inspirations have dominated memorial art, which has yet to produce any work of originality as fit epitome for contemporary ideologies.

Ledger. Recumbent slabs of stone, usually rectangular, performed the double office in churches of commemoration and paving and, in the latter respect, are often found in churchyards throughout Cheshire, Lancashire and the West Riding. In most cases, however, they were laid on a low base, or formed part of chest and table-tombs. Lancashire early ledgers were often like flagstones, long and narrow, with merely initials and dates for record (see example at Wigan, 1506, with incised cross).

A formal design, widely used in the late seventeenth century, consisted of an arch supported on pilasters with angels' heads on the spandrels. This device occurs on the most elaborate series of early ledgers found in the West Riding, of which the best are at Morley and Lightcliffe, ranging from 1667 to 1742, together with a central panel composed of a lyre-shaped scroll-pattern set between initials and dates, the whole enclosed in borders of strapwork and floral growth. Such details, including the floriated letters derived from Dutch "blooming-initials", while obviously derivative from Jacobean furniture design are vital expressions of a local folk-art. The slabs to Henry and Mary Greetheed, 1722, at Morley, with its fantastic sunflower angels and comic cadaver at the base, and Judith Goodall's at Lightcliffe, 1715, with fine border and central panel, are among the best of these remarkable stones (Plate 1).

Heraldic ledgers, usually in black or grey marble, form a distinct class, and are found both in churches and on churchyard tombs. Their high standard, both of armorials and lettering, suggests they were the work of carvers who worked in association with the official Heralds and made this work their speciality. They appear never to have been signed and seldom show any local difference of style.[57]

Bodystone, Coffin-Stone, Coped Stone. The form of the grave-mound was sometimes made into a permanent feature by means of a bodystone of stone, brick, or tile, coped or semi-cylindrical in shape. In the South-east and Home Counties these were laid either directly on the ground or on low bases and have no headstones. Elsewhere the medieval precedent of the coped stone was adopted in the seventeenth century, with the inscription spreading the length of the slab, as can be seen at Yarm

11 (left). *Cleeve Prior (Worcs.), Michael Campden, 1747: Forest of Dean headstone, 51 in. high, 42 in. wide, by John Laughton of Cleeve;* (right) *Egloshayle (Cornwall), 1827: Delabole slate headstone by Robert Oliver of St Minver (photograph by Mr Eric Brown). Here text and ornament are framed by formal architecture; in the first instance apparently derived from the contemporary door or window-case; in the second, more remotely, from wooden panelling of the early seventeenth century.*

12 (left). Ketton (Rutland), Robert Hibbins, 1865: a large Gothic Revival monument in stone and marble to a member of a local family associated with stone-cutting and quarrying for over two centuries; (centre) design for a monument by John Gibbs of Oxford (plate 37 from Designs for Christian Memorials, Oxford, 1868). The Ketton monument is obviously influenced by such designs and appears to be based on plate 33 of this pattern-book, which was one of many published by Gibbs; (right) Barnwell St Andrews (Northants), 1846: Ketton headstone to three children of Daniel Stevens, a member of a local family of stone-carvers. An original Gothic Revival design showing the characteristic Victorian gravestone flora of lilies and ivy.

(Yorks.) 1617 (also engraved with a halberd); Barrowden (Rutland); Old Weston (Hunts.); Barton (Cambs.); Standlake (Oxon.).[58] In the same area, where the echoes of Gothic seem as universal as the overtones of bells, are tombs of some size, with a single or double gable, such as a small group at Weldon, 1653, 1715; Isham 1656; Rushden 1656, 1669 (all in Northants.); another is to be found on a high plinth at Langham (Rutland) to Thomas Beaver, 1653, and a similar one with the addition of a cornice at St Ives (Hunts.) 1657, in a monument approximately of the same size, 6 feet long by 3 feet high. Bovey Tracey

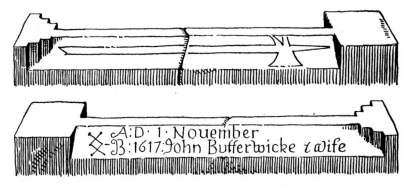

FIG. 38. *Coped stone (Yarm, Yorks.), 1617, 77½ in. long, 9½ in. high.*

(Devon) has a more ornate tomb to Maria Gardyner, 1655, with three small obelisks cresting the gable, separately carved with a rose, mermaid and thistle, and their respective legends of *Surgam*, *Vivam* and *Canam*, together with armorials and mortality emblems on the base. Yet another central Midland tomb-type (which as Gough first observed, a cursory glance would classify as medieval) occurs in the area between Rutland, Lincoln and Huntingdon; it consists of a tapered slab with convex upper surface on which is a shield in very low relief, its ends sometimes ornamented with scroll-work or an angel's head, placed either directly on the ground, or supported by transverse slabs in table-fashion. They range in date from the seventeenth to nineteenth centuries and in some churchyards are quite numerous: Carlton Scroop and Belton (Lincs.) having seventeen and twelve respectively, while Old Dalby (Leics.) has a strange triple-ridged example which resembles a bellows.

Apart from such scattered exceptions, coped stones only appear again when the Gothic Revival restored them to favour. They are then usually placed on decorated bases, with gables or hipped roofs of varying degrees of pitch, sometimes topped with moulding or cresting, with a cross on the gable. A popular type resembled a miniature cruciform church (based on medieval examples at Bredon and Hauxswell), but for the most part they were usually combined with a headstone cross. More magnificent examples emulated shrines, being carved with angels and heraldry under housings, with tiled and crested gables, such as Solihull (Warws.) 1861.

Coffin-shaped slabs, of some bulk, without supporting head and footstones are rare. Late seventeenth century examples occur in the vicinity of Olney (Bucks.), and at West Knoyle (Wilts.), while Baslow (Derbys.) 1702, has a realistic reproduction of a coffin, complete with ring-handles and mortality emblems on the lid. As previously noted, it was customary in Essex and Hertfordshire to link the head and foot-stones with a coffin-shape, sometimes deliberately mimetic, as at Maldon (Essex), where the monument to William Raymond, 1812, is equipped with alternate paterae and handles. At Great Bradley (West Suffolk) are four coped and coffin-shaped slabs with head and footstones of the late seventeenth century, two of them with grisly cadavers in bold relief on the ridge.[59]

Chest-Tomb. Continuing the tradition of the medieval tomb-base, chest-tombs in an infinite variety have persisted in popular use since the Reformation, their greater bulk associating them with a social importance superior to that of the headstone. At their simplest, they were given during the late sixteenth and early seventeenth centuries the ponderable quality of megaliths, consisting of a base in ashlar or brick set upon a plinth, with a massive cover-slab moulded or chamfered.[60] Arising from the usual method of construction as a cist or box of four slabs, it became natural to work the transverse ends into the form of pilasters, balusters or consoles, thus giving the illusion of corner supports with intervening panels—the eighteenth century standard type, of which most churchyards possess at least a single specimen.

It was mainly in the Cotswolds, in the area bounded by the Windrush, Severn, and Bristol Avon that the chest-tomb developed its greatest magnificence, and at Burford and Painswick its characteristics can best be seen. The older monuments in the latter churchyard show the ends of the chest-tombs made into vigorous consoles, giving the typical lyre-shaped silhouette reminiscent of the Italianate form of sarcophagus, such as five tombs to the Poole family, 1658–1798. By the mid-eighteenth century side panels were often recessed, and the ends buttressed by a single scroll, as in the Palling tomb, with its rococo cartouches and lozenge patterned borders of quasi-Gothick flavour.

Bale-Tomb. At Quenington (Glos.) 1697, placed on the ledger of such a console-tomb, can be seen a semi-cylindrical grooved capping-stone, which in its mature form at Burford, Swinbrook, Fulbrook, Standlake, etc., has received the name of bale-tomb, perhaps by association of ideas, as so many of these ornate memorials commemorate mercers whose riches came from the Cotswold flocks. Traditionally its shape is said to represent a wool-bale, although comparison with the remaining metal hearses placed above tomb-effigies, such as the Beauchamp monument at Warwick, shows its true derivation.[61] Its simplest form is a smooth half-cylinder, but it is usually deeply grooved, either lengthwise, transversely or spiraliform, with skulls or shells inset at the ends. Finally it appears as if bound together by three hoops or bands supporting vases or finials, set upon a high chest-tomb, divided into panels by mouldings, pilasters or consoles, lavishly decorated with swags, festoons of fruit and flowers and rich cartouches, as in the memorials to Harman Fletcher at Asthall, 1730 and Robert Aston, Innholder, 1698, at Burford (Oxon.). Nostalgic echoes of style are sometimes apparent in these monuments. At Bourton-on-the-Water (Glos.), where the brook runs limpid through its cresses down the village street, John Jordan's bale-tomb bears medieval weepers, while in contrast an adjacent memorial is decorated with Ionic pilasters set between semicircular arched panels containing tulip sprays, a derivation from Jacobean wood screen-work. The Morgan tomb at Shipton-under-Wychwood (Oxon.) 1727–59, is a sort of grandiose three-decker, with its high base divided longitudinally by a pie-crust moulding (Plate 15).

A later development of the bale-tomb can be seen at Witney in particular—and in other churchyards extending into Berkshire, such as Coleshill—where the capping-stone has been reduced to a series of mouldings like the coved lid of a casket, and the decoration of the chest-tomb has more delicate arabesques. Fairford, which contains both sorts of tomb, has also an unusual "sport": the Harvey tomb, *c.* 1826, a plain chest-tomb with flat ledger supported by four female caryatids with flimsy draperies and Egyptian head-dresses, similar to one at Kingston Bagpuize (Berks.). Churchyards in the Severn valley also contain splendid chest-tombs, with interesting varieties of weepers, such as Hardwicke (Glos.) 1675, where they hold mourning scarves, or at The Lea (Herefs.) 1742, where they are dressed in loose oriental robes with pantaloons. Finest of all, and remarkable for its imagery, is that to Arthur Knowles (Plate 16), 1707, at Elmore (Glos.) with its allegorical

FIG. 39. *Chest-tomb* (*Darley Dale, Derbys.*) *with weaving implements, c. 1640.*

figures in contemporary costume clinging to the scriptures for salvation, flanked by the grim personages of Time with his customary scythe and hour-glass standing on a wheel, and Death as a cadaver holding his dart trampling a globe.

In other districts the direct tradition of the Gothic tomb-base with traceried sides was still retained. Darley Dale (Derbys.) has two such tombs, of 1631 and 1640, the latter being completely covered with tracery, the former decorated with patera, Tudor rose, heart, darts and a chalice. Nearby, by the same hand, is a unique tomb commemorating a weaver, carved on all faces with shuttle, tenter, loom, spinning wheel and warping-mill (Fig. 39). In Somerset in particular the older tradition persisted, for at Closworth, 1711, Thomas Purdue, a well-known county bell-founder, had his high tomb carved with a bell.

Such tombs are, of course, exceptions to the ubiquitous classical norm, which with its moulded ledger and plinth, and chest decorated with panels flanked by simple pilasters or squat balusters, remained in common use during the first fifty years of the eighteenth century. After that date, affected by ideas diffused by the Adam revival, it took on a greater elegance, the panels becoming recessed, or given a concave sweep, the ends made convex, and the base and plinth often swept into a graceful curve. A similar treatment was accorded to the ledger, sometimes given a pie-crust moulding, and topped with a graceful urn or vase. At this stage it had completely shed all medieval derivation and reverted to the classical prototype of cippus and pedestal monuments which, for the sake of introducing order into chaos, are described separately in the next section.

By the turn of the century, particularly in the London area, the classical form of bath-tub sarcophagus appears, oval in section, its sides or ends covered with strigilations (Kensington, 1784); or the *arca*, a coffer in the shape of a truncated pyramid, with triglyph pilasters topped with acroteria and ending in lion's feet (Plate 14).[62] The Roman couch derived from the Scipio Barbatus type also makes its appearance; Thomas Warmington made two fine examples in Leamington parish churchyard, *c.* 1850; while at Upton (Bucks.) 1849, Merryman of Windsor perched one over a base supported by Doric columns. Highgate and Kensal Green in particular, and others among the older London cemeteries, are the best places in which to see the various manifestations of this purer *gusto greco*, impeccably expressed in white marble.

With the Gothic Revival the tabernacled tomb-base was reinstated, and in the more elaborate monuments given the architectural proportions of a shrine or building, being made both with solid or pierced walls, complete with buttresses, gablettes and pinnacles. During the present century, owing to the ground space it occupies, this tomb has fallen out of fashion, but the inspiration for its occasional use has been the similar seventeenth century type of plain chest, with heavy chamfered ledger, such as examples designed by Eric Gill, which are lettered around the edges of the slab.

Pedestal-Tomb. The proportions of the chest-tomb emphasize length, the pedestal-tomb its height, often rising from a plan dictated by the variations on a square rather than a rectangle. The contrast between the earlier Cotswold chest-tomb with consoles and this later variation in form can best be seen at Painswick, where the unique collection of these monuments has been ascribed on circumstantial evidence as the work of the Bryan family.[63] These are square, circular or octagonal in plan, with straight or concave faces, the corners buttressed by luscious scrolls or consoles ornamented with angel-heads or bat-winged skulls (Plate 15). Some have domical tops, Hindu in feeling rather than classical; others are pyramidally built up into mouldings, with bands of lettering in relief set amid delicately chased bands of ornament. The work is difficult to date with precision, as all are family tombs, but the majority would appear to belong to the latter part of the eighteenth century.

In the villages along the Severn valley this tradition of large pedestal-tombs, square, rectangular or oval in plan, with bold cornices and domical finials was developed into the nineteenth century by other local masons such as John Pearce of Frampton-on-Severn, whose work can be recognized by characteristic drooping sheaves of foliage set over oval letter-tablets. The imagery has more variety than at Painswick, and with boldness and vigour it shows cherubs weeping beneath stalwart oaks, robust nymphs with blowy drapery contemplating urns by decollated trees, together with a wealth of trophies, bows and arrows and quivers, flaming hearts, doves and sunbursts—extracted second-hand from Jesuit pattern-books and blandly applied to Augustan use.

Such domical or tent-like capping-mouldings were often topped with an urn[64] (as in a fine series by Colecom of Merstham at Banstead (Surrey) and belong to the end of the eighteenth century. At their best, as in the Anthony tomb at Beaconsfield (Bucks.) 1800, Fyfield (Glos.), or Wootton (Surrey) 1718, where the Glanvil tomb has a graceful vase upon a column,[65] their stance is charming, seen against the churchyard's boskage; at their worst, like the graceless pile at South Mimms (Herts.) 1741, or Morden (Surrey) 1755, with its peculiar three-sided vase, they are but oddities of masonry (Plate 15).

The sarcophagus was also placed above a pedestal, a herculean specimen being designed by James Wyatt, for Gray's monument in the fields by Stoke Poges church where the Elegy was inspired; or, in a more swashbuckling style to Captain Day, 1790 at Cirencester (Glos.); or at Melton Mowbray (Leics.) 1747, flanked by graceful urns, one of the products of the local Staveley family. Nearby, at Burton Lazars, can be found one of the most ambitious churchyard monuments of the

Georgian period, about which we have some all too rare literary evidence retailed in this case by those gossiping Leicestershire historians,
Nichols and Throsby.[66] The tomb commemorated William Squire,
1786, a weaver who left half his little fortune of £600 to be spent on
the monument. Some 20 feet high, it is made of several types of stone
and consists of a buttressed rectangular base, finished at each end by
cylindrical piers topped with celestial globes entwined by serpents, and
decorated with the emblems of the constellations. Resting upon this is an
arca supported on brackets, carved with oval plaques representing Peace
and Time, and edged with a pie-crust moulding. Next follows a
pyramid with concave faces resting on four iron balls, its pierced oval
centre enclosing a vase, with seated figures of Faith and Hope, topped
with a finial sphere, which originally bore an eagle wrestling with
snakes. Its ornament is lavish and well-carved, including trophies of
mortality and various passion emblems. According to Nichols, it was
painted to imitate marble, and also gilded, which explains Throsby's
gibes of its being "a pretty painted thing" and "a gingerbread tomb"
(*Hist. of Leicestershire*, vol. 2, p. 181). The device of a pyramid tempting
gravity by resting on four spheres was derived from Jacobean decoration, and examples of its use can be typified by such monuments as
those to Waller, the poet, at Beaconsfield (Bucks.), now picturesquely
shaded by a great walnut tree; in Bunhill Fields to Joseph Collete, 1725;
at Buckden (Hunts.) 1799; or the graceful example with large mourning
nymph and leafy garlands at Reigate (Surrey) 1825 by James Colecom.
It was carved in relief on headstones and large wall-monuments during
the latter part of the eighteenth century, where, topped with an urn or
pineapple, it made a decorative finial to a supporting tomb on these
architectural frontispieces. Thus it can be seen at Hallaton (Leics.) to
George Fenwicke, 1760 (Plate 14); on the exterior of nearby Kings
Norton, to the Smalley family, *c.* 1772, and to the builder of the
church, William Fortrey, 1783, in monuments which probably came
from the same workshop.[67]

Actual pyramids for monuments are not unknown, like John Bryan's
at Painswick, 1787. They are usually sharply pointed, following the
Roman prototype of Caius Cestius. In this fashion the local mason
Smithe in 1810 made the monument to that twenty-two stone
"Hippopotamus", John Fuller, buried in Brightling (Sussex) in 1834.

"Mad Jack" was a patron of Turner and amateur astronomer, who had his Observatory and Rotunda at Rosehill, Robertsbridge, designed by Smirke, and decorated his estate with architectural fal-lals such as the mock spire or Sugarloaf at Dallington, an Obelisk, and a Hermit's Tower. At Sharow (Yorks.) under a model of the Great Pyramid topped with a cross lies Charles Piazzi Smyth, whose measurements of the Ghizeh original induced his belief in its being an esoteric means of prophecy; while on Worvas Hill, overlooking St Ives (Cornwall) is a granite pyramid 50 feet high, set up in 1782 by the eccentric John Knill for his remains, which, however, he eventually left for hospital dissection.[68]

The short-lived Egyptian style, which followed the discoveries of Napoleon's archaeologists, had some slight effect upon our native building and was used by Stephen Geary for the entrance to the Catacombs at Highgate cemetery in 1838. It was occasionally adopted for small mausolea, of which various examples can be seen in London cemeteries, particularly in Kensal Green, such as those to Thomas Farrant, 1847, and Henry Adderley, 1875. Its most bizarre manifestation in the latter cemetery was the tomb to Andrew Ducraux, the equestrian, 1837, whose performances at Astley's Amphitheatre had made him an idol of the day: a theatrical hotch-potch of Graeco-Egyptian, replete with winged Bucephali and four sphinxes skulking amid the elder undergrowth.

When George III's daughter Sophia was buried in Kensal Green in 1848, her interment not only established this new cemetery as both respectable and fashionable, but led to her eminently Augustan casket-tomb on its high plinth designed by Edward Pierce being frequently copied by lesser cemetery statuaries such as Brine and Lander. A few yards from Ducraux's monstrosity is Robert Sievier's Lysicratean monument housing a statue of Hygeia, to the eminent quack John St John Long, who for a brief time was John Martin's only pupil and himself died from the tuberculosis he affected to cure. Less orthodox is the Holland sarcophagus by Digby Wyatt and Roulton, 1856, with its Greek nymphs holding reversed torches supported on the crouching backs of cruelly-beaked griffins (Plate 17); or Major-General Casement's four life-sized Sikhs who act as the caryatids to his monument, 1844.

In work of the Gothic Revival the obelisk was illogically adopted by

John Gibbs, although he disguised its pagan character by interpolations of crosses, topping it off with capitals or cresting, angels or busts. In Smith's designs it grew nearer to a spire, springing from a traceried base with gablettes, a form of monument which when in local stone has a pleasant aerial character in contrast to the usual mass of earth-bound chest-tombs, but like them the pedestal-tomb has proved too cumbersome a memorial for the taste of the past fifty years.

Table-Tomb. This type of monument consists of a ledger or thick slab on supports, either in the form of transverse slabs at each end, or as upright blocks or columns, usually four or six in number. Although it had a medieval precedent in the solitary example found in the burial-ground at Old Sarum, its use is practically confined to the northern counties, where it would seem to have originated during the seventeenth century. An early example at Upleatham (Yorks.) to Henry Rice, 1687, is supported on four posts, and variations can be seen at Guiseley, Keighley, Ripley, Tickhill, Wadsley (West Riding), Easingwold, Hovingham, Scarborough, Whitby (North Riding), High Coniscliffe (Durham), etc. At Yarm, 1784, the ledger has six Doric columns for supports, and at Aycliffe (Durham), more precariously, merely three; in many cases these are turned balusters reminiscent of wooden originals. At Kirkleatham and Brompton (Yorks.) in particular, *c.* 1790–1860, the supporting convex ends are joined together by a central slab, giving the illusion of a chest-tomb with deeply recessed sides, the ledger being sometimes additionally sustained by delicate balusters. This imitative form of construction is reminiscent of the Sussex stone styles but seems due in this locality to some obscure derivation from furniture design, of which there are other traces apparent in North Riding headstones with occasional Chippendale Gothic strap-pattern borders.

Mausoleum. When congestion made it impossible for important families to bury ancestral remains within churches, they established vaults or mausolea within churchyards or upon their own estates. The greater ancestral tomb-houses of this kind were often designed by architects, such as Castle Howard (Yorks.) by Hawksmoor, or Cobham Hall (Kent), 1783, and Brocklesby Park (Lincs.) 1787–94 by James Wyatt, Dulwich Art Gallery by Sir John Soane, 1812, the ingenious Turner mausoleum at Kirkleatham (Yorks.) by Robert Corney, 1763, or J. B. Papworth's mortuary in memory of Mrs Lytton at Knebworth (Herts.)

1816, to put a few examples in a sliding scale of splendour. Best-known of all is the extraordinary Dashwood columbarium at West Wycombe (Bucks.), romantically sited by the church on the hill beneath whose chalk labyrinth the Hell-Fire Club members were reputed to disport themselves. Also in the same county at Hambledon is a square domed gazebo to the Kendricks, which Horace Walpole thought worthy of a sketch; while at nearby Fawley, hidden in its fold of the hills, are two mausolea in a single churchyard—the circular Freeman tomb modelled on that of Cecilia Metella, *c.* 1750, and the Mackenzie edifice, sombre in granite, evocative of Dracula, 1852.[69] Curious rustic emulations of this form of monument are the barrel-vaulted oven-tombs peculiar to Kent (such as at Bethersden, Smarden etc.), entered by a doorway at one end, with ledger inside on which coffins were placed; or the town equivalent in such catacombs as Highgate or Liverpool.

Monumental freaks are confined mainly to recent times and cemeteries, although earlier work in churchyards is not exempt from eccentricity. In Richmond (Yorks.) is a chest-tomb with fragments of Robert Willance's leg-monument upon it. He was a merchant, who fell 200 feet on horseback, but miraculously escaped death at the cost of an amputated leg, which he buried separately and commemorated by a stone in 1606. On his death in 1616 both monuments and the corpse were united. An ex-voto of a different kind was the iron dish originally fixed to the headstone of William Symons, 1753, at Woodditton (Cambs.), his epitaph quoted so often as "the man that loved a sop in the dripping pan". Unobtrusive and eminently economical are the two mill-stones used by Robert Fincher, millwright, at Hertford for memorials to himself and his wife, 1777. With less reticence J. C. Loudon, the landscape designer, commemorated his father at Pinner (Middx.), 1809, by a large pyramid with arched recess, above which a classical sarcophagus seems to have extruded itself from the interior, and which has given rise to an inevitable local legend. At Otley (Yorks.) is a model of the tunnel built at Bramhope in the construction of which the workmen commemorated lost their lives, and in the same county a model of an organ at Kildwick to John Laycock, a local organ-builder. At Hampstead cemetery is an even larger instrument in white marble 8 feet in height, and at Hammersmith a respected member of the Borough Council erected a chair for his monument, and at Mortlake

Sir Richard Burton suitably reposes beneath an Arab tent hallowed by a crucifix. Lawnswood, Leeds, is somewhat our equivalent of Père Lachaise in Paris, which has eccentricities enough to delight the collector of such trivia, while our own cemeteries have anchors, epicene angels, rusticated crosses and blasted trees enough and to spare. Even Barnack contains such a *tour de force* of mimicry: a fallen palm-tree cut from an immense monolith of Ketton stone.

Monuments in cast iron, made at the first centres of smelting in the Weald and Shropshire, have already been mentioned, and they continued to be turned out by local founders during the nineteenth century.[70] Examples are to be found, for instance, throughout the Midlands, products of the Etna forges, or at Leiston (Suffolk) where Messrs. Garrett first established their foundry in 1778. At Witham

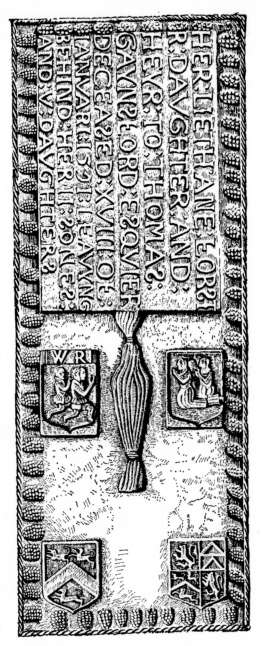

FIG. 40. *Cast-iron grave-slab (Crowhurst, Surrey), 1591.*

(Essex), a complete chest-tomb is panelled with quatrefoils; and the great iron-master John Wilkinson was commemorated by a large cast-iron obelisk near Lindale (Lancs.). The most ambitious use of the material, however, was in two churchyards in Kent. At Shoreham (put up a few years before Palmer settled there) stood until a few years ago the memorial to Ann Medhurst, 1820, over 12 feet in height, consisting of a large circular plaque rising from a base decorated with Gothic and classical ornament, supporting a tall Ionic pilaster topped with an urn—a considerable achievement in casting. At Chelsfield nearby the Rev. Robert Cottam's monument of 1828 formerly existed, a small Greek pavilion having a pediment crowned with a serpent-entwined urn, supported by pilasters and a railing, which deserve to be painted and kept up as an elegant bygone. Are sports contagious? For, in conclusion, Brasted houses a "ready-made" to Francis Crawshay of 1896; an obelisk of granite surrounded by a rail composed from actual ship's anchors and davits looped with chain.

FURTHER READING

H. Batsford and W. H. Godfrey, *English Mural Monuments and Tombstones*, 1916; W. Brindley and W. S. Weatherley, *Ancient Sepulchral Monuments*, 1887; H. M. Colvin, *Biographical Dictionary of English Architects, 1660–1840*, 1951; K. Esdaile, *English Monumental Sculpture since the Renaissance*, 1927, *Monuments in English Churches*, 1937, *English Church Monuments*, 1946; R. Gunnis, *Dictionary of British Sculptors 1660–1851*, 1953; D. Knoop and G. P. Jones, *The London Mason in the 17th Century*, 1935; Henriette s'Jacob, *Idealism and Realism, a study in sepulchral Symbolism*, Leiden, 1954; W. T. Vincent, *In Search of Gravestones Old and Curious*, 1896; L. Weaver, *Memorials and Monuments*, 1915; A. Whittick, *History of Cemetery Sculpture*, 1938, *War Memorials*, 1946.

Notes

1. The earliest burials belong to the Upper Palaeolithic period, with the remains often buried in red ochre, as in the ritual skull-burials at Ofnet, Bavaria, or our native example from the Paviland cave, Gower peninsula. Mesolithic burials in Brittany, with ritual hearths over the graves, include at Teviec rough stone mausolea, among the earliest identifiable commemorations. Later carved stelae found in the Bouches-de-Rhone district in France, the design of which shows similarities to cult objects distributed throughout France and Spain, may have had a commemorative function.

2. The popular names which have been given to megaliths relate them to fairies, wizards, giants or heroes, or to a diabolic origin. Superstitious belief in the spiritual power of stones is still evident in the respect accorded to such a palladium as the Stone of Scone in the Coronation chair, or that of Blarney Castle.

In 1851 a stone idol was being worshipped in the islet of Inniskea, off the Mayo coast; fifty years later Breton peasants were still anointing menhirs (a practice which Gaulish church edicts had forbidden centuries before). The Ram Feast at Holne on Dartmoor, where villagers on May Day slew and ate a ram on a menhir, persisted until the mid-nineteenth century. In 1859 a Manx farmer offered a heifer to prevent ill-luck after his opening of a tumulus, an act which was probably the last sacrifice in Europe. Oaths were sworn upon stones, they were used as oracles, to cure diseases or confer fertility. The older gateposts in Cleveland were made with a difference of shape that gave a male and female significance to each pair, and in other parts of Yorkshire certain menhirs are still called "The Old Wife".

3. Cp. headstones to John Reeve, 1772, Loddington (Leics.) inscribed "The grave is call'd a bed of rest"; and Dr John Gardner, 1807, St Leonard, Shoreditch, his "last and best Bedroom"; the couch form of classical tombs shown on the Etruscan symposium type; the early sarcophagus to Scipio Barbatus in the Vatican Museum; and Greek precedents such as the elegant couch-tomb in the Ceramicus cemetery, Athens.

4. At Barca (East Slovakia) remains of Aurignacian pit-dwellings with traces of supporting posts are probably the oldest discovered architectural remains. Similar post-rings which suggest temporary tomb-houses have been found both in early and mid-Bronze Age barrows, such as Bleasdale (Lancs.) "where a pair of cremation urns in a central pit were surrounded by a ring of massive oak posts, a ditch with an entrance causeway, and a large outer circle of posts linked with palisading" (J. and C. Hawkes, *Prehistoric Britain*, p. 82).

5. A local method of cist building in the early nineteenth century in Wexford was recorded in *Folk-lore Journal*, vol. 7, p. 39. Graves were cut 6 feet deep, with a 2 foot high wall at the head and foot, the space between being lined with sods. The body

was brought in a coffin and laid on this turf, planks were placed to rest on the walls and covered with a long sod, grass side down. The grave was then filled in, and the coffin left in the churchyard.

6. Burials followed the usual practice of lining the roads to town approaches. Most notable are Watling Street, where they are almost continuous from Blackheath to Canterbury; and between Kingsholm and Wotton (Glos.). Cemeteries occur outside towns, such as Baldock (Herts.), Ospringe (Kent), Hassocks (Sussex), while villas had their private burial grounds. Bodies were usually oriented, the head at the west. Charon's fee of the coin in the mouth was comparatively rare in Britain. Examples have been found at Baldock, and from tumuli at Rougham (Norfolk).

7. See B. Ashmole, *Catalogue of the Ancient Marbles of Ince Blundell Hall*, 1929, also F. Poulsen, *Greek and Roman Portraits in English Country Houses*, 1923. This collection, housed in a gallery which was built specially for its display, has become the property of a religious order and is in danger of being prized from its setting. Several rich dilettantes during the eighteenth century formed such collections to embellish their country houses. Their taste and pertinacity are exemplified by Lord Elgin, who thus preserved for public enjoyment the Parthenon sculpture, and Thomas Hope, who housed his great collection of antique marbles at The Deepdene, Dorking, and through a series of books on interior decoration, admirably illustrated by his protégé Henry Moses, helped to create the Regency Style.

8. For Roman barrows, see *Antiquity*, 1927, vol. 1, p. 431; and their relation to the masonry tomb in *Arch. Journal*, 1922, vol. 79, pp. 93–100.

9. One of the finest post-Reformation reproductions of a Roman altar with its bucrania and festoons is the Dormer monument in Wing (Bucks.) 1552. Such sacrificial heads were replaced in classical times by the cherub's head. The arrangement of such festoons, cherubs and letter-tablets on some Georgian headstones, particularly those from the Hornton workshops, is remarkably Roman in feeling and, when one sees stelae in natural surroundings, as in the Museum of Antiquities in Rome, it requires little imagination to transmute them into English headstones.

10. The anxious terror of these days is vividly shown in the monk's poem:

> Bitter is the wind tonight: it tosses the ocean's white hair;
> Tonight I fear not the fierce warriors of Norway:
> Coursing on the Irish Sea.

Finds in Norwegian tombs provide evidence of piracy. It is ironical that the indigenous art-style of the invaders, such as the monuments at Jellinge, was influenced by this plunder, and that English missionaries in the tenth century helped in the conversion of Norway and Sweden. In the twelfth century a group of fonts in Vastergotland show the influence of contemporary Anglo-Norman work, as do headstones and grave-slabs in the same district (H. Wadsjo, *Gravkonst*, 1930).

11. Cp. a fragment from Pontardawe (Glam.) showing a figure similar to the St Matthew symbol in The Book of Durrow, where the torso resembles a metal plaque with protruding head and feet; a motif not unknown in Irish metal-work, and probably originating from anthropomorphic boulders of Gaulish-Celtic type such as Fermanagh (F. Henry, *Irish Art*, pp. 5–7).

12. The dial on the cross is the earliest example extant. See A. R. Green, "Anglo-Saxon Sundials", *Soc. Antiq. Journal*, 1928, vol. 8, p. 489. The example at Kirkdale ends "Haward me wrohte and Brand priest", while at Great Edston (also in Yorkshire) the mason's name, Lothan, is included.

13. Such as the example found in St Cuthbert's coffin at Durham, and others from Wilton and Ixworth (D. M. Wilson, *The Anglo-Saxons*, 1960, illus. 40–42). Absolution crosses of lead, sometimes engraved with the appropriate formula, were buried both in English and French graves during the eleventh and twelfth centuries. The practice became obsolete *c.* 1300 (*Antiq. Journal*, 1940, vol. 20, p. 508).

14. The funeral procession on the base of the north cross at Ahenny shows an ecclesiastic carrying such a cross. Staff-roods ending in a spike, as if for planting in the ground, occur on slabs at Clonmacnoise, Trowbridge (Wilts.), in East Wales, etc.

15. It has been suggested that the cylindrical stone shafts from Reculver (Kent) and Wolverhampton (Staffs.) may have been church columns, of a type found on the Continent. Crosses in Wessex are rare, but there is a delightful shaft at Codford St Peter (Wilts.) where a man holds up a bough of vine in a characteristic Anglo-Saxon attitude.

16. The six coffin shapes cut in the rock at Heysham (Lancs.), five of which have loculi at the head of each recess, are unusual, both for their shapes, and also this latter feature. Each is rebated to receive a coffin-lid. Burial scenes are not infrequent in contemporary MSS. which show the shrouded figure being deposited both in graves and stone coffins, usually with a coffin-slab or coped stone. Cp. Matthew Paris, *Chronica Minora*, MS. Royal 14, cvii, ff. 112, 198, 213. For the most part, such drawings are purely conventional and afford no additions to our knowledge, except the frequent use of polychrome; also shown on French monuments such as those in the Gagnieres collection, Bodleian Library.

17. *Antiq. Journal*, vol. II, 1931, pp. 133–35. For list of known examples in Ringerike style, see *Proc. Soc. Antiq.*, xxvi, pp. 60–72.

18. S. O. Addy, "House Burial", *Derby. Arch. Soc. Journal*, vols. 41, 42, 62, gives a good account of the historical development of the "soul-house" in relation to primitive hut-urns and later buildings such as the unique Teapot Hall at Scrivelsby (Lincs.), inhabited up to twenty years ago.

19.   Two wooden coffins of seventh century archbishops were discovered at Canterbury by St John Hope and reconstructed by him (*Arch. Cantiana*, vol. 32, p. 22). One had a gabled roof of steep pitch; the other, a hipped roof of convex section and flat ridge set upon a base. St Cuthbert's oak coffin at Durham, *c.* 700, had a flat top and was decorated with incised figures similar in style to those of the Lindisfarne Gospels. Its original contents included the Saint's pectoral cross, ritual comb, portable altar and tiny chalice. Compare the latter with examples at Hexham and the "Trewiddle Hoard" (which also included the unique silver scourge).

20.   E. Kurth, "The Iconography of the Wirksworth slab", *Burlington Mag.*, 1945, vol. lxxxvi.

21.   Used by Professor T. S. R. Boase in his *English Art* 1100–1216, 1953. "They are the images of an age hardened to unalleviated pain, to the wearing pangs of undiagnosed disease and its no less agonising attempted cures, to wounds and blows ..." p. 89.

22.   Reported in *Proc. Soc. Antiq. London*, 2nd series, vol. 26. For Strata Florida see S. W. Williams, *The Cistercian Abbey of Strata Florida*, 1889, p. 204.

23.   C. Fox, "Anglo-Saxon Monumental Sculpture in the Cambridge District", *Camb. Antiq. Soc.*, 1922, vol. LXXI, pp. 15–48.

24.   Another local group at Oxted, Tandridge, Titsey (Surrey) and Brasted (Kent) bear plain, spindly crosses devoid of decoration.

25.   *Marigold* is the technical name given to those multi-lobed patterns which can be easily inscribed within a circle by using the compasses set at a constant radius. They are the inveterate doodlings of this instrument, and ubiquitous as graffiti. As decorative devices they were common in Visigothic art, and on Merovingian sarcophagi, and occur on post-Roman Christian stelae at Whithorn and on a discoid at Maughold (I. of Man). Anglo-Norman masons similarly constructed their three or four-lobed knot patterns and headstone crosses.

26.   In the fine Norman chapel of Steetley (Derbys.) a slab has two circular crosses and a representation of an altar-slab supported by three pillars on which rests a chalice and paten, with hand in act of benediction. Other slabs of twelfth and thirteenth century date showing the rite in this cryptic manner occur at Barnard Castle; Newcastle St Andrew (Durham); Sproatley (Yorks.); Kirby-in-Ashfield (Notts.).

27.   Nash-Williams, in his *Early Christian Monuments of Wales*, 1950, suggested that Merovingian influence probably affected Wales in late eleventh–twelfth centuries, and detected it on monuments at Newcastle Bridge End, the cart-wheel crosses peculiar to south Glamorgan, and such cross-slabs as Meifod (Montgoms.) which he compared

with work from Poitiers in eighth century. Several features on these foreign slabs can be compared with native work, e.g. the interlinked chain-pattern (Llantwit, Glam.), the transverse bars (the Cambridge group) and above all the rosette device mentioned here, used on a fine group of thirteenth century slabs in Herefordshire.

28. This churchyard contains two separate plots, each with three monuments, of which five have head and footstones linked by slabs. Two of these are coped and bear crosses, the remainder have the half-effigies described, including a single diminutive example without head or footstones. The latter, except for two rectilinear footstones are all discoids, their edges decorated with herringbone pattern. The monument to Griffith Grant, 1591, in the same yard was evidently imitated from these medieval stones (*Arch. Cambrensis*, vol. 3, p. 318).

29. Expressed in that ubiquitous epitaph and its English variations: *sum quod eris, fueram quod es.* The macabre effigy, as well as the weepers carved upon the tomb-base, were derived from French sources, where in the early fifteenth century there was an obsession with the themes of the Quick and the Dead, and the Dance of Death. This emphasis on fleshly corruption as opposed to the salvation of the soul is found mainly on monuments to ecclesiastics, of which the most gruesome are Abbot Wakeman's at Tewkesbury, where worms, lizards, frogs, mice and snails batten on the corpse; and the Rev. Ralph Hamsterley's brass, c. 1515, at Oddington (Oxon.) with its writhing worms.

Such emphasis on mortality survived the Reformation, finding expression in the work of the metaphysical poets and carvers of the seventeenth century, and in later graveyard poetry. Colt's monument at Bishops Hatfield (Herts.) gave it noble and original form, and it remained dominant in graveyard imagery until the Gothic Revival.

30. About a hundred wooden effigies of the medieval period have survived, the majority belonging to the period 1280–1360. During the sixteenth century, owing to the best alabaster working out, there was a revival of their use. Towards the end of the fourteenth century it became customary to bear a dressed-up effigy in the funeral procession of important people, and to place it temporarily in the church beneath the hearse. Such wooden puppets, with portrait-masks of wax or plaster, are best seen at Westminster Abbey and have been restored within recent years.

31. Ancaster church porch contains some unfinished effigies, showing that in some instances at least (as at Corfe and Chellaston) work was prepared at the quarry site.

32. The custom of placing figures representing mourning relatives on the tomb-base, first used on the tomb of St Louis at St Denis, 1260, appeared in England on the monument to Lady FitzAllan, Chichester, 1275. It was popularized by the alabasterers from the end of the fourteenth century, who introduced the variant of angels holding shields. Later Burgundian influence (from the tomb of Philippe le Hardi, Champmol,

c. 1412) introduced the hooded type of mourner, seen on the Beauchamp tomb at Warwick. The theme survived the Reformation, when defunct members of a family were signified by a skull held in the hands. It is found on Cotswold tombs of the seventeenth and eighteenth centuries, such as Hardwicke (Glos.), to Thomas Smith, 1675, where figures hold mourning scarves and handkerchief to eyes, like the disconsolate widow of the late Georgian period.

33. One of the principal quarry-owners, during the early fifteenth century at Chellaston, was Thomas Prentys, whose workshop turned out ornate tombs for Midland and Southern patrons at comparatively low prices. Richard Parker of Burton made the tomb of the first Earl of Rutland, Bottesford (Leics.) for £20 16s. 8d.; Richard and Gabriel Roiley had a prolific Midland output; while the last products of the alabaster men were coarsely incised effigial slabs, common in Derbyshire and Staffordshire.

34. Incised effigies were also cut during the Middle Ages, such as the military examples at St Bride's (Glam.); Avenbury (Herefs.) and Bitton (Glos.). Early fourteenth century examples include those to the master-mason William de Wermington, Crowland; the foreign merchant Wisseins de Smalenburgh, Boston, 1312; and Wyberton, 1325 (all in Lincs.). A slab at North Stoneham (Hants.) 1491, with the Imperial Eagle and Evangelist symbols, marks the common burial-place of a gild of Slavonian merchant-sailors.

35. At the beginning of fifteenth century the most expensive brass and its matrix cost from £10 to £15, and the cheaper sorts £5. After 1460, as both size and craftsmanship declined, prices ranged from £1 to £3, thus opening up a wider market. Even before this, there is evidence of shop methods, standard products being produced prior to commission and stock-piled (Stone, *Sculpture in Britain*, p. 179).

36. Both heart and viscera were sometimes separately buried and commemorated, especially when the deceased died abroad. The remains of Nicholas Longspee, Bishop of Salisbury, d. 1237, were interred at three places in Wiltshire; viscera at Ramsbury, body at Salisbury, heart at Laycock-on-Avon. For heart burials of various dates refer *Dorset Nat. Hist. Notes*, vol. 46, pp. 38; *Proc. Yorks. Arch. Soc.*, 1936, vol. 2, no. 4, p. 9; C. Bradford, *Heart Burial*, 1933.

37. Brass-making increased *temp.* Elizabeth, when the material was first made in England. Small inscribed mural tablets continued to be made up to the eighteenth century, and the engraver's art was also used on coffin plates [see Rhuddlan (Flints.); Dolgelley (Merions.); Huyton (Lancs.)]. In Cotswold and North Yorkshire in the Georgian period it became customary to fix inscribed plates on plain external stoneledgers. See Stroud where the local masons Cook, Franklin, Freebury and Hamlett signed many examples. Cast-iron grave-slabs were produced by Wealden iron-founders; the earliest known is at Burwash, fourteenth century, sixteenth century ones are

at Rotherfield and East Grinstead while Wadhurst contains thirty, 1614–1790 (all in Sussex). Anne Forster, 1591, at Crowhurst (Surrey) shows a shroud, kneeling relatives and shields within a vine-border (Fig. 40, p. 139).

38. Most common are pastoral staves, chalices and patens to ecclesiastics; various weapons for knights and men-at-arms; shears for wool-staplers; bugle and bow for forest ranger; horseshoes and tongs, blacksmith; square and compasses, mason, etc. Unusual examples include bellows at Papplewick (Notts.); bagpipes, Ford (Northumb.); bell and crucible, St Dionys (Yorks.); knife and dredging-box to William Cannyngis' cook at Bristol; cross-bow, Wentworth (Yorks.); fourteenth century ships in Doncaster crypt and St Hilda's, Hartlepool.

39. Cp. the U-shape devices on Anglo-Norman iron work on doors at Woking (Surrey); Staplehurst (Kent); and the thirteenth century masterpieces by Thomas de Leighton (maker of Queen Eleanor's tomb-grille at Westminster Abbey) on the church doors at Turvey, Eaton Bray and his birthplace, Leighton Buzzard (Beds.).

40. Time-lags in design are notable on sepulchral monuments. Cp. slabs from Valle Crucis and Gresford (Denbighs.); the first, thirteenth century, shows interlacing ending in dragons; the latter, fourteenth century, has a background of oak leaves disgorged by a mask, combined with palmettes of Anglo-Norman type. See J. Evans, *Nature and Design*, 1933, for the French originals of the English naturalistic style.

41. Cp. contemporary burial-wishes in wills. John Cook, 1502, Bury St Edmunds: wooden crosses at head and foot carved with arms and prayer for his soul; John Skarpe, 1532, husbandman of Felsham (Suffolk): leaving 8s. for stone crosses; John Greenhill, 1536, Romney: pair of stone crosses for 10s. and body-slab for 33s. 4d. carved with arms, and prayers.

42. Astbury (Cheshire) has a fourteenth century canopied tomb in its churchyard. Effigies were also placed in gabled recesses of the church wall, such as Great Brington (Northants.), 1275.

43. Burial in shrouds of fabric or leather was the usual practice, as coffins of stone, being monolithic, were expensive. These usually taper and have a recess for the head. Probably the finest is to Prince Llewelyn, 1240, at Llanrwst (Denbighs.) with quatre-foiled sides. Lead coffins were occasionally used in the medieval period (Kings Langley, Herts.), but more often in post-Reformation family vaults, where they were made like mummies, with anthropomorphic features. Cp. vaults to the Cliffords at Skipton (Yorks.); Barnadistons at Kedington (Suffolk); the Harveys at Hempstead (Essex), where there are fifty-one coffins, 1655–1830; Lucas at St Giles, Colchester. Coffin-plates and tablets were also plumber's work; cp. Burford (Salop) 1516; Windsor (Berks.) and West Grinstead (Sussex), eighteenth century.

44. At Sleaford (Lincs.) a fine half-effigy has three apertures, head and feet being in circles, folded hands in a vescica. Stone monuments at Bredon and Halesowen (Worcs.) show obvious similarities with contemporary bracket-brasses, as both include crucifixes, combined in the first with busts under canopies, and in the latter with a kneeling figure. Apart from the sixteenth century stone at Llantihangel Abercowin previously mentioned, late examples of the half-effigy occur at Elford (Staffs.) *c.* 1450, and three illusionist monuments cut horizontally between wall-arcading in Lichfield Cathedral. The unusual use of the demi-figure in effigial sculpture can be seen in those to Aymer de Valence, *c.* 1261, Winchester Cathedral, and Sir Godfrey Foljambe and his wife, 1377, at Bakewell.

45. Among contemporary carvers who have produced monuments of rare distinction, one should mention in addition to Eric Gill, Joseph Cribb, Richard Garbe, Alan Howes, Eric Kennington, David Kindersley, Gilbert Ledward, Herbert Palliser, John Skelton and Freda Skinner.

46. Mrs Esdaile was of the opinion that the footstone anticipated the headstone and instanced the ballad in Hamlet, IV, v, in illustration: "at his head a grass-green turf At his heels a stone".

47. The churchyard scenes carved on the base of a number of headstones found in the Sussex churchyards of Horsham, Hurstpierpoint, Shipley, Steyning and Thakeham, etc. (probably the work of Gregory Page of Horsham), include both a wooden grave-board with elaborately moulded posts, as well as a Sussex type with connecting stone rail. The account-books of May and Parsons, Lewes, show that this firm were making such latter memorials, *c.* 1800, at a cost of just over £5, the term "rail" being used for the connecting slab. The posts were given great variety of shape and were usually linked to the board by brackets. Horley (Surrey), and Cowden (Kent) to Flora Turner, 1884, contain examples with large wooden scrolls joining the posts. Surrey Archaeological Society is compiling a list of the surviving grave-boards in the county. The body stones of the Home Counties are often decorated with ribbing or bands which may be intended to represent either the shrouded corpse or the brambled and withied grave-mound. Earlier examples are rounded in shape like a "fish-tail" coffin; later they have angled shoulders. For the making of such coffins see G. Hogg, *Country Crafts and Craftsmen*, 1959.

48. In North Riding and Durham backs of stones are sometimes panelled like wooden door frames or, as at Youlgreave (Derbys.), claw-tooled into simple patterns resembling pargetting. Headstones at Preston Capes, Abthorp (Northants.) and Blockley (Worcs.) 1715, have hood-moulds supported by cable-twist colums.

49. For a good account of these Kent–Sussex stones see: Innes Hart, "Rude Forefathers", *Architectural Review*, November 1939, pp. 185–8.

50. Discoids or markers occur at Lower Swell (Glos.) 1628, as head and footstones; Langham 1650; Upper Hambleton (Rutland) 1656; Chartham (Kent) 1663; Wansford 1672; Kingscliffe (Northants.) 1779; Lingfield (Surrey) 1674; Over Silton, seventeenth century; Upleatham (Yorks.) 1680; Woodplumpton (Lancs.) 1689; Fyfield (Essex) 1690; Buckden (Hunts.) 1691; Knaresborough (Yorks.) 1706; Durham Cathedral, 1697, 1706; Bishopton (Durham) 1711; East Harlesey (Yorks.) 1720; Glentham (Lincs.) 1774.

51. Christopher Staveley's finest slate engravings commemorate James Rubins, 1765, Grantham; Robert Wing, 1770, Denton (Lincs.) (Plate 4). See Hibbins's work at Ketton; also at Great Casterton (Rutland) rococo freestones of 1791 and 1803 signed by John Holmes and John Haines of Stamford, who repaired the tower and spire of St Mary, Stamford, to Staveley's designs c. 1787 for £293 (Colvin). Cleeve Prior and Pershore (Worcs.) have finely engraved architectural frames to Michael Campden and Andrew Blizard, 1710–66, by their fellow masons, the Laughtons of Cleeve. Robert Oliver's slate to James Hawke, 1827, Egloshayle (Cornwall) in his *chef-d'oeuvre* (Plate 11.)

52. A slate headstone, Melton Mowbray (Leics.) to the Ferman family, 1749, by Stephen Staveley has four tondi, only one of which has been filled. A single stone with twin tablets to husband and wife saved the cost of separate commemoration; the second inscription was added when appropriate and signed by the mason responsible. Many Midland slates, therefore, bear double signatures. William and James Hill of Great Easton (Leics.) framed their double or triple letter tablets with bold rhythmic stems sprouting marigolds and tulips, as at Great Easton, Caldecott, Hallaton and Medbourne, which includes two lovely tablets inside the church to the Goodman family 1728, and 1767, the former signed by William, presumably the father (Plate 2).

53. Towards the end of the Georgian period, slabs were often large; as in Rutland at Liddington, 70 by 36 inches; Manton, 65 by 39 inches, 1848; or at Childs Wickham (Glos.), 84 by 48 inches. Slates were often 7 to 8 feet in length with 3 feet allowed for fixing in the ground. Cookham (Berks.), has six head and footstones, 1778–1807, 81 by 36 inches, with curious silhouettes reminiscent of chairbacks. At Tingewicke (Bucks.) an unusually broad stone, 5 feet wide, 1694, to the four children of John Russe, is decorated with five arches supported by caryatids. At Coningsby (Lincs.) 1800, the letter-tablet is a large urn with a skeleton arm snuffing its Quarles-derived candle. Saffron Walden, 1791, has an elevation of a chimney-piece for its letter-tablet.

54. Unorthodox treatments of the letter-tablet include the arbitrary division of tondi into two segments, a feature of work by Samuel Andrews of Wisbech, and other Fenland masons; the curious scooped-out irregular backgrounds blending into linear arabesques, and ogival-framed panels on headstones in the vicinity of Olney (Bucks.), for some of which, James Andrews, Cooper's one-time Michelangelo, may

have been responsible. The stone to Charles Morgan, 1791, at Olney, and to Mary, the wife of Charles Drew the mason, at St Paul's, Bedford, are unusual, at this date, for their free pictorial treatment of figure work.

55. Other pattern-books include: George Smith, *A Collection of Ornamental Designs after the Manner of the Antique for the Use of Architects, Ornamental Painters, Statuaries, etc.*, 1812; George Maliphant, *Designs for Sepulchral Monuments, c.* 1828; Stephen Geary (designer of Highgate and other cemeteries), *Designs for Tombs and Cenotaphs*, 1840; William Thomas of Leamington Spa, *Designs for Monuments and Chimney Pieces*, 1843; Edward Trendall, *A New Work on Monuments, Cenotaphs, Tombs and Tablets, etc.*, 1850, 1858; J. B. Robinson, *Gravestones, Tombs, Monuments, Crockets, Alphabets, etc.*; William Borrowdale of Sunderland, *Monuments, or Designs for Tombs, Wall Monuments, etc.*, 1867, *Original Designs of Headstones and Crosses* (includes rustic crosses and kerbs), 1881.

56. Various local foundries also turned out cheap cast-iron markers or plaques fitted with prongs so that they could be thrust into the ground. J. Jacques of 4 Long Lane, London, whose Architectural Composition Ornament, Projecting Letter and Chimney Piece Manufactory was in existence for over forty years in Holborn and Long Lane, claimed to be the inventor of those three-dimensional or Stereographic letters for fascias that are today a commonplace. About 1819 he issued *Headstones, Tablets and Monuments* as a puff for his pre-cast reliefs in lacquered iron which could be fixed as ornaments to monuments. These rusty paterae, angels' heads or mourners can still be found in churchyards, mainly in the London area, although some are as far afield as Chatteris (Cambs.) and Banbury (Oxon.).

57. Up to the seventeenth century the Heralds were responsible for checking the designs, inscriptions and heraldry of tombs; and the College of Arms was still influential in the early years of the eighteenth century. Afterwards, despite the work of Herald Painters, such as Randle Holmes (who published his *Academy of Armorie*, 1688), the quality of design deteriorated, as in hatchment limning [although Compton Wynyates, (Warws.) has a fine series].

Local masons were often painters and responsible for the lettered boards of local charities and Creed and Commandment tables, that had been statutory church equipment since Elizabeth I's enactment. James Sparrow, for instance, painted the sentences and a charity board at Radcliff-on-Trent 1757 and 1760. John Burton of Somerby, who signed a fine heraldic ledger to Ann Wigley at Scraptoft 1786, was also a painter and seems to have been a local man specializing in heraldic work, of which there are fine examples on Swithland slate headstones. (See N. E. Toke, "Heraldic Ledgers in Kentish Churches", *Arch. Cantiana*, vol. 41, p. 187, etc., listing 160 examples in 50 churches.)

58. A local coped stone presumably of eighteenth century date served as inspiration for Philip Webb's delightful memorial to William Morris in Kelmscott churchyard (Oxon.); it is shaped like a curved roof with eaves, supported on two transverse slabs.

59. Up to the end of the eighteenth century the poor were usually buried only in a shroud tied head and foot, carried to the grave on a parish bier, and interred without a coffin. A higher rate was charged for coffin-burial; cp. these differences:

Birchington (Kent) 1638: 8d.–6d.   Caistor (Lincs.) 1717: 1s.–4d.

At Wootton (Oxon.) 1758, a coffin cost 8s. See William Andrews, *Burial without Coffins*. In Devonshire about a century ago, the use of a ridged coffin was general among poorer burials (*N. and Q.*, vol. 8, p. 104). The following items of parish burial furniture are still extant in the following churches: parish coffin, Easingwold (Yorks.); coffin-trestles, seventeenth century, Chenies (Bucks.); coffin-stools, Beddingham (Sussex); parish biers, Broughton, 1653, Hardmead, Ludgershall (Bucks.), Great Samford (Essex), Bledington (Glos.), Weston-on-Trent (Derbys). 1653. Pinchbeck (Lincs.), Walpole St Peter (Norfolk) and Wingfield (Suffolk) each possess a "hudd", or tall sentry-box to protect the parson from bad weather when reading the Burial Service.

60. Throwleigh and South Tawton (Devon) contain such ponderous examples. The base was sometimes insignificant, the thick cover-slab having complex mouldings, e.g. Chop Gate 1727; Great Ayton 1750 (Yorks.).

61. The *herse* was usually a gabled framework garnished with tapers, over which was spread the pall, for the temporary housing of the corpse or funeral effigy of important individuals during the funeral service. It was sometimes made of metal and fixed over the tomb as a permanent feature: West Tanfield (Yorks.); Spratton (North-ants.) 1371. Weever described it as "a temporary monument set over a grave", but a few years later it had fallen into disuse, for *c*. 1670 the word had taken on its modern meaning of a carriage for the corpse's conveyance. Like the Cotswold bale-tombs the curious hooped covers or barrel-vaults to chest-tombs of seventeenth century at Dyserth (Flints.) and Beaumaris (Anglesey), may be derivatives of the older herse. Childwall (Lancs.) has a "hearse-house", *c*. 1810, in its churchyard.

62. Stuart and Revett's first volume of *The Antiquities of Athens*, 1762, was the founda-tion of the filigree style popularized by the Adam brothers, but it was not until the turn of the century that neo-Hellenism made itself felt. The contrast between the Adam and Greek styles is clearly shown on two adjacent tombs in Fairford Congre-gational Chapel yard: one with light arabesques and pilasters, the other having stocky Doric columns, heavy pediment and cornice, 1849.

At Yarm (Yorks.) there is an unusually early use of Doric columns on a tomb of 1784, as well as a Greek Revival sarcophagus as late as 1887. Doric columns were first used by Bonomi on Great Packington church (Warws.) 1790.

63. The brothers John and Joseph Bryan, as well as general masonry, made a good many fine interior tablets (see Gunnis). One of John's daughters married into the local Painswick family of Loveday, who have a characteristic tomb in the churchyard. James Castle, mason, is also buried here.

64. Cp. Thomas Hood's *Tom Tatter's Birthday Ode*:

Here's young Squire Ringwood's health, and may he live as long as Jason,
Before Atropos cuts his thread, and Dick Tablet, the bungling mason,
Chips him a marble tea-table, and a marble tea-urn a-top of it.

65. See Woodford (Essex), a large column of jasper with Corinthian capital, which cost £1,500, set up by Sir Robert Taylor to his benefactors, the Godfrey family. The broken column was probably introduced *c.* 1815 by the statuary J. B. Papworth, and much used by Flaxman. An early churchyard example occurs at Strensham (Worcs.) 1837 by the local mason, Bell. It came into general cemetery use later.

66. This monument was partially restored recently, through help given by the Georgian Society, by Mr A. S. Ireson of Stamford, members of whose family have been associated with the craft of stone for generations, and who is himself also Secretary to The Men of the Stones, a local body which has done much useful work by precept and propaganda in helping to protect fine buildings and monuments in the Midlands from neglect or destruction. At Barrow-on-Soar (Leics.) the lower part of this tomb has been duplicated, minus the pyramid, on a tomb of 1796. In 1961 a fund was inaugurated for the repair of chest-tombs in Gloucestershire, and a group of similar monuments in Corsham (Wilts.) were restored through the help of the Pilgrim Trust.

67. Mr Fortrey's two Gothic churches of Galby, 1741, and Kings Norton, 1775, were built by architects named Wing, father and son, the latter also designing East Carlton in 1788 (see Colvin and Gunnis, under Wing).

I believe this family, members of which worked at Leicester and later Bedford, originated from Hallaton (Leics.). John Wing of Hallaton was appointed July 24, 1775, to repair Kettleby Bridge (Melton Mowbray Town Records) and three years later he was described as a stone-cutter of that village on his son Vincent's indentures. Elizabeth, wife of John Wing, d. October 25, 1778, aged 55, is buried in the churchyard, where headstones of 1813 and 1828 are signed "Wing", as well as a cross of 1863, "Hinton, late Wing, Bedford". In 1772 the churchwardens of St Martin, Leicester, agreed that "Mr Wing should repair the four middle windows on the spire for £11" (Churchwardens' accounts). Slate headstones signed by John Wing of Leicester have been recorded there at St Margaret and St Martin; Birstall (Leics.); Maidwell (Northants.) 1782 to 1792.

68. Knill left a bequest for its perpetual upkeep and also provided that every five years ten little girls should dance and sing the Hundredth Psalm before it; for this they, along with local fishermen and net-makers, received money gifts. The custom is still in force, with the added dignity of Mayor and Town officials, and winds up with a civic dinner.

At Farley Mount, near Hursley (Hants.) a pyramid commemorates the fantastic leap of Paulet St John's horse in 1733, which earned him the name of "Beware Chalk Pit".

69. Mausolea and tomb-houses occur also at Lowther (Westmd.); Warham, Bracon Ash, Heydon (Norfolk); Turvey (Beds.); Wargrave (Berks.); Hursley (Hants.); Blandford (Dorset.); Littleton (Middx.); Ockham (Surrey). In the same county, at Weybridge, within a small domed and castellated chapel attached to the Roman Catholic church of St Charles Borromeo, reposes Louis Philippe, "citizen king" of France and other royal personages. Although no mausoleum, the magnificently sited Doric temple known as the Penshaw Monument, deserves mention—now overlooking the coalfields and shipyards of north-east Durham, and put up by county folk to the first Earl of Durham, c. 1840.

70. West Country work includes the fine series of armorial ledgers at Burrington (Herefs.), 1619-1754; also memorials at Bridgenorth, Broseley and Madeley (Salop). At Soham (Cambs.) cast iron slabs are signed "G. Lever"; at Amersham (Bucks.) an iron memorial in the churchyard, 1834, and a tablet on the Baptist Church are signed "H. How Chesham"; and another slab in the churchyard 1842 by "Jones, Manufacturer, Brick Lane, St. Luke, London".

3

Design of Monuments

SYMBOLISM; SOURCES OF IMAGERY; ORNAMENT; LETTERING; INSCRIPTIONS AND EPITAPHS

BEFORE analysing the decoration of memorials in historical sequence under the separate headings listed above, some general comment on design in its wider sense is necessary, both in respect to individual monuments and their setting.

A broad distinction can be made between the design of churchyard and cemetery memorials which is intimately connected with the changes in working practice which took place during the nineteenth century. The arrangement of the first has been based on current architectural proportion and is essentially a formal and symmetrical decoration of surfaces; the latter, being three-dimensional, belongs technically to the category of sculpture.

The separation from this architectural canon, which for centuries established a harmony between the various crafts, has gradually widened ever since. During the present century the trend in architecture has been largely functional and anti-ornament, and the Georgian revival in monumental design is perhaps symptomatic of a nostalgia for this lost tradition. On the other hand, insular characteristics of restraint and formality have inhibited the development of that type of design depending upon balance rather than symmetry, and consequently modern memorials show no inspiration from those abstract conventions that have revolutionized art-form since World War I. Reckoning also with the present reaction against large and ostentatious memorials, and restrictions imposed not only on size, but even upon text and imagery, it is evident that a deliberate reassessment of monumental design is overdue. Yet the present mood within the craft is one of apathy and confusion, with a conflict of self-interest rather than co-operation. The organization of a conference (on the lines of that promoted by the British Institute of Industrial Art and the National Association of Monumental Master Masons in 1925) between representatives of the monumental craft, diocesan architects, and cemetery authorities might well help towards a solution of this problem.

The need for design is implicit not only in the individual shape and pattern of memorials but also in their collective arrangement within the boundaries of the garth or cemetery. In the past the church acted as a focus around which monuments were placed with little more arrangement than into rows following a north–south alignment, but with the establishment of large tracts of land for cemeteries their potential increase in number made necessary some degree of order in relation to site. Here was an opportunity to devise an ideal necropolis, in which monuments could be disposed according to the principles of landscape gardening, and which would have been in effect a translation of the planned park of the great country estate to a truly democratic use. Admittedly much credit is due to early cemetery designers such as Stephen Geary, whose lay-out included entrance lodges, chapels and catacombs linked by walks and avenues, but it would have required the far-sighted genius of a Repton to have risen fully to the occasion.

It has been left to America in our own day to devise such a form of memorial park in which individual monuments freely designed are grouped within a formalized landscape setting. Such a conception, it may be argued, is possible in a country of broader acres than our own in which building congestion and high land-values put a premium on ground space. The problem, however, is by no means academic, for we shall soon be placed in the same dilemma as a century ago, when it became necessary to close metropolitan burial grounds, and establish cemeteries in what were then considered the outskirts of building expansion.

Therefore, unless gravestone commemoration ceases as a custom within the next generation or two, the larger cities will find it necessary either to make wholesale clearances of existing cemeteries in order to provide room for new burials, or else establish grounds well outside the city-limits. The former remedy seems too drastic to be put into full effect because of the inevitable tenderness of public feeling, so the latter must be considered, for only by immediate preparation and long-sighted planning can the mistakes of the past be avoided.

To conclude this foreword, an extract is given from recently published suggestions as to the ideal constitution of a memorial park. The writer, after suggesting that in suitable cases, the large country house and its grounds, rather than go under the hammer, might be adapted for such purposes, goes on to describe its arrangement:

The house would be used not only for the administrative offices of the Park, but as a county or borough museum and gallery—for local archives —and refreshment rooms—thus uniting a number of functions. In the offices dealing with the cemetery proper, would be a comprehensive plan of the grounds, with a card index of burials, which the public would be free to consult; an enquiry office where advice on all questions pertinent to burial, cremation, and the choice of a monument, would be available; and a hall where masons could exhibit specimens of their handiwork. In contrast to this exhibition of contemporary memorial carving, a small museum would house photographs and actual specimens of traditional gravestones, together with genealogical information concerning the men who made them.

Nearby would be a sculptor's yard, which the public could visit to see the various processes in the making of a monument. The mason-in-charge would be elected by competition, and hold his post for a limited period. Working under this master would be a number of apprentices and trainees holding special grants to enable them not only to learn their craft, but to study memorial art in its contemporary and historical aspects. It is to be expected that under such conditions of study, experiments in design might well lead to the establishment of a local style in monumental carving.

In control would be the Master of the Park, his duties involving a rather special talent; being a liaison officer between Diocesan and County Architects, religious bodies, individual masons and their trade organizations— and needing to possess an extensive knowledge of horticulture and the historical and practical aspects of masonry.

The majority of the ground staff would be housed on the estate, among them a number of old-age pensioners able to carry out light duties.

The layout of the Park, designed through the collaboration of gardeners and architects, would include both natural and formal elements, a blend of nature and art, which would afford continual surprises to the visitor because of its variety of prospects. The particular plots and positions for monuments would be pre-determined, some being set out in a regular formation, others disguised or hidden by screens of trees, banks, and valleys, and each self-contained—so that cremations, white marble monuments and those of native stone assumed definite patterns of colour and shape. There need be few restrictions upon monuments other than those of good design and workmanship, for their type, size, and character would be specified in general terms on the initial plan.

Architectural devices such as porticoes, terraces, façades, gateways, etc., used as settings or surrounds to the individual plots, could also have tablets or monuments built into their fabric. There would be ample opportunities for memorials of a different character—gifts of portions of the fabric, individual trees, groves or parterres; and for those unable to afford a memorial-stone, the record of their names on some pavilion or arbour about the burial-place. In contrast, the wealthy could erect mausolea upon commanding positions of the terrain, where they would give scale and punctuation to its perspectives.[1]

The utilitarian reaction to such proposals is easily forecast: houses for the living should have priority before houses for the dead. On the other hand, the issue seems plain. If commemoration *is* to persist, then the standard of design in sepulchral monuments should be high enough to accord them lasting virtue, not merely as ephemeral private mementoes, but as works of art which will become an essential part of the heritage of the community, and, equally as important, their setting should be so devised as to provide free access for the public enjoyment of these amenities.

SYMBOLISM

ROMANO–BRITISH

Standing figures or groups are usually set within a semi-circular headed niche, which gives them the illusion of architectural statuary. This may have a purely decorative border, such as the wavy-leaf pattern on the stela to Marcus Favonius, the Colchester centurion, shown holding his wand of office, or a simple cable-mould accompanied by abstract doodles, as on that to Pervica's daughter in Blackgate Museum, Newcastle. More elaborately, it is flanked by pilasters and a low pediment in the form of an exedra; the finest example of this sort commemorates Regina, the British wife of Barates from Palmyra, shown seated in a large wicker-chair with a jewel-box and basket of worsteds at her feet (South Shields Museum). At Tullie House, Carlisle, and Lincoln cloisters, similar façades frame a woman holding a large circular fan, with

FIG. 41. *Headstone to Regina of Palmyra (South Shields Museum), 49½ in. high, 28¼ in. wide.*

a child stroking the dove in her lap and a young man holding a hare in his arms. Other figure subjects include an armourer with his hammer and tongs, and Flavia Augustina with her husband and two infants at York; the boy with his toy whip from Old Penrith ; and the piper and figure holding a bunch of poppies, both at Carlisle.

Simpler slabs have a quasi-architectural framework, usually with a decorated gable, such as that on the stela to Titus Valens (British Museum), which is enriched with a trident and dolphins, symbolic of his overseas service. Simple paterae or sexfoils are also common ornaments, as well as the nondescript ragwort foliage that often does duty to fill a spandril, as on Marcus Petronius' memorial in the same collection.

Two stock allegorical themes of Roman funerary art are both represented: the Conquering Hero and the Sepulchral Banquet.[2] The first, invariably used for the memorials of cavalrymen, showing the rider with horse rearing over the body of a barbarian crouched upon his shield, is of doubtful origin but can be compared with the Dexileos stela of the fourth century B.C. in the Ceramicus cemetery at Athens. Our best native examples commemorate Flavinus, the standard bearer, at Hexham Priory, and Longinus at Colchester. The second scheme shows the deceased reclining on a couch as at a banquet or symposium, attended by members of his family (Julia Velva, at York); or being proffered refreshment by an attendant (Victor's well-carved memorial at South Shields shows the servant as an homunculus and himself holding a cup and bunch of leaves). Tombstones are sometimes crowned with a triple finial consisting of a central sphinx or harpy flanked by

FIG. 42. *Roman headstone (Colchester Museum); the "Conquering Hero" type, 72 in. high, 30½ in. wide.*

FIG. 43. *Roman headstone (South Shields Museum); the "Sepulchral Banquet" type, 39 in. high, 23 in. wide.*

lions devouring human heads or serpents, which like a Medusa head from a broken stela at Chester probably represented funerary divinities or the disembodied shade. Such devices, along with that emblem of fertility, the fir-cone,[3] have been credited with Mithraic significance, although they occur on tombstones to women as well as men. Scallop shells—a common decoration on leaden coffins where they are accompanied with sticks of bead-and-reel moulding—had also a symbolic connotation and, along with funeral garlands and festoons and the groovings or strigillations found on sarcophagi, later became part of the post-Reformation repertoire of classical ornament.[4]

ANGLO-SAXON AND DANISH

The monumental carving of this period both in form and detail is compounded from several art-styles. In early Northumbria the menhir-form of the high crosses derives from Celtic sources; the figure-work is related to Syrian or near-Eastern influences and expresses Irish themes which are themselves linked with Thebaid monasticism; the ornament is derived in part from similar origins but borrows as well from native pagan metal-work or jewellery, and takes its ubiquitous plait-patterns from Mediterranean sources. During its middle period it became more directly enmeshed with Carolingian art-forms, while its ornaments, losing their original Eastern flavour, grew increasingly affected by the barbaric elements in Scandinavian design, which itself had filched decorative motifs from Scythian prototypes. In a word, these six centuries witnessed a contest between the Nordic and barbaric taste of Scandinavia, and the humanistic trend from the Mediterranean; a struggle which has proved to be perennial, in spite of temporary successes on either side.

The most important figure-work (at least on sepulchral monuments) is found on the high crosses, particularly those of Ruthwell, Bewcastle and Easby, the shafts of which are divided up into panels filled with ornament and imagery. The iconography derives from no known source but at Ruthwell seems to extol the contemplative and ascetic side of the Christian faith. The panels show St Mary Magdalene washing Christ's feet; St John the Baptist, St Paul of Thebes and St Anthony, all eremetic individuals; Christ worshipped by the beasts of the desert; and a tentatively introduced Crucifixion, to which the poem inscribed upon the monument gives the nature of an heroic contest. Only the front of the Bewcastle shaft bears imagery, but on its three panels, the subject of Christ and the Beasts occurs again, together with St John the Baptist with a lamb, and his namesake evangelist with customary eagle. At Easby, the style is sophisticated and Carolingian in taste (accounted for possibly by the Francophile Alcuin of York), the main

13. Title page and plate 1 from one of several pattern-books issued by Theophilus Smith of Sheffield c. 1864. Smith's designs are conspicuous for their use of cast-iron railings to emphasize the privacy of the grave-plot. Incidentally, these designs show that "brambling" graves was still customary at this date.

14 (left). Hallaton (Leics.), the Rev. George Fenwicke, 1760: wall-tomb on northern exterior of chancel, 14 ft. high, 8 ft. wide; a large architectural tomb in alto-relief, admirable in proportion and detail; (above, right) Worth (Sussex), Robert Norman, 1813: chest-tomb in the shape of a classical arca, 6 ft. wide, typical of many South Country monuments of the Regency period, spartan in form and ornament; (below, right) Horsted Keynes (Sussex), a seventeenth-century translation in stone of the wooden grave-board, once the characteristic monument of the south-east counties and now becoming extinct.

theme being a Christ in majesty with a series of ingeniouslyc arved busts of the Apostles set beneath arcading, whose smooth modelling suggests an inspiration from ivory-carving.

In complete contrast to these major works, the cross-fragment from St Andrew Auckland (Durham) has flat figures with incised drapery, two of which, representing Ecclesia led by an angel, suggest an Eastern Mediterranean influence from some Syriac source. Recondite imagery is also evident on the Wirksworth coped slab, a work of little artistic merit, but one which has the largest collection of subjects of any monument of this period. These include the Annunciation, Nativity,

FIG. 44. *Anglo-Saxon coped stone (Wirksworth, Derbys.).*

Massacre of the Innocents, Burial of the Virgin, the Washing of the Apostles' feet, grouped about a Greek cross on which is placed a lamb; all are themes derived from feasts of the Byzantine calendar, and presumably copied from some imported manuscript or ivory.

The architectural shrine-tomb from Peterborough, known as the Hedda stone, is a native Mercian treatment of an early Christian sarcophagus, on which standing figures are set beneath an arcade, similar to sculptural fragments from Castor nearby, and also Fletton, Breedon-on-the-Hill, and the figure of Christ holding a book in Eastern style on the Lechmere headstone. This device of the figured arcade persisted throughout the Middle Ages, being the most convenient way for organizing a procession in a formal manner, where it is used to shelter the weepers or attendant angels on the tomb-base.

On the later Gosforth cross is to be found a Crucifixion combined with pagan Norse mythology, in a flat, barbaric treatment similar to a shaft at Aycliffe (Durham), which has the traditional scene with its witnesses of sun and moon, and the attendant soldiers Longinus and Stephaton.[5] Above this panel are triplet figures, which also occur on a stone from Gainford in Durham Library, reduced to a completely formal pattern of interlocking limbs. This dehumanised treatment is carried over into the Anglo-Norman period and can be seen in the Virgin and Child puppets at Shelford (Notts.), or more markedly on a totemic figure at Buckland Norton (Dorset), also of mid-eleventh century date. Such stones show a latent pagan element, a folk-art opposed to orthodox imagery and boldly expressed in the numerous fertility carvings or sheela-na-gigs built into church walls, and particularly common in the West Midlands, one of which is a phallic caricature of the Deerhurst angel.[6]

During the early years after the Conquest, Scandinavian influence was still paramount, and even its latest style (taking its name from the Norwegian church of Urnes), which dominated Irish art of the eleventh century, can be seen mingled with continental cross-currents on various West-Midland churches such as Kilpeck, or a slab from Jevington (Sussex) where Christ is shown treading the asp and the basilisk beneath His feet.[7] It was, however, the older Ringerike style, modified by manuscript illumination, that reflowered ironically enough in those northern districts which the conquerors had devastated a century before. Its scroll-work, refloriated and issuing in a decorative spray from the monstrous heads of cats or lions, was used both on architectural ornament and tombstones; such as the slab from St Peter's, Northampton, and the coped stone at Conisborough. To its motif of the Great Beast the Anglo-Norman carvers added fresh ideology through the cult of St Michael, whereby the older animal combat, ubiquitous as a surface decoration, was personified into a fight between the saint and the dragon, a common feature upon tympana, and found again on the hotch-potch imagery of the Conisborough monument. New themes derived from liturgical calendars, such as the Zodiac signs, Labours of the Months, or the Battles of Virtues and Vices, borrowed from *Psychomachia*, became common decoration on fonts and church doorways. Such imagery has an allegorical rather than religious significance; but an important theme of the latter kind is shown on the Tournai marble slab at Ely, where the soul of the deceased, carried in a napkin, is being taken into the charge of the guardian angel. This symbolic translation was adopted as a device by the medieval carver and was later reissued in classical guise on post-Reformation tombstones.

Refurbishings of oriental themes, with which the carver may have become familiar through the traffic in eastern textiles, can be seen in the Gilgamesh-stance given to David and the Lion which had already appeared on Scottish cross-slabs at Nigg and Aberlemno; the Tree of Life motif, on the Bishopstone slab, where the birds sipping from a vase signify the remission of sins via the sacraments; or the bird-beasts of Sassanian art at Dewsbury, which became transmuted into the wyverns or griffins of medieval heraldry.[8]

Traces of Merovingian influence, the result of a familiar western searoute of trade and culture, can be seen in some isolated cross-slabs of the Fenland area, and also in South Wales, where the use of ornamental rosettes made up of broken rings, in lieu of conventional cross-heads, developed into a sumptuous series of thirteenth century memorials in Herefordshire. Love of pattern for its own sake is evident on the simpler tombstones, which in many cases are decorated with geometrical motives only, such as the repetitive semi-circles at Oxford Cathedral; or Trowbridge with its half-rings and chip-carving; the formal architectural arcading of the Fordwich shrine-tomb, and in the various technical experiments made on the discoids to devise illusory forms of cross.[9]

MEDIEVAL

A series of churches in Herefordshire show the existence of a school of masons in this area, who borrowed design elements from western France and Scandinavian inspired Irish metal-work for the rich adornment of these buildings. Their local successors produced a series of fine coffin-slabs, distributed in villages of the same county, which have spiraliform scrolls sprouting from a central stem in an intricate series of curves that not only show an evolution from Merovingian sources but are reminiscent of contemporary ironwork. They represent a decorative treatment of the sacred emblem, not as a formal representation of a processional standard or metal pectoral cross, but as the Tree of Life, which was to persist, with appropriate changes of foliage, throughout the Middle Ages. In a sense it was no new conception, as presumably the Anglian high crosses with their decoration of inhabited scrolls had a similar implicit meaning and, although the shape, no less than the pattern of Scandinavian types such as the Gosforth cross, is evocative also of the Norse Yggdrasil, its ultimate origin lay in Iranian renderings of the World-Tree of the Paradise Garden.[10]

Apart from these specimens, the majority of the numerous medieval coffin-slabs, either incised or in relief, bear some variety of Latin cross with the arms decorated heraldically in the form of a cross-fleury or some minor architectural enrichment. Towards the end of the fifteenth century, in imitation of brass-design, the cross may be shown in perspective, but its general tendency is towards a new austerity of shape, which in the case of a series in Devon show certain eccentricities, such as cross-triplets joined to the main stem (Drewsteighton); or crescent projections on the shaft (Inwardleigh, Sheepwash).

The practice of combining with the cross-symbol tools, weapons or emblems to signify the deceased's profession or trade, first seen on Anglo-Norman slabs, became one of the most popular forms of monumental expression during the medieval period. Originally drawn from classical sources, the practice might well be adopted today, as an expression of pride in work or leisure interests, as it involves none of the doctrinal objections that are apt to be roused by the cult of personality.

The first effigies of the Anglo-Norman period were imported Tournai slabs in high relief, usually to prelates, holding in static poise their pastoral staves beneath an architectural or floriated canopy; these were to be succeeded in the thirteenth century by the designs of the Purbeck marblers, who developed the effigy in the round and gave to a fine series of military figures a variety of lively poses, which in the hands of the alabaster carvers relapsed to a recumbent posture with the hands either folded in prayer or, in the case of husband and wife, love-linked, as Donne described them in *The Ecstasy*.

In the thirteenth century, in succession to gabled shrine-tombs, usually decorated with a network of quatrefoils, it became customary to place the effigy upon a decorated base divided up by architectural tracery or recesses, in which were placed figures of weepers, angels and finally shields; above it was erected first a gabled, then later a magnificent fretted and pinnacled canopy, and finally a horizontal cornice, embattled or vaulted, which during the first period of Italian and Flemish infiltration shed its Gothic dress and changed pinnacles and buttresses for pilasters supporting arched soffits. At this time the ornament of the greater tombs was a mixture of classical imagery corrupted by Dutch extravaganza, the beginnings of the sixteenth century hybrid style, which although as eclectic, was less aesthetically satisfactory than previous work on the Northumbrian crosses, which had shown similar tendencies. Churchyard tomb-chests of this period, in contrast to slabs, are invariably covered with architectural pattern. Loversal, the earliest, with its unique collection of window designs, may well be the perpetuation of a master-mason's notebook, but in fifteenth or sixteenth century work the surface is monotonously divided into either traceried panels or the original grouping of quatrefoils, with a massive covering ledger, either chamfered or moulded with a bold cavetto.

The obsession with mortality shown in cadaver-effigies of the early fifteenth century was perhaps the most important of the medieval trends in design which persisted after the Renaissance. It is evident in the work of the metaphysical poets and tomb-makers' funerary imagery and remained as the main motif on churchyard headstones into the mid-eighteenth century and is found in isolated cases as late as the Regency period. Belonging to the same time as these first charnel exercises was a sadistic preoccupation with blood and martyrdom, which devised the Passion emblems as part of the heraldry of Christ. These are sometimes to be found on tombstones, along with the Sacred Heart—both, curiously enough, becoming part of the ornamental scheme of post-Reformation monuments when the cry of "No Popery" had become a common catch-phrase.

POST REFORMATION

The imagery on post-Reformation monuments is mainly concerned with the expression of the three themes of Mortality, Resurrection and the means of Salvation which, broadly speaking, develop in point of time in that order and can be summarized as follows:

(a) *Mortality.* Up to the beginning of the Georgian period the obsession with Death and Time is shown in terms of a simple charnel imagery such as skull and bones, the tools of the sexton, and the hour-glass, sundial and candle.

(*b*) *Resurrection*. During the major part of the eighteenth century, combined in its early years with these mementoes of death, the grow-ing emphasis on the resurrection of the body is expressed by means of the ubiquitous angel's head, representing this metamorphosis as the soul, together with other classical imagery significant of death, time and eternity.

Fig. 45. Headstone (Rotherfield, Sussex), 1778; the Resurrection, with falling tower and Christ in Limbo.

From the last quarter of the century until the end of the Georgian period, the central motif becomes the urn, adapted not for any doc-trinal reason or change to cremation, but simply as being the most conspicuous item in this pagan repertoire of ornament, made modish through the initial antiquarian researches of Stuart and Revett, and popularized in decoration by Adam.

(*c*) *Means of Salvation*. During the last fifty years of the Georgian period new allegorical personages such as Faith, Hope and Charity, largely superseded the older stock characters of Death and Time, and a number of pictorial subjects, of which the Last Judgement and the General Resurrection are most frequent, appear together with textual material derived from the Bible; this can be related to the develop-ment of education, and the influence of Methodism.

Finally, coinciding with both a change towards ritualism in religion and the Gothic idiom in architecture in the beginnings of the Victorian period, the Cross was reinstated as the central motif on monuments, but after reigning alone for a comparatively short time became again absorbed into a broadening eclectic scheme of imagery which levied toll on almost every known art-style of the past.

Although this brief analysis shows the restricted field of the general iconographical scheme, its hackneyed items were used with extraordinary versatility and freedom of treatment, so that in this vast amount of admirable carving actual replicas in design are unusual.

The classical motifs are invariably cut with care, although in some cases it is obvious that the carver was ignorant as to their proper function, and it is likewise certain that the more recondite imagery he used was scarcely intelligible to country folk, although they were no doubt satisfied enough with it, as being part of the one art-object they could lay some claim to possess.

SOURCES OF IMAGERY

While the gravestone-makers borrowed from building practice and the designs of the statuaries the two main devices of the architectural surround and floriated cartouche for the display of their text and imagery, any direct imitation of the elaborate symbolism used by the latter craftsmen is conspicuous by its absence. The churchyard carvers seemed content to use their own modified range of emblems, and it was not until the end of the eighteenth century, when they ventured in some districts to use pictorial treatments, that we can detect the rare influence of isolated tombs upon their work. The most conspicuous example, itself a *tour de force* of dramatic symbolism, was the great Nightingale monument in Westminster Abbey by Roubiliac[11] which, together with its companion-piece to General Hargreave, John Wesley reckoned as the only monuments in that fane "worthy the attention of a Christian". The imagery of the Nightingale monument, however, showing the collapsing Tower and the grim struggle of the protagonists Death and Time, was only a sophisticated rendering of a scene that was already familiar to thousands among the piously literate, derived from the emblem books that were printed time and again throughout the eighteenth century, and from which—along with the architectural

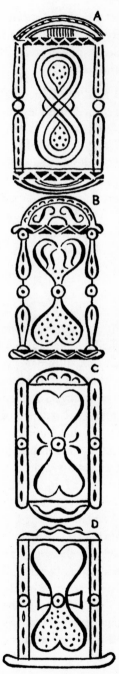

pattern-books by Dieterlin and De Vries in the sixteenth and seventeenth centuries, and by Englishmen such as Batty Langley and William Halfpenny—monumental masons derived a good deal of inspiration. Among the English writers of these emblem books the work of Francis Quarles was most popular, his *Emblemes* and later *Hieroglyphics of the Life of Man*, being first printed together in 1639. Quarles' illustrations (described by Pope in *The Dunciad* as his redeeming feature) were derived from two Jesuit books, Hugo's *Pia Desideria*, 1624, and *Typus Mundi*, 1627; and it was the theme of his *Hieroglyphics*, in which man's life is compared to a burning candle, that was freely adapted by monumental masons. One of the scenes, in which a skeleton arm emerges from clouds to snuff the candle occurs at Coningsby (Lincs.) 1800; but the most familiar is that showing Time with his hour-glass and Death as a skeleton with dart about to put out the candle held in its peculiar vase-like container.[12]

HOUR-GLASS

The same play of design is to be seen in treatments of the hour-glass. In early examples it appears as a cup, without its supporting stand (Bletchingley, Surrey, 1697), and again in Kent takes on a variety of conventional shapes ranging from inverted triangles diabolo-fashion, to double hearts. Chronos, or Father Time, is also personified separately and invariably carries his scythe and hour-glass but may also hold a candle-snuffer or a flaming lamp. Usually con-

FIG. 46. *Decorative treatments of the hour-glass from Kentish gravestones, early eighteenth century.*

ceived as a muscular old man, he is shown to best advantage at St Mary Castro, Leicester, 1799, where, in a plaque cut by William Firmadge (Plate 22), he stretches at ease amid clouds, or at Holy Trinity, Wolverton (Bucks.) 1714, dangles his leg over the letter-tablet. He lolls, full-paunched, at the base of slates by Samuel Turner of Market Harborough at Desborough (Northants.) 1791; or in work by James Coles of Thrapston, at nearby Titchmarsh in the same county, pours his sand over a medallion-portrait of the deceased; similarly he is emptying his hour-glass over skulls and bones at Chadwell (Essex) 1786; and Cowfold (Sussex) 1807. At Ripley (Yorks.) 1897 he stands inexplicably upon an upturned boat.

SUNDIAL

The sundial is used less often than the hour-glass and is usually shown with the gnomon fixed to a globe; at Quorn (Leics.) 1800, a skeleton examines one, holding a long scroll lettered "Put thy house in order, thou shalt die and not live". Gravestone-makers also made dials, and Samuel Turner, who did much work in this way, made the central feature of his headstone in St Mary Arden, Market Harborough, into an actual dial with a metal gnomon.[13]

CLOCKS

Hour-glasses are common, clocks rare, although Quarles had used the image in *Hieroglyphics*, IX. 6:

> Our Life's a clock, and every gasp of breath
> Breathes forth a warning grief, till Time shall strike a Death.

Time and Death were often used on clock-faces, and Erasmus Darwin describes one in *The Loves of the Plants*:

> Here Time's huge fingers grasp his giant mace,
> And dash proud Superstition from her base:
> Rend her strong towers and gorgeous fanes, and shed
> The crumbling fragments round her guilty head

—a passage which gives a new meaning to the motif of the falling tower. A clock-face was used as the central feature of headstones at Newnham, 1725, combined with hearts and diamonds; Barnwell St

169

Andrew, 1764, cut by Daniel Stevens (both in Northants.); Bidford-on-Avon (Warws.) 1706; and Cranbrook (Kent) 1791.

Candlesticks set with lighted tapers are also common enough, used to convey the passage of time or imminence of death, if snuffed. They are placed on coffins, trestles, tables, altars, hugger-mugger with other emblems, or combined (as at Sherington, 1733) with a weeping child holding a reversed torch, the classical version of Thanatos or Death that only became popular later in the century.

By a modification in design these personifications of Death and Time are brought into the dying man's bedchamber, and the scene becomes an assassination, Death plunging his barb into the man's breast while Time starts back aghast as witness to the act. This scene, with variations, occurs in village headstones in the vicinity of Olney (Bucks.), at Lavendon, Lathbury, Ravenstone and Sherington, which are traditionally attributed to James Andrews (1735-1817), a local stonemason, who during Cowper's residence at Olney, gave him lessons in drawing. John Campion's headstone at Sherington (Plate 20) shows the dying man in bed with curtains drawn back from the tester, a bureau by its side, and a hanging wall-clock, above which angel-heads in glory subtend rays of light upon the *coup de grâce* dealt by the skeleton, who snuffs the candle with his other hand, while Time falls back dropping his hourglass. A variation at Ravenstone, 1786, shows Death emerging from behind an altar or tomb spearing a heart upon it, flanked by attendant weepers and a trumpeting angel in the sky with the crown of life. At Olney, Sherington and at St Paul's, Bedford, Death is given the guise of Atropos and cuts the vital thread with shears. Elsewhere Death lurks behind a curtain, (Orlingbury, Northants.) 1775, or a coffin (Lavendon), accompanied by setting suns and the pyramid of Eternity. In a small South-Country group at Iping, 1773, Haslemere 1794, Cocking and Easebourne, the grim figure becomes an archer and the scene is enacted beneath an arcade. At Bingham (Notts.) 1816, the dying man in bed has a scroll with "Reader, behold thy Fate" thrust on him by the skeleton, from which his wife cowers upon a chair; and at Whatton, 1813, the grisly scene is set within one of Wood's idyllic landscapes, a church, house and grazing sheep amid its meadows. A draped urn is the central feature, and here Death hurls his dart at fleeing Time, whilst Faith and Hope flank the scene. At Great Thurlow (Suffolk) 1797,

Death is a swordsman; while at Lutterworth, on the headstone to the
mason William Kilpack, 1782, the scene has become a representation
of the Christian's "good fight", in which a nude figure, armed with
sword and buckler, has put on "the whole armour of God" and
tramples Death down. At St Margaret's, Leicester, 1776, there is a literal
illustration of Mark 8: 36, for here Death offers the dying man in his
nightcap and gown a globe in his bony hands (Plate 20).

Apart from such pictorial scenes, Death and Time are frequently
personified with their appropriate emblems of dart, scythe and hour-
glass, particularly on the Swithland slates throughout the Midlands. At
Plungar (Notts.) 1785, the carver William Barnes has given Time an
explanatory text "Time flies, our Glory fades, and Death's at hand" and
placed him with a serpent-encircled globe, Death holding his dart and
snuffer ready. Kimcote (Leics.) 1813, has one of the not infrequent
triple plaques found upon these slates; in the central tondo Time holds
a serpent and scythe and is swathed with a vine and acanthus surround;
the smaller flanking reliefs include Death with a spade and a serpent-
globe with the inveterate text "Time how short, Eternity how long".
The deceased kneels before Death at Broadway (Worcs.) 1685; Time
stabs him with a trident at Wartling (Sussex) 1733; at Gedney (Lincs.)
a figure dressed in shirt and breeches aims a gun at the fell poacher;
and at Ringmer (Sussex) he lies in a shroud pierced with his own darts.
Probably the finest carvings of these personages occurs on the magnificent chest-tomb of Arthur Knowles, 1707, at Elmore (Glos.), with
Time standing on his wheel, and Death, splendidly anatomized, on a
globe (Plate 16).

There are many examples of cadaver, often accurate in anatomy,
such as the chest-tombs at St Gregory, Sudbury, 1669; or St Nicholas,
Ipswich, 1790, where a skeleton sits within a coffin holding a large book;
some are fantastic and horrible, such as those at Great Bradley in the
same county of Suffolk; others frankly comic to our eyes, such as the
grinning little puppet with plus-fours pelvis at Morley (Yorks.) 1722,
with its head-panel of Struwelpeter angels holding a crown (Plate 1).
The same variety is to be found in skulls and bones, these simpler
devices being used to convey the mortality theme. In the London area
skulls are often excellently cut, as at Greenford, 1663, or West Wickham, where the thickness of the headstone has been unusually worked

into little death's-heads, and the cartouche has a mask inspired by Tijou's iron-work. In other cases, in the yard of Epsom for instance, the mason certainly worked by inspiration rather than knowledge.

Throughout Kent and parts of Sussex death's-heads are often incised on those characteristic headstones which resemble wooden prototypes and show an extraordinary range of design, being often half-bone, half-mask, and almost negroid in their barbarity. Some have merely circles and triangles for features, others an engrailed surround resembling a shroud, or even a nightcap, made into a composite glyph by bones and darts placed in saltire behind them. In other cases the teeth have become a chevron pattern and, in examples at Brede, Salehurst and Ewhurst with a mouth above this band, it has been suggested that the type was developed from imitating local medieval carvings representing heads with forked beards. The monument like a gate-post at Loose (Kent) 1712, has such masks engraved upon its finial.

The skull was also shown enwormed; enclosed within the serpent of Eternity; bat-winged; crowned; garlanded with wheat-ears, flowers or laurel leaves; and combined with the scythe, spade and mattock of the sexton in mock heraldry such as Long Sutton (Lincs.) and Ightham (Kent) 1712. In Norfolk, following the model initiated by the tomb-maker Nicholas Johnson, it is placed upon the winged hour-glass to make a single ideograph.

FIG. 47. *Death's-heads from Kentish headstones, early eighteenth century.*

ANGELS

The variety given to full-length figures is indeed entertaining; buxom, bucolic, majestic, ethereal, with the features of plump dowagers or the inhuman gaze of cult figures, they float, lumber or cavort with their trumpets of doom, palms of victory, crowns of glory, or scrolls of admonition. The isolated cherub's head representing the soul also gave the designer an imaginative freedom which he indulged to the full. In the absence of signatures local treatments of the theme are often some guide to the work of local masons, whom it would be attractive to define in this way. We could speak of the Master of the Tulip Angel, whose apocalyptic angels of the north Norfolk coast are dressed in ample skirts; the Master of the Sunflower Seraph, such as the fantastics in the West Riding; and we could distinguish others by the bat-winged sprites of Weldon (Northants.), the double-headed Janus angel at Winslow (Bucks.), angels in surplices at Long Sutton (Lincs.) along with fat *putti* burdened with heavy crowns, the angel blowing two trumpets at once at Nutfield (Surrey) 1760, etc. When they approximate to the Palladian norm, as Joseph Batt's own accomplished headstone at Epsom, 1763, they are perhaps most removed from our present taste, which prefers folk-art types, such as those with cap of curls and triangular pinions on the Vale of Belvoir slates or feathered examples in the Cotswolds carefully designed to fit lunettes, or follow the curves of subtended festoons. Apart from their apocalyptic duties, angels are also shown carrying the departed soul as a child in their arms, at March (Cambs.) 1790, or Steyning (Sussex) 1792; or again in the guise of guardian embrace the deceased at Hemel Hempstead (Herts.) 1738, while bunches of them appear within clouds amid rays of light, symbolizing the presence of heaven.

Towards the end of the eighteenth century the conception of the angel as the classical winged genius, with negligent robes and great vans for wings, is given majesty in Van Gelder's monument in Warkton (Northants.) designed by Adam, or in Richard Westmacott's noble figures.[14] The difference between this majesty and mawkishness can be seen in the cemetery white marble angels, which followed the same tradition to the letter, but unfortunately missed its spirit. In fact the dress of angels is an amusing study: long albs or feathered tights in

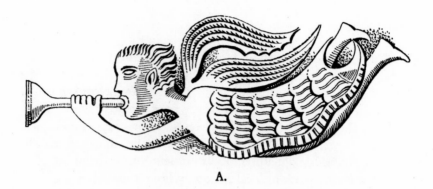

A.

FIG. 48. *Angels from headstones*: A. *Weldon, Northants., 1792*; B. *Blakeney, Norfolk, 1787*; C. *Egloshayle, Cornwall, 1776.*

B.

C.

the medieval period, surplices or skirts in the Georgian, succeeded by the loose chiton, and finally the Victorian nightgown.

URN

In many cases it is obvious that the precise use of the urn was a mystery to some country masons who regarded it as an ossuary, as can be seen in several cases stretching from the Fens to Bedfordshire, where angels lift lids from urns with the air of inspecting cooks, to reveal the traditional skull and crossbones within. A flame-burst too is often shown as issuing from it, but here, rather than ignorance, the deliberate use of an illustrative convention is likely, similar to putting wings upon it (Wanstead 1780), or rendering it as a sort of lamp, although the usual form of the latter was the customary gravy-boat shape which had been in use on interior tombs since the seventeenth century. While the tea-urn type (satirized by Hood) became established as the elegant norm of this emblem, the influence of such pattern-books as James Pain's *Decorative Details* can be seen when the handles are turned into serpents (as at Turvey, Beds., 1813) or in a fine cluster of classic revival work at Clewer (Berks.), probably the work of Merryman of Windsor.

It is often draped with a festoon, surrounded by a garland or wreath, partially shrouded with drapery, or tied up with ribands, in the more delicate examples and, like so much gravestone imagery, starting late it died hard—persisting well into the 1850s by which time its shape has often become brutish and heavy.

As well as these stock centre-pieces, other items of imagery were used in endless and often arbitrary combinations, some of them in general use, others the result of local invention. These, for the sake of clarity, are

FIG. 49. *Angel from headstone (East Peckham, Kent), 1822.*

listed separately, before proceeding to describe the allegorical and pictorial work of the last fifty years of the Georgian period.

BOOK

This emblem seems to have several shades of meaning; it could signify Prayer, or Knowledge, or Memory (where it is given a dog-eared page), as well as its inveterate role of being the Book of Life in the shape of the Bible. Many Cotswold tombstones and chest-tombs show half-length figures or busts holding books, and in some cases, such as Thame (Oxon.) 1765, the surface of the headstone is conceived as an opened book, a double-page spread in publishing terms, which appeared in numerous cheap editions in the Victorian cemetery and is still a popular trade monument today. In its capacity as Book of Life or Common Prayer, it is usually placed on an altar, often with a crown above. Towards the end of the eighteenth century a female figure may be shown "searching the scriptures", as in many Sussex examples, while at Hadlow (Kent) 1782, two young girls reading books have profiles cut with a purity of line that resembles Renaissance medallions (Plate 19).

BUTTERFLY

This classical symbol for the soul might well have been used as an emblem of the Christian life, but its use seems limited to a few headstones in Evesham, now illegible, *c.* 1820, in which it is being attacked by birds—or on a tablet at Patrishow (Brecon), where it is decorative rather than symbolic.

CADUCEUS

An emblem of the classic revival, it is comparatively rare in churchyards, except for those in the London area and the South. It was used

15 (above). *Shipton-under-Wychwood (Oxon.), bale-tomb, 1727–59, to members of the Morgan family: a grandiose version of a type of monument peculiar to the Cotswolds; (below, left) Painswick (Glos.), Gardner family tomb, c. 1765. While at Burford several varieties of bale-tomb can be seen, Painswick can show not only characteristic Oxfordshire chest-tombs, but tall pedestal monuments which are reputedly the work of the local Bryan family; (below, right) Beaconsfield (Bucks.): contrast in styles. In front, a nineteenth-century wooden grave-board, behind it an eighteenth-century pedestal tomb to the Anthony family, built in several stages and topped with an urn, and near it the slender pyramid in Portland and marble to the poet Edmund Waller, restored in 1862.*

16 (above). *Elmore (Glos.), Arthur Knowles, 1707, 82 in. long, 44 in. high: a magnificent chest-tomb in high relief, carved on the north and south faces with figures of Death and Time, angels and weepers in contemporary costume, with heraldic panels on the scrolled ends;* (below) *The Lea (Herefs.), Stephen Yearsley, 1742: a chest-tomb of similar form and dimensions, with angels in exotic costume.*

by Henry Hind on a tombstone at All Saints, Leicester, as early as 1754, and at Great Chesterford (Essex) 1811.

CHILDREN

The untimely deaths of many poor innocents are reflected in gravestone imagery. Figures of babies reposing in cradles or on a bier are found on two fine stones from Sawtry St Andrew's (Hunts.) of 1728 and 1736 accompanied by attendant mourners, and at Chatteris (Cambs.) 1738, where an apocalyptic angel hovers over the child. At Crick (Northants.) 1785, Frances, the child of the local stone-mason Benjamin Button, is shown kneeling in prayer, like the famous Reynolds' portrait. Parents mourn over the encoffined bodies, as at Wendover, 1708, and High Wycombe (Bucks.) 1746, where the little coffins are placed upon trestles. At Towcester, adjoining the headstone to the mother who had quads, is an unusual carving of a nude mother embracing two children in her arms. Ursule Claridge, 1696, on a wall-tablet with appropriate epitaph at Horley (Oxon.), is shown suckling her baby; at Fairford, 1708, a nurse in contemporary dress dandles an infant in swaddling clothes; Cwmyoy (Mon.) 1821, has a full-length figure of Jane Thomas clutching her child, while guardian angels, bearing the soul in the form of a child to heaven, are also found. Mourning figures, both adults and progeny, can also be seen in contemporary dress. At Falstone (Northumb.) 1779, there are two full-length figures of sisters; at Sutton Valence (Kent) 1835, the son and daughter of John Brinkworth, dressed in simple gown and frilled collar with Eton jacket, grieve over their father's tomb; others at Minster-in-Sheppey, 1849, sit with a harp, handkerchief to eyes. A monument of great dignity is the exquisitely carved slate relief at Desborough (Northants.) 1796, cut by Henry Clay of Leicester, where the figures of Ann Holmes and her daughter Harriet lie side by side in death (Plate 18).

COLUMN

Columns surmounted by urns occur among the incidental monuments carved upon headstones, but the broken column, first used by J. B. Papworth in 1815 and later popularized by Flaxman, is rare. It is shown on a headstone at Strensham (Worcs.) 1837, carved by the local mason J. Bell, but it was not until the advent of cemeteries that its use becomes frequent, when it is usually shown girdled with flowers. In this respect, however, it was often used as an ornamental feature on late Georgian headstones.

CORNUCOPIA

These horns of plenty are often used in quasi-decorative fashion in the ornamental surrounds to headstones, along with the usual displays of flowers and fruit, such as Whittlebury (Northants.) 1837, where they emit roses and wheat-ears, or in Sussex examples at Bosham, Midhurst and Singleton. At March, 1812, a winged figure representing Pomona or Abundance holds the emblem, while in the same churchyard, 1816, a nymph bears a reaping-hook and sheaf (Plate 22).

CROWN

Symbolic of honour or glory, but in its usual sense referring to Paul's metaphor to the Corinthians (1 Cor. 9: 24-27), when he compared the athlete's award in the foot-race to the immortal crown of the Christian Life.

It is often shown set amid clouds in the sky, offered by angels to the mortal below, proffered by a hand from heaven, or held in the grasp of a detached arm (Hayes, Middx., 1766).[15] While common in association with other emblems, it is more rare as an individual feature, such as Rolvenden, 1740, where it appears in the star-tipped heraldic variety of celestial crown, or Shoreham (both in Kent), 1760, in medieval shape. Elsewhere, it is the arched or hooped variety, adopted since the days of Henry VII, often ludicrously perched on the polls of the fat little angels of the Fenlands.

DOVE

In the same area, the dove, as the Divine Spirit in a glory of light, is a central feature on headstones during the last quarter of the eighteenth century. As Noah's dove it flies over the waste of waters at St Mary's, Ely, 1800, and in this aspect, with an olive sprig in its beak, it presumably signifies Hope or Promise and is common enough. At Wooburn (Bucks.), 1744, together with angels, doves kiss one another; they are associated with hearts at Stokesley (Yorks.) 1696, and at Chaddesley Corbet and Charlecote (Warws.) 1684, are made to flank a central shoot or spray, in a pose reminiscent of earlier Byzantine imagery. In scriptural allusion, doves are also shown with serpents, or with an eagle at Leigh (Surrey) 1789, where the appropriate reference may be Psalm 103: 5, signifying the renewal of life.

GARBE

The heraldic term for the sheaf of corn, which is a common feature on headstones to yeomen farmers and is found in all districts. It was a former country custom to send a sheaf to relatives on the death of a farmer. Apart from its use as an occupational emblem, wheat as well as the vine has its obvious sacramental significance, and both sprays of corn, and harvest-knots are used in decoration. In some cases, it signi-fied the good seed in the parable of the Sower. At Burnham (Bucks.) 1789, for instance, William Grover's headstone shows a central garbe, and skull and book set amid springing shoots (the word of God taking root); and at Long Sutton (Lincs.), accompanying an urn full of bones, a line of young corn blades springs from the furrow below.

GARLAND

The wreath of leaves or flowers is not as frequent as one might suppose, considering the variety of actual tokens set upon graves for remem-brance. It was used about the turn of the seventeenth century and then seems to have lapsed in popularity until the classical revival. For instance, on a chest-tomb at Langney (Glos.) 1695, it is carried along with skulls in the hands of figures; at Wellingborough and Great Harrowden (Northants.) 1717, it encloses flaming hearts, and even as late as 1878 a Gothic headstone at Horsham (Sussex) shows a hand holding it as the crown of victory.

As decoration however it was used as an edging to ornamental plaques or letter-tablets and on early work was highly formalized, such as the running-scrolls used by the Webbs at Linton (Herefs.) 1720, or the Brute's bold gouged lobes in the Llanbedr district (Plates 2, 3), changing later from a neatly-plaited roll of leaves to more naturalistic sprays bound with ribands, like the ubiquitous festoon, which shows to great floral advantage on headstones at Hayling (Hants.) and in the neighbourhood of Portsmouth. At Husbands Bosworth (Leics.) 1821, her father carved an elegant Flora for his daughter Ann Peck, a female figure holding a shattered festoon of flowers and letting fall its blossoms from her hand, as an image of untimely death.[16]

HAND

The disembodied hand or arm is used in a variety of ways; as an admonitory finger it may be a naïve pointer to some part of the text, or to heaven, as at Stamford, where it forms the finial of an obelisk. Like the medieval Divine Hand, or *Dextera Dei*, it may signify the Divine Presence, as at Chop Gate (Yorks.) 1749, with the inscription: "Prepare to meet thy God"; or Stoke-by-Nayland (Suffolk) 1824, where a hand from clouds points to a Bible with the terse admonition "Read - Mark - Learn". Its association with the heart is an emblem of Charity, as on John Colt's monument at Toppesfield (Essex), or on headstones at Aycliffe (Durham) and Eton, 1832. Clasped hands signify friendship or brotherly love, as in the particular case of a contemporary David and Jonathan in Hereford Cathedral, 1691, where a ledger is inscribed "Conjuncti in Mortem"; and on headstones at Padbury, 1808, and Maids Moreton (Bucks.) 1811, and Wilsford (Lincs.) 1847. The four hands clasping cross-wise in fireman's lift fashion at Hertford, 1783, is an unusually early example of this device which was to be used in Victorian times in connection with Tennyson's line, "O for the touch of a vanished hand".

LAMB, SACRIFICIAL

The lamb, stretched on an altar amid blazing faggots as a burnt-offering, is found at Long Sutton and Chatteris, 1754; and as the apocalyptic Lamb from which issue streams of living water, at Longborough (Oxon.). In the form of the *Agnus Dei*, with cross and banner, it occurs at Wisborough Green (Sussex), 1729 and 1753, and at Great Harrowden (Northants.) 1790, and becomes more frequent on Gothic Revival monuments. The deceased appear in the guise of lambs at West Peckham (Kent) 1869, and Haversham, (Bucks.) 1800, where a child also holds a lamb; while William Innocent's headstone at Whatton (Notts.) 1811, shows a child and lamb, inscribed "Suffer little children ...", Thomas Wood obviously fitting the imagery to the name. This mason's pastorals, unique in gravestone imagery, are described more fully later. The theme of the Good Shepherd is not so popular as one would expect, considering its Biblical and rustic connotations, appearing mainly in the Fenlands and southern counties, such as Wisbech St Mary, 1840, Pulborough, 1798, or on a "folk-art" slate at Poundstock (Devon) 1860. Monuments to shepherds, showing pictorial scenes of folded flocks, occur at Olney (Bucks.) 1779, to William Langley "pasture keeper", which together with Hobday's relief of David as a shepherd at Church Honeybourne (Worcs.) are now unfortunately illegible.

MIRROR

It is associated with books on a pedestal tomb, *c.* 1750, at Fairford (Glos.), where the meaning intended is probably Truth and Knowledge. On a headstone at Beaconsfield (Bucks.) 1763, a hand-mirror is bound-up with palm branches and may possibly refer to 1 Cor. 13: 12; "For now we see in a mirror, darkly; but then face to face" etc.

NEPTUNE

On a headstone at Stokesley (Yorks.) 1783, to a master mariner, little devices of Neptune with a trident, an anchor, and the traditional puffing-cherub representing the Wind are shown. Maria Gardyner's shrine-tomb at Bovey Tracey (Devon) 1655, includes a mermaid, and these creatures are used as supporters to a cartouche on a vast headstone at Manton (Rutland) 1752.

PALMS

Palm-branches, traditionally associated with Easter, are symbols of Victory over Death and are common everywhere. The use of the palm-tree, however, is unusual. At Lewisham, 1781, there was formerly a relief showing a pick and spade at the foot of the tree, expressing Victory over Death in somewhat *Treasure Island* terms; at Wisborough Green (Sussex) 1790, it accompanied a cherub with reversed torch. The invidious *tour de force* cut out of a Ketton monolith at Barnack of 1847 has already been mentioned.

PINEAPPLE

After the introduction of the pineapple into England during the reign of Charles II, its shape often modified that ancient fertility-emblem the fir-cone, in common use as a gate-post finial. Its only use on headstones

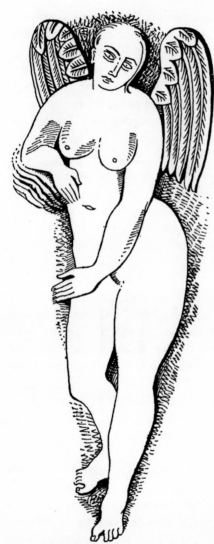

(where it was presumably chosen for its exotic appeal) seems to be the splendid fruit carved by Wood at Lowdham, 1816, flanked by figures of Faith and Hope (Plate 27). The three little pot-plants at Middleton Cheney (Northants.) 1770, may be either pineapples or thistles.

PSYCHE

Kibworth Harcourt (Leics.) 1789, has a delicately carved slate relief, showing a nude winged figure that must have prompted some bucolic witticisms. At March (Cambs.) on an early nineteenth century headstone, Venus with a dove hands an arrow to Cupid.

PYRAMID, FALLING

The standing pyramid or obelisk was used by Shakespeare as a symbol of Eternity, but when toppling in fragments, as by Roubiliac on the Hargreave monument, and suggested by Erasmus Darwin's lines previously quoted, it probably refers to Superstition or Pride. It is to be found in Last Judgement scenes in Kent and Sussex (which will be later described).

FIG. 50. *Relief of Psyche, 7½ in. long, from slate headstone (Kibworth Harcourt, Leics.), 1789.*

SERPENT

In the circular form of a serpent engulfing its own tail it represented Eternity and often enclosed other emblems within its bound, such as

Cleeve Prior (Worcs.) 1797, with an hour-glass, and the inscription "Time is encircled with immense Eternity". At Doddington (Lincs.) and Pulborough (Sussex) 1794, figures holding crowns and palms of victory are shown trampling on serpents and, rather than a recrudescence of the older theme of "bruising the serpent's head", this may refer to Luke 10: 19 or the Pauline ejaculation "O death, where is thy sting," etc., of 1 Cor. 15: 55. At Romaldkirk (Yorks.) 1825, mortality emblems combined with doves and serpents point the text of Matt. 10: 16.

FIG. 51. *Relief from slate headstone (Penshurst, Kent), 1842, representing the Serpent of Eternity and the Poppy of Sleep.*

At Kensal Green the headstone to Mrs Sarah Ride, 1851, is encircled by a carved serpent.

SHELL

Conventional representations of the scallop shell had been in common use for the decoration of niches or semi-circular hood-moulds over doorways since Roman times, and its use on tomb-stones seems to be decorative rather than symbolic. As fertility or life-symbols, however, shells, varying in type from cowries to cockles, have been found in prehistoric burials and up to recent times have been used for the decoration of graves in ways that suggest a remarkable persistence of folk-memory. In Anglesey, for instance, where several megalithic tombs on the island have been found to contain shells, sea-shells and white pebbles have been used to decorate modern graves. An article in *Chambers Journal* in 1859 described shell decorations on the graves of the poor in Bow Cemetery, where names and texts were picked out in shells; conches were similarly engraved, and various possessions, such as children's toys and walking-sticks were also present. "On many graves we found the little white Cupids that many Italian boys carry about on their heads for sale. They were doubtless taken for infant angels by the ignorant love which placed them there ... here the infant Cupids were exchanged for the Child Samuel kneeling in prayer." The fondness for the cheap Italian statuary shows how easily the imported white marble monuments from the same source were able to establish a firm hold on popular taste.[17]

TORCH

The emblem of the flaming torch was derived from the classical games, where it was handed on to successive runners in the relay race and has become familiar today in the traditional opening of the Olympic Games. In this respect it signified Life, as opposed to Death when reversed, drooping from the hand of a cherub in the classical representation of Thanatos or Death, or from the grasp of a disconsolate mourner.

TREE

The tree as related to the message of the Fall and Redemption has already been mentioned, but in simpler terms it signified Life when verdant and Death, if lopped or blasted. Such emblem imagery is clearly expressed in a monument to Sir Gilbert Prynne, in Chippenham (Wilts.) 1620, where a Tree of Life is inscribed: "Each man's a plant, and every tree, like man is subject to mortalitie". The idea was similarly shown in Cowper's lines: "Like crowded forest trees we stand, and some are marked to fall; the axe will smite at God's command, and sore shall smite us all"—as at Braintree (Essex) by a hand emerging from a cloud and chopping down a tree.

On the monument to Elizabeth Sharpe, 1752, in Bunhill Fields, a vine-plant was cut down by a skeleton wielding a scythe; while at Walberton (Sussex) 1767, a fine headstone to Charles Cook, shows his death through a falling tree, with a bust of Christ the Judge within a wreath of clouds from which is suspended a pair of scales. It was not until the end of the eighteenth century that the willow was used on sepulchral monuments as a sign of mourning, and then usually with a figure of Hope, or the grieving widow or weeper clinging to the urn beneath the arching boughs of the tree. At Linslade (Bucks.) 1810, a fine Greek revival headstone expresses the idea of grief, mortality and resurrection by a willow tree with its female attendant; an urn and a scythe; and an obelisk set within a flower-garland emitting rays of light

FIG. 52. *Headstone to Robert Gurney, 1810 (Linslade, Bucks.).*

(Fig. 52). At Frampton and other villages along the Severn Valley, local masons such as Pierce, Wilkins and Bennett were fond of the theme, carving it in alto-relief on pedestal tombs, and drooping its long fronds over their letter-tablets. At Fladbury (Worcs.) 1836, Laughton made it the sole feature on a headstone; and in the North Riding, during the 1850s, its arched shape bent over a tomb was made to fit a lunette (such as Dalton's headstone to Thomas Fawcett, 1859, at Brompton), becoming conventionalized almost out of recognition. The oak is sometimes introduced in a Life-Death antithesis, as on nineteenth century chest-tombs at Coxwold, in the same district, where urns diapered with fleurs-de-lis are disposed among branches of oak and willow.

FIG. 53. *Angel from headstone (Melbourne Baptist Chapel, Derbys.), 1845, by Samuel Bagnall.*

TRUMPETS

Trumpets take on a variety of shapes, varying from post-horns to bugles, and are frequently found, either combined with contrasting mortality emblems, or in the hands of apocalyptic angels. Their meaning, compounded of Victory and Resurrection, can be related to Paul's great declaration in 1 Cor. 15: 51-57. These angelic trumpeters would make an interesting study in themselves. One can discover such robust wenches as those by the younger Firmadge at All Saints, Leicester, 1782 (Plate 18); Samuel Bagnall's cherubs at Melbourne Baptist Chapel (Derbys.) 1845, carrying their little garlands; suave seraphs at Bletchley (Bucks.) 1734, their long trumpets decked with bannerets; the droll bambini with loin-cloths in the Crickhowell vicinity; naïve ones in Cornwall, arrogant ones in Fenland, and blowing two trumpets at once, like the Greek aulos, at Swanage (Dorset) 1781.

WEEPERS

This medieval term seems most convenient to describe the various standing or seated figures in the charade of mourners. On many Cotswold tombs are figures which, both in stance or costume, might well be medieval, such as those on John Jordan's chest-tomb of 1774 at Bourton-on-the-Water; or at Hardwicke, 1675, where demi-figures draped in mourning scarves press handkerchiefs to their eyes. For the most part they appear in the guise of amorini, sometimes following the ancient practice of holding skulls to denote their demise, slouching disconsolately with guttering torches, or wiping their eyes on the drapes of a curtain-fall. Towards the end of the eighteenth century they were ousted by the female mourner, who may rest her foot on a globe, despising the pleasures of the world, or contemplate a skull—but is usually found either embracing or sitting beside an urn, under the drooping boughs of a willow. In similar fashion she may be shown reading the epitaph on her mimic memorial or, most often, from a book, presumably searching the Scriptures for consolation. In later cemetery monuments she is made to cling passionately to a pillar, anchor, cross or crag, in allusion to Toplady's popular hymn, *Rock of Ages*.[18]

Following this summary of the stock emblems used during the seventeenth and eighteenth centuries, later allegorical figures and scenes from Biblical sources, used during the last fifty years of the Georgian period, can now be discussed.

The more recondite allegorical figures used by the tomb-makers of Shakespeare's day, which inspired his metaphor, "She sat like Patience on a monument, Smiling at grief," were seldom adopted by the grave-stone-makers, who contented themselves with Death and Time. But towards the end of the eighteenth century, following the precedent of such devout statuaries as John Bacon, personifications of the triple virtues of the Christian Life—the Faith, Hope and Charity of the Pauline epistles—became popular. Their symbols of cross, anchor and heart had been used in emblem imagery, but they were seldom assembled in one group (as at Weybourne, Norfolk, 1740), and the same is true of the allegorical figures, of whom Hope is by far the most common.

FAITH: THE CROSS

The fears of possible Roman Catholic ascendancy in England left its mark on Georgian symbolism, so that, in an officially Christian country, we find a virtual absence of the Cross as the prime instrument of Salvation, and an anomalous preference for the use of pagan imagery.[19] Ironically enough, the Jesuit iconography on which Quarles founded his work, at a time before mysticism was replaced by an orthodoxy that abhorred "enthusiasm", became absorbed into the symbolic scheme, so that passion emblems and esoteric imagery are by no means rare. Indeed the evidence of gravestones shows the English reluctance to put theory into rigid practice and the freedom of worship tacitly permitted in exceptional cases. In the next village to Olney, where Cowper and his friends were serving one religious interest, his neighbours and future landlords, the Throckmortons of Weston

Underwood, practised the older faith, as can be seen in the memorials of their dependants—circumstances repeated at Coughton (Warws.) where another branch of this family worshipped and buried in a remote village.

There are about a score of monuments at Weston in which the Cross is prominent, either alone, or in combination with the skull, angel-heads or passion emblems.[20] Others have been given a pictorial treatment in delicate relief, showing the cross with a skull at its foot set in a realistic landscape. A few miles away, at Holy Trinity, Wolverton (Bucks.), a headstone to Mark Elmes, 1797, shows an almost complete collection of passion emblems, including the cross, crown of thorns, ladders, spear, reed, cock, chalice and ewer, set amid sprays of wheat-ears and grapes, with a pelican in piety nested on the cross (Plate 25).[21] This stone was originally highly coloured and has a counterpart at Dunchurch, near Rugby, of 1793. At Little Gaddesden (Herts.), a headstone of 1836 has a vine-leaf border, with winged heart, three nails, crown of thorns and cross in a lunette, flanked by a reed and lance, and at its base a tomb with the stone removed, and the thirty pieces of silver.

Trophies of passion emblems were used as decoration on the Burton Lazars tomb and others in the Cotswolds, but it is on the Swithland slates, combined with mortality emblems, that a more esoteric imagery was devised which has hitherto escaped notice. For instance, the headstone to Richard Denshire, former Mayor of Leicester, at St Margaret's in that city, 1761, cut by Robert Kinnes, depicts the Death and Resurrection theme (Plate 25). In the centre rests a cadaver within a tomb, on which is placed a book inscribed: *Per Serpentem Mors; Per Christum Vita.* To its left lightning blasts a withered tree set in a graveyard with crumbling tombs, a skull and serpent at its foot, and spear, scythe and spade at its side. To the right is a tree in full leaf extending rays of glory in which float cherubs, together with a cross and chalice into which drip three gouts of blood from the sky. In the same yard a slate by Firmadge, 1773, shows three spandrils containing chalice and palm-branches, an anchor and a serpent, cross and dart entwined between a crown and hammer: while another by Riley, 1804, has a dove rising from a sarcophagus with a spray of olive, flanked by a spade, scythe and dart, with a serpent and tree, cross, sunburst and chalice. The same mystic relationship between the trees which occasioned the Fall and the Redemption is shown at Burton Overy to John Voss, 1766. Here a central book is inscribed *Ad Arborem Aspice en Lethū; Ad Crucem Aspice Ecce Salutem*, with a skull, scythe, dart, spade, tree of knowledge and serpent, and a radiant chalice, with hammer, sponge, cross and spear. The symbolic intent is made clear at Narborough, 1825, where a sarcophagus with "Sin gave the wound and Christ the cure" is flanked by a tree, skull and crowned cross, showing in symbolic terms the old and new dispensations. A pictorial treatment of the same idea was carved by Ballard at Childs Wickham, 1801, and South Littleton, 1804 (near Evesham), where the risen Christ is shown above Adam and Eve and the Tree of Knowledge, with an angel and Death with his dart (Plate 6); and at Church Langton (Leics.) by William Platt, 1777, where Adam and Eve and the Tree with its serpent are accompanied by mortality emblems and the angel with the flaming sword. Adam and Eve in Paradise is to be found at St Lawrence-in-Thanet, 1756, and Wadhurst (Sussex) 1789; the Expulsion at Cleeve Prior, 1793, and Coughton (Warws.) 1794 by Thomas Laughton of Cleeve.

HOPE: THE ANCHOR

The figure of Hope with her anchor, derived from early Christian symbolism related to Hebrews 6: 19, is common, either alone or in connection with Time, from the end of the eighteenth century up to the Victorian period, when the anchor set within a pile of rocks becomes a frequent device on white marble monuments. This symbol, because of its seafaring connections, is often found in coastal districts; and a curious late example of 1842 at Stockton Holy Trinity (Durham) shows its tine stuck into a cloud, with fallen leaves and a lopped stock of a tree below, apparently intended as a literal rendering of the Pauline text, contrasted with the tree of death. At St Peter's, Sudbury (Suffolk), 1800, are three headstones with large figures of Hope and an anchor in a flat archaic style, but usually the device is treated with sophistication, as on the Midland slates with their robust wenches, or on delicate Portlands in Sussex. Typical examples of this draped female figure set within a niche can be seen at Shoreham and Broadwater; elsewhere in the county, as at Pulborough, 1763, she stands by an urn pointing to a crown of glory or is replaced at Billingshurst by a naked cherub (Plates 19, 23). More elaborate twists of imagery occur on an interior tablet at Metheringham

(Lincs.) 1763, where Hope presents a flaming heart to Cupid; or Bishops Tachbrook (Warws.) to Thomas Ashton, 1809, by J. Shearsby, where the emblem is flanked by angel-heads, with Moses' staff and serpent and the *Agnus Dei* in borders, an unusual use of an old type and anti-type motif.

CHARITY: THE HEART

The more precise meaning of Charity, greatest of the Pauline virtues, was expressed in emblem literature by the heart, put through fantastic interpretations by Quarles, and accorded devotion as the Sacred Heart of Jesus through the visions of St Marguerite Maria Alcoque; this cult was established in 1675 and the heart was depicted with flames to signify the fire of Divine Love.[22]

Hearts are not infrequently found on seventeenth century head-stones, where they are pierced with darts, crowned, held in hands, or later associated with Biblical texts, such as John 14: 1, 27, at Cold Brayfield (Bucks.) 1755; or Matthew 5: 8, at Cuckfield (Sussex) 1764. The flaming heart is found at Wellingborough (Northants.) 1717, and even as late as 1862 at Leake in the North Riding. It is common on Cornish slates, and also in Cotswold, where its characteristic association with other emblems can be seen on such a tomb as to Christopher Minchin, 1756, at Quedgeley (Glos.) which includes also dove and palm branches, bow, quiver, dart, sword, shield, club and reversed torch, together with angel-heads in a glory. The personification of Charity as a mother nursing two or three children is comparatively rare. Jona-than Harmer of Heathfield, however, included the device among the various terracotta plaques which he used to apply to headstones; and it was exquisitely cut in slate by Christopher Staveley at Burton Lazars, to Mary Blower, 1781 (Plate 23). To William Firmadge its symbolism was poignantly apt, for he used it on an interior tablet to his first wife and three children who died in infancy at Scraptoft (Leics.) his birth-place, in 1793.

This representation of Charity, along with other figures of Pomona, Flora and Vertumnus, that are occasionally found on churchyard memorials, was derived from the main source of general imagery, Cesar Ripa's *Iconologia* published in 1603, which was much imitated, and generally plundered by designers. George Richardson, who designed Stapleford church, built by Stavely, *c.* 1783, published his own two volume work entitled *Iconology* in 1779, which contained over four hundred figures derived from Ripa and may well have been familiar to the Leicestershire mason.

LAST JUDGEMENT

Doomsday and the General Resurrection are usually suggested by apocalyptic angels blowing trumpets, but complete renderings of this complex scene are understandably rare. One of the most remarkable carvings can be found at East Dean in West Sussex, to Richard Vallar, 1776, which shows Christ as Judge, holding a book and sword within a semi-circular mandorla of cloud, beneath which is suspended a balance (Plate 21).[23] To left and right seraphs swoop down blowing trumpets over skeletons struggling from their coffins amid flames, accompanied by Time and Death. Next to this stone is another by the same hand to John Vallar, 1779, with the same bust of Christ in glory, but beneath it is a figure of the deceased in contemporary dress lolling on a tomb-chest, together with a garbe and serpent of eternity.

At Broadwater in the same county, the headstone to Elizabeth Penfold, 1793, has less merit but is unique for showing both land and sea giving up their dead. Christ, seated amid clouds and holding a cross, is flanked by two trumpeting angels. Beneath is an expanse of sea, with boats and cadavers tossing in the waves, and a churchyard, with church tower riven in twain, the boundary nearby paled with rails and various monuments revealing their dead. Hind of Swithland carved an oval relief at Rothley (Leics.) 1794, with a representation of the last event taking place within his own churchyard (Plate 21). Here the figure of Christ holding a great trumpet and scroll (inscribed with text from 2 Thess. 1: 7, 8) is supported by cherubs amid a mass of cloud subtending lightnings, which have cloven the spire of Swithland church, toppling it down over the graves and their occupants. The additional interest in this carving to the local antiquary is its representation of the Danvers Chapel, built in 1727, before its restoration. The Last Judgement (now sadly worn) at Queenborough in Thanet, 1784, was the most ambitious figure composition attempted by a gravestone-cutter during this period and can be compared with Wesley's sermon on the Great Assize of 1758, "I saw the dead great and small, stand before God." A gigantic angel strikes down amid the dense crowd of figures with an open book in one hand and trumpet in the other, the sky being full of angels in clouds bearing trumpets, along with figures of Time and Death. A similar design, slightly less elaborate, is to be seen at Minster nearby, to Thomas Crayden, 1756.

GENERAL RESURRECTION

Kent and Sussex contain fine examples of this theme, showing treatments similar to the Hargreave monument by Roubiliac, with trumpeting angels, fallen tower, the deceased risen from the tomb, and the figures of Death and Time. In the former county they are to be found at Borden, Capel, Darenth, Horton Kirby, Gillingham, Newington, Plaxtol, Sittingbourne, Speldhurst and Trottiscliffe, ranging from 1731 to 1821. At Cowfold, 1798, there is a spirited composition where the scene is enacted in a country churchyard. A man triumphantly flings back his shroud at the angelic summons, while a mother and her two babes rise from their tombs; Time stands over the prostrate figure of Death beneath the collapsing tower. The same confident carving of figures on a small scale can be seen at Newhaven, 1768, where a mother and child leap up at the trumpet's call, Death falls before them, and Time snaps his dart over his knee.

At Steyning, West Grinstead, Horsham, Thakeham and Shipley, c. 1794, there are a number of large stones, usually with dual letter-tablets, and obviously the work of a single craftsman, possibly Gregory Page of Horsham. They all have a brace of seraphs with trumpets and palms flanking an open book, while beneath the letter-tablets is a delightful panorama of a country churchyard, showing a church with aisles and tall shingled spire, various monuments including chest-tombs, dead-boards and Sussex style-stones, with the deceased in the centre tossing back his grave-clothes, surrounded by a clump of trees, and a Chinese wicket-gate beneath evergreens. The poetic quality of these minute landscapes is only exceeded by the pastorals of Thomas Wood of Bingham (1760–1841), "Well known for more than half a century as an ingenious Carver of Tomb and Gravestones", whose delicate reliefs, probably inspired by chap-book illustration, are usually framed in lunettes and have a central urn or memorial upon which reclines a female figure. At each side is a landscape of undulating hills with clumps

17 (above). *Reigate (Surrey), tomb to Rebecca Waterlow, 1869, 15 ft. long, 10 ft. high: the architectural base of Portland and granite has inset reliefs of the Sacrifice of Isaac and the Good Samaritan and supports two life-size angels seated on a sarcophagus flanked by bronze tripods. The work of Samuel Ruddock of Pimlico; (below, left) Kensal Green cemetery: Robert William Sievier's memorial to John St John Long, 1834, an adaptation of the Choragic monument of Lysicrates complete with statue of Hygeia; (below, right) Kensal Green cemetery: the Holland family tomb, c. 1856, designed by Digby Wyatt and carved by W. Roulton in the guise of a Hellenistic sarcophagus, decorated with angelic caryatids, garlands and guttering torches, supported on the backs of griffins.*

18 (left). Desborough (Northants.), Ann and Harriet Holmes, 1796: Swithland slate headstone by Henry Clay of Leicester. The figures of the dead mother and her child, 9 in. long (right, above), are carved with great delicacy and feeling. The monument was cleaned and its lettering gilded some ten years ago; (below, right) All Saints, Leicester, John Bracebridge, 1782: detail of Swithland slate headstone by William Firmadge of Leicester, which has a pair of these buxom angels, 18 in. wide.

and coppices of trees, amid which are half-concealed country houses and a spired church (Plate 27). At ease in these pastures lie down together various cattle, horses, sheep and cows, breathing the air of a "peaceable kingdom" and carved at about the same time as Blake was engraving his illustrations to Thornton's *Virgil*.

Other good representations of this scene could include two stones to Mary Chessell, 1773, and William Cooper (set in ornate baroque scrolls) at Brading (I. of Wight); Braunstone (Leics.) 1787, 1795; Hurstpierpoint (Sussex) 1791; Uffington (Berks.) 1829; Holt (Norfolk) 1809, where the trumpeting angels in this area are rustic beauties with bare breasts and blowing skirts, carrying scrolls inscribed with the verse from 1 Cor. 15: 52.

Midhurst (Sussex) 1763, shows other apocalyptic imagery, where the doom angels make their summons beside a cross from which drips blood or flames with the earth burnt up below. Wendens Ambo (Essex) 1814, has the Recording Angel holding a large scroll and pen and ink, amid a chalice, wheat and grapes; at Stoney Stanton (Leics.) 1785, Christ as Judge with a blazing sun overhead points to a book marked Omega, which at Clare (Suffolk) is placed on the altar as the Book of Life. The pile of human heads, flanked by two extremely dumpy and repellent angels at March (Cambs.) may be intended for the Numbering of the Righteous.

RESURRECTION OF CHRIST

Apart from these scenes of the Last Days, there exist a few representations of Our Lord's personal resurrection, shown in the medieval manner holding a long cross-staff. At Rotherfield, 1778, He appears in the scene with the falling tower, but separately at Ewhurst, 1774; West Grinstead (Sussex) 1787; East Ham (Essex) 1781; Fladbury (Worcs.) 1807; Great Casterton (Rutland) 1811. At Callington (Cornwall) He tramples on the recumbent body of Death; while at Bretforton, Thomas Laughton of Cleeve shows Him standing in a chest-tomb set in a little landscape with a careful rendering of a Gothic church.

BIBLICAL ILLUSTRATION

Pictorial scenes of Biblical incidents are to be found in two main areas, the eastern counties of West Suffolk, Kent and Essex, and the west Midlands, the latter being the products of a group of masons working in the villages near Evesham, such as the Laughtons of Cleeve Prior, Ballard and Wheeler of Littleton, Hobday of Honeybourne, Davis of Bidford and Crisp of Badsey, all identifiable because of their habit of signing

FIG. 54. *Central panel of headstone (16 in. diameter) representing the Fall of Man (South Littleton, Worcs.), 1804 (see also Plate 6).*

work. Not least among the beauties of these carvings are the ornamental arabesques which surround the imagery—miniature gardens and orchards of flowers and fruit, redolent of their fruitful Vale. Unfortunately, owing to the poor weathering qualities of the Forest of Dean stone used, this major contribution to the sepulchral art of the early nineteenth century is likely to become illegible within the next fifty years. Although its merit was recognized over thirty years ago, it is deplorable that nothing has been done in the way of record or preservation.

The subjects of the Western group include the Fall and Redemption; Expulsion from Paradise; Sacrifice of Isaac; David as Shepherd; David

FIG. 55. *Central panel of headstone representing Joseph's Dream (Ashton-under-Hill, Glos.).*

and Bathsheba; Joseph's Dream; Balaam and the Ass; Isaiah and the Burning Coal; Elisha and the Shunamite; Annunciation; Flight into Egypt; Good Samaritan. The Flight; Good Samaritan; and Sacrifice of Isaac are common to both groups. The Woman of Samaria at the Well, Christ washing the Apostles' feet, Noli Me Tangere, and Agony in the Garden are peculiar to the Eastern section. Several of these scenes are rare in English iconography, and the reasons for their choice enigmatic. The series as a whole bears no relationship to any known traditional scheme, and one can only assume that in most cases the choice was arbitrary, though to some extent influenced by the details of country life included in the particular incident and their appeal to a rustic patronage.

The only truly allegorical scene is an interpretation of 1 Cor. 15: 21, 22, found at South Littleton, and Childs Wickham (near Evesham) and Church Langton (Leics.) 1777. Here Adam and Eve are shown by the Tree of Knowledge and its serpent, dressed in leafy skirts; an angel admonishes them, while Death directs his dart at Adam below a figure of the risen Christ (Fig. 54). One of the most elaborate of the Evesham reliefs was Joseph's Dream at Ashton-under-Hill (Glos.) 1800, now practically illegible. The scene has fused Joseph's two dreams into one; and the explanatory text is from Genesis 37: 7. In the sky is a great blazing sun, moon and eleven stars, with Joseph below sleeping beneath a tree, a dog at his feet. Reapers are at work amid the corn, where the eleven sheaves are bowing to the central garbe; the sweep of field is bordered by a Cotswold drystone hedge, with a church, mill and castle on the horizon (Fig. 55).

In addition to such Biblical scenes, these men also used the stock "antiques" of the time on their simpler headstones, as well as a few reliefs showing the deceased's occupation; such as the hairdresser's tools at Broadway (Worcs.) 1786; the harp at Harvington, 1830, by Davis of Bidford; the fine plaque by Hobday at Shrawley (Worcs.), which shows a gamekeeper with his pointer, shooting at a brace of birds in a style reminiscent of a sporting-print. Such insets were merely the centre-pieces of these astonishing headstones, which are carved with a lavish arabesque of natural and artificial foliage that will be discussed later under the heading of ornament. Space prohibits further mention of their figure sculpture, but its excellence merits urgent record in face of its lamentable weathering. It should be possible for local committees to list each maker's products, photograph the best and, in certain cases, remove them into the church for safety.

Among the Biblical illustrations of the Eastern group, stretching from Holland to Sussex, the most popular scenes are the Sacrifice of Isaac, the Good Samaritan and the Woman of Samaria at the well. While the figure-work is somewhat less naïve than that of Evesham, the carved scene is usually self-contained, without any floral surround to give it an overall elegance.

SACRIFICE OF ISAAC

The most elaborate example of this theme, at All Saints, Kings Lynn (Norfolk) 1833, is unfortunately badly worn. It shows all the essential items of the scene: the two young men with the ass, a tree with a vase of water and fire at its foot, the central scene with Abraham and Isaac prostrate on the pyre, a seated angel holding an explanatory scroll, and the angel of the Lord appearing in clouds above the ram caught in the thicket. The attendants occur also at Great Casterton (Rutland) 1803, and Gillingham (Kent) 1795, but are often omitted, the scene being confined to the main figures, as at Margate (Kent) 1797, where Isaac stands beside his father after his release, and also on a large Portland headstone at Pulborough (Sussex) 1792; also at Rusper, 1791, where the two figures stand stiffly each side of a Roman altar, the scene being enclosed by the serpent of eternity. At Wisbech St Mary, 1828, the letter-tablet is decorated with a chalice, wheat and vine, thus relating the scene to God's own sacrifice (Plate 24).

GOOD SAMARITAN

East Peckham is a typical churchyard in which to study the ornament and imagery used by Kentish gravestone carvers and is notable for the use by a local craftsman of low relief backgrounds of domed, spired and castellated buildings intended to represent Jerusalem. William Martin's headstone of 1781 shows such a silhouette behind the Samaritan who, dressed in feathered bonnet, doublet and trunk-hose, complacently pours oil into the wounded man's arm (Plate 24). Behind him is tethered his horse; to the right amid trees stands a contemporary farmer with cudgel, and the Levite in clerical garb. The curious trees with horn-like shoots, together with the dress of the Samaritan, suggest a borrowing from engraved illustration.[24] The same scene occurs at Woodchurch, 1782, and there are similar examples at Capel, Cranbrook, Smarden, Speldhurst and Westerham. At Shorne, 1760, in the same county, and Stapleford Tawney (Essex) 1781, the scene is limited to the two main figures and grazing horse with the legend, "Go thou and do likewise".

CHRIST AND THE SAMARITAN WOMAN

This scene no doubt appealed because of its everyday country theme. The two figures are grouped about a well-head, Christ seated beneath a tree, with the woman resting her water-pot on its rim, preparatory to giving Him refreshment. Most of the examples occur in Suffolk, and it is interesting to note that on a headstone to Charles Tooke, 1859, at Wrentham, the panel shows signs of being a separate tablet let into the surface; this, together with replicas built into the walls of an alley in Woodbridge, associates it with the name of a local maker of artificial stone, James Pulham, whose tomb is in Woodbridge churchyard.

NOLI ME TANGERE

This scene has been found only in Kent and Sussex, at Borden, Boughton Monchelsea, Hadlow and Oxney from 1762 to 1788; and later in Sussex at Horsham, Pulborough, New Shoreham and West Grinstead, from 1801 to 1823. At Hadlow Henry Kipping's headstone of 1784 (Plate 24) shows Mary Magdalene with her vase of spices kneeling before Christ, who holds a spade, flanked by the other two Maries who stand by a church; the two crosses remain on Golgotha, with Jerusalem in the background and watchful angels in the sky.

AGONY IN THE GARDEN

This scene where an angel supports the figure of Christ is identified at Hunton, 1787, by its inscription from Luke 22: 42, 43, and is repeated at East Peckham where, on a stone to Ann Long, 1779, the central group is flanked by Christ holding a cross and a mourning attendant, with the Jerusalem prospect behind. Here the Sully headstone of 1784, which also shows the Good Samaritan, may refer to the text of Matt. 4: 11, when angels ministered to Christ after His temptation in the wilderness, an apposite comparison to the parable; it resembles a delicate tondo at Cowfold (Sussex) 1817, where Christ falls prostrate over a rock or tomb, supported by two angels, one of whom holds a crown.

FLIGHT INTO EGYPT

Mary and the Divine Child upon an ass led by Joseph are to be found on stones at Capel, Mayfield, Milton Regis, Pembury, Plaxtol and Sittingbourne, all in Kent, ranging from 1719 to 1760. The only other example known is at Fladbury (Worcs.), carved by Thomas Laughton of Cleeve.

The bulk of this illustrative work therefore was local and produced mainly during a period of about fifty years; its only counterpart lies in the scenes of Biblical inspiration found on the Anglian crosses of the seventh and eighth centuries.

Considered in retrospect, the narrow scope to which gravestone imagery has confined itself is remarkable, and its rejection of many themes that would seem to afford appropriate material often inexplicable.[24] Our present range of knowledge, one would think, should lead us to a greater exploitation of symbolism, yet this is far from being the case, and contemporary imagery remains for the most part conservative and imitative. There is an opportunity here to devise a new iconography suitable for our intellectual and spiritual needs.

ORNAMENT

Our surviving Roman-British monuments bear comparatively little ornament as distinct from symbolic imagery, certainly none of the exuberant repeating-patterns or borders used, for instance, by the workers in mosaic. Much of it is quasi-architectural, in the form of a façade or exedra framing the figure-groups by means of an arch or pediment supported by pilasters, which in the case of the simpler stelae breaks down into geometric patterns. The treatment of foliage such as the acanthus is stiff and formal, appearing at its worst as a species of ragwort doing duty for spandrils. Architectural mouldings are reproduced with little specific accuracy, although sticks of bead-and-reel combined with scallop-shells are a common form of applied decoration on leaden coffins, and the shallow S-shaped groovings or strigillations are usually used to pattern the surface of sarcophagi.

In contrast the ornament of the Anglo-Saxon and Scandinavian period has an intense life of its own, existing apart from the didactic elements or imagery with which it is associated. With the exception of the chequer-board patterns on the Bewcastle cross, probably derived from the art of the metal-worker, the majority of the ornament used during this period falls into two categories. The first is pure plait or interlace, found also in contemporary manuscripts and metal work, the second a vegetable scrollwork in which both birds and animals and later monsters play a decorative role.

The origins of the latter can be related to Hellenistic and Roman arabesques which became adapted into grotesques after the Renaissance; and a fragmentary stone of this sort, carved with a cherub and animals set amid the coils of a vine-scroll, has been found at Hexham and may have been part of Wilfrid's original church, cut by his imported work-men. However, the more conventional treatment of this vegetation among the branches of which birds and animals are engaged in pecking fruit, a motif to which the name "inhabited scroll" has been given, is more nearly related to Syrian or Alexandrian sources of the sixth century. It occurs on the great crosses of the early Northumbrian period in bold relief and subtle modelling. At Jedburgh (Roxburgh), there is a variant with central stalk and side-branches, which is distinguished from a similar example at Croft (Yorks.) by its parrot-like birds, which have analogies with Coptic decoration. An exception to these aviaries is the double-interlacing vine-scroll with grape-bunches on the Acca cross, which is devoid of such creatures. At Melsonby (Yorks.) along with simple interlace and vegetable spirals there is an inhabited scroll of a different sort, in which lizard or seal-like beasts blend their tails into the scrolls and thus make their own perches. A heraldic treatment is to be noticed at Ilkley, where the pairs of beasts confront one another, and the same flat style, which is now expressed in lower relief and empha-sized silhouette, occurs on a cross-shaft put to use as a font at Melbury Bubb (Dorset). Traces of the Carolingian influence evident in Wessex carving is to be seen in this combat of a hart and a dragon, symbolic of the Christian struggle, which developed in animal terms the contest of good and evil and would thus be intelligible both to Christians and the Norse invaders. It was to persist in the form of a dragon gnawing the root of the Tree of Life well into the thirteenth century.

A reversion to the zoomorphic plaits which had previously appeared in Northumbrian and Irish manuscripts is symptomatic of fresh Scandi-navian influence; the modelling of these creatures becomes flat and ribbon-like and is reduced to an interlace in which they are barely intelligible. They also developed as an isolated portrait pattern, a type of "Great Beast" characterised by double contours, spiraliform jointed limbs, and enmeshment within its own coils, such as that at Colerne

(Wilts.). This new conventional creature is usually classified as the main feature of the Jellinge style which, rather than being imported, seems to have matured by a mutual interchange of ideas in England. A representative example of the later treatment given to this beast can be seen on a slab at Levisham (Yorks.), where it is separated from its background, and the interlace tends to bud into spirals and volutes. This burgeoning of the interlace, which eventually sprouts new elongated leaves reminiscent of the acanthus writhings of the Winchester style of

FIG. 56. *Coffin-slab (Levisham, Yorks.), 50 in. long, 18 in. wide.*

book production, is a feature of the succeeding Ringerike style, evident on monuments during the period of Danish ascendancy, and persisting with its scenes of animal combat into the Anglo-Norman period. Its most lively monument is the Guildhall tombstone, which evidently represents a stag and serpent in agitated struggle, and whose mannerism has suggested an influence from Scythian art transmitted through Viking-controlled Kiev to the West. The more typical features which the style was later to develop can be seen on the Bibury slab where the ribbon-band ends in lion or cat-headed terminals.

Apart from these zoomorphs, pure geometric interlacings and other abstract ornaments were used in carving of this period. Various forms of interlace had been devised by our native workmen on similar lines to those of the Lombardic carvers of the eighth century, who derived them by migration from Hither Asian sources. They can be divided into four classes: continuous plaits; plaits twisting at regular intervals into knot-work; individual knots, triple, quadruple or circular; and chain-work.

At first the interlace was organically arranged to follow the under-over meshing of its wire-plait or manuscript derivatives, but later work can be detected by an irregularity and neglect of this principle. This is a characteristic trait of Welsh cross-slabs (in contrast to their Scottish equivalents) which also show separate knot and key-patterns, all of which continued to be used in the Anglo-Norman period. Chain-work, a Scandinavian device, occurs on the Gosforth cross and is a particular characteristic of Manx decoration, where it is usually defined by beading.

The tendency for pattern to break down in the Anglo-Norman period into abstract ideograms can be seen on work in Northumbria, Galloway and Anglesey, where the crude spirals, rustication and lozenge diapers found upon tombstones seem to be vestiges of the Anglo-Saxon heyday. On the Welsh crosses in particular the slovenly treatment of these traditional motives is a noticeable feature, and they finally relapse into knot-units and two-strand plaits. Such work was easy to set out and execute, and remained popular well into the twelfth century. It can be seen to advantage on the pseudo-coped slabs of the Cambridge group, where the plaits form neat regular backgrounds to these typical cross-framed monuments.

During the course of the Middle Ages the majority of minor sepulchral monuments were cross-slabs, which in the virtual absence of inscriptions can only be loosely dated according to the style of their foliated crosses. In these vegetable renderings of the Tree of Life, one can thus separate the rhythmic lobes of thirteenth century foliage from the realistic leaves of the succeeding century, until the force of the symbolism spent itself—for during the hundred years previous to the Reformation the cross became formal and heraldic.

Simple traceried niches or quatrefoils were the usual decoration of the chest-tombs of the time, and such Gothic features continued to be used well into the seventeenth century, and after new Renaissance patterns had become absorbed into the gamut of ornament. Our native love for the Garden was then beginning to express itself in a richly-charged language in which fruit and flowers were given symbolical significance, an imagery shared between poetry and the plastic arts, and finding a fresh outlet on sepulchral monuments. In the Midlands and parts of Wiltshire, the floral decoration is incised, with S-scrolls, paterae, and daisies in combination with fleurs-de-lis, Tudor roses, marigolds and tulips; whilst the Hornton work is in relief, spilling masses of fruit and flowers from cornucopias or enscrolled sheathes. The love of tulips was early expressed in Parkinson's *Paradisus* of 1629; John Tradescant grew fifty varieties of the flower for Charles the First; and in Holland *c.* 1640 tulipomania was in full flower. Probably Addison's satires in *The Tatler* of 1710 prevented its resurgence in England, nevertheless, although tulips

FIG. 57. *Initials with tulips and knot-work (Kimcote, Leics.), 1713.*

are seldom mentioned in eighteenth century poetry, in applied decoration their use was paramount and remained conspicuous on gravestone decoration until the early years of the eighteenth century. Along with our native love for the rose, this flower is often found amid the curlicues of initials on early incised slates combined with sunflowers, or put into little vases, such as Upper Winchendon, Ellesborough (Bucks.), and Wroxton (Oxon.) 1698; or doing duty as spandrils in the various tablets by members of the Brute family found in churches in the Southern Welsh Marches. It is common on the chairback designs found on West Riding ledgers (Plate 29), occurs in association with the thistle at Wantage (Berks.) 1689, and is set within borders of Flemish strap-work at Hambleton (Rutland). Great fleshy tulips and marigolds were used by the Hills of Great Easton for their cartouche surrounds; while Francis Lamb of Bottesford, at Farndon (Notts.) 1758, used sprigs of Tudor roses that seem to be derived from brass-engraving and occur as late as 1777 at Thirsk (Yorks.). Formal Tudor roses, combined with a free treatment of pseudo-acanthus and anthemion, decorate the headstone of Robert Hockham, 1829, at Stow-on-the-Wold (Glos.); while the chased and shaded roses familiar on Swithland slates seem to show borrowings from textile designs and damasks. Although the lily, along with ivy, only became popular in Victorian times, it is early shown at Bidford (Warws.) 1710, combined with a rose and death's-head, and the cut lily, signifying early death, at Dartford (Kent) 1755. In similar fashion the plucked flower is found as early as 1630 on a tablet in Newton St Cyres near Exeter, while the later rose-slip severed by a sickle occurs on a tablet by Nicholas Read at West Horsley (Surrey) 1767, and on headstones at Penshurst (Kent) and around the Reigate area in Surrey in the early nineteenth century. By the 1730s, this formal and heraldic decoration began to be replaced by more artificial and exuberant designs showing the influence of rococo. Henry Copland (who is traditionally associated with Chippendale's furniture designs) was the first to introduce rococo into England, in his *New Book of Ornaments* published in 1746, and began the

FIG. 58. *Panel from headstone showing the theme of the severed flower, a violet, in the foreground (Penshurst, Kent), 1830.*

fashion for the ornate craftsman's trade-cards which were perhaps the direct sources of inspiration for gravestone carving in this style. By 1760–80 gravestone-cutters both in slate and freestone throughout the Great Stone Belt from Wash to Severn were producing immense numbers of ornate stones in which rococo elements were paramount. In particular, the slate-engravers, borrowing elements from medieval brasses, introduced a Gothic flavour into their rococo, using an elaborate technique in which incision, relief and gouged lines enabled them to exploit its resources to the full. The more particular influence of rococo furniture design is shown on remarkable headstones such as Elizabeth Brooks, 1777, at Wisbech (Cambs.) and a group at Fulham,

1753, and Bishops Stortford, 1756, Saffron Walden, 1764, Epping Up-land, 1772, and Roydon, 1779, in Essex (Plate 9). Not least of the fascinations of gravestone ornament are the ways in which individuals imposed their own inventive faculty on the current idiom of pattern, freely adapting the often recondite models which sparked their inspiration. In this way William Walker of Market Harborough devised intricate calligraphic garlands to his text. His headstone to Elizabeth Tayler, 1739, at St Mary Arden, Market Harborough, is obviously related to patterns used by metal-chasers and bookbinders in the seventeenth century and seen in such writing-manuals as Richard Gethinge's *Calligraphotechnia* of 1619.

With few of the resources available to the contemporary designer, past craftsmen must have attached a greater value to whatever models they used and derived from them a livelier mental stimulus. Their books were scanty, and a stone-mason of the calibre of Jonathan Harmer of Heathfield, with intellectual and Republican sympathies, owned only half a dozen, apart from his own notebooks.[25] Working drawings and designs were kept and handed down in the family, and masons presumably compiled their own pattern-books, although, as these were usually thumbed to pieces through continual use, existing specimens are virtually unknown.

Thomas Wood of Bingham, as a professional gravestone-maker, used a wide range of ornamental devices, some of them unique, such as the great pineapple at Lowdham (Notts.) 1826, which is shown with its original leaves, suggesting that he had seen a growing plant, which he must have deemed a rare exotic (Plates 27, 28); or the pheasants (as a change from doves), holding sprigs of olive in their beaks and a loop of label, their tails blending into an arch to receive the superscription. He seems to have been the only slate-cutter to use cavo-relief for the well-observed animals placed in his pastoral landscapes, whose foliage and banks of ground are shaded into a semblance of tone by a series of flecks similar to Chinese stone engravings. His more conventional ornament is neo-classic, but the various ways in which he manipulated shield-shaped cartouches, spindly pilasters and various design elements, show a natural ability as a designer of great merit, although he was merely a country mason who worked in his native village all his life. Some craftsmen were sufficiently versatile to adapt their style according to the changing fashion, and James Sparrow (another mason whose main output was tombstones) shows the gamut of folk-art Georgian, baroque, Gothic-rococo and, in his last years, neo-classic influence. Others, such as the Brutes of Llanbedr or the Hills of Great Easton, were more conservative. The work of succeeding generations with their changing outlook on design can in many cases be compared in a single churchyard, such as Linton (Herefs.) or Scraptoft (Leics.) in the case of the Webb and Firmadge families.

From Langhorne's

> Nature deigns to sympathize with art
> And lead the moral beauty to the Heart.

it was but a step to considering natural abundance as a manifestation of divine bounty, following Shaftesbury's dictum identifying the Beautiful with the Good. The introduction of more realistic detail into the artificial arabesques of conventional ornament that is to be found on some gravestones in the latter Georgian period reflects this consciousness of plenitude, the crowning achievement of the rustic year in harvest festival. This is indeed characteristic of the Evesham masons, who mingled urns, acanthus and wreathed columns with flowers and fruits of the English field and farm, hops, corn, vine, convolvulus, roses and pea-pods, along with winged serpents and hydras vomiting flames. It can be seen throughout Rutland and Sussex, where panniers of flowers so often form the centre-pieces; in the profuse festoons cut with great virtuosity by the Moor family in Havant and other churchyards in South Hampshire; in the Severn valley, where the earlier pompous scrollwork was succeeded by fragile sprays of olive and myrtle, roses and wheat-ears; in Wood's bryony and acorns; Richard Phipps's woodbine, and Pearce's willow-fronds.

Alas, in a few years these Gardens of Adonis had withered, to be replaced by prim conventional Gothic foliage, and later by meagre strands of ivy, impoverished bouquets of lilies and forget-me-nots, and those last arid vestiges of the language of flowers, the immortelles.

LETTERING

Within recent years handwriting and typography have engaged a good deal of critical research, and the influence of such masters as Edward

Johnston and Eric Gill has had its effects on public taste. The older mercantile copper-plate has been ousted by the humanist script, and a purist zeal for classical forms has led to a canonization of the Trajan Column alphabet. In typography, on the other hand, and largely due to the nostalgia aroused by the Festival of Britain, Victorian jobbing-types once decried as bad taste have become acceptable for use in both commercial art and fine printing. Carved letter-forms and their relation to type and calligraphy, however, are a branch of this subject that has not received sufficient attention for, besides their architectural use, it is on gravestones that they were mainly employed. Even the most casual student of this vast output of lettering on churchyard monuments throughout England cannot fail to be impressed with its remarkably high standards of taste and execution. Being ubiquitous, it has to all intents and purposes been ignored; yet in two areas alone, in Cornwall and the Midland counties, where the material is impervious slate, the complete history of post-Reformation letterforms is available for inspection. Ironically enough, the pattern-books from which much of this text was derived are now rarities for the bibliophile or the major library. An appreciation of lettering is perhaps a specialist taste, and space

FIG. 59. *Devices from Kentish headstones, based on a coin of George I, showing gradual deterioration of pattern; from top to bottom: West Malling, 1735; Sandhurst, 1713; Seal, 1757 and 1761.*

prohibits more than a brief analysis of the subject here, yet it is to be hoped that some awareness of the value of these monumental inscriptions may stimulate some systematic and regional research before they fall victims to corroding Time.

Although most lettering on Roman-British tombstones is of moderate provincial merit, it is invariably redeemed by the classical norm of spacing and proportion. Square capitals are invariably used, sometimes compressed in width, with linked and encircling letters used as decorative tricks of spacing. The largest and perhaps finest inscription is that on the tomb of the Procurator, Julius Classicianus. Anglo-Saxon inscriptions are few and laconic; those on the pillow-stones of Northumbria have the square form, half-uncial in character, derived from bookwork, while the inscription to Herebericht at Monkwearmouth is more ample and monumental. Welsh crosses at first show the influence of Irish half-uncials, which were later supplanted by mixed square and rounded letter-forms introduced from the Continent. During the period of Scandinavian influence both Latin and Runic were used together, Manx inscriptions being confined to the Nordic script entirely.

Apart from large tombs, inscriptions on Norman as well as medieval monuments are rare, the rank and file being anonymous. They are usually placed as borders to the tapering coffin-slabs, or lengthwise on the stone, as in the Anglo-Norman inscriptions to Gundrada at Lewes, *c.* 1100, or Maurice de Londres at Ewenny, 1150, which show the decorative letter-forms that were common to Western Europe at this time. During the thirteenth century carvers adopted from manuscript illumination the brush-stroke versals or Lombardic letters which, as well as being incised, could also be recessed for filling with insets of brass or lead. This type of letter continued as an anachronism on Scottish and Irish memorial slabs and English bell-founders' stamps until the sixteenth century, but it was generally superseded by black-letter or Gothic script towards the end of the fourteenth century. The tomb of Richard II in Westminster Abbey has one of its finest treatments. Up to this date majuscules or capital letters only had been used, but future inscriptions follow the modern method of combining lower and upper-case characters.

Both on brasses and tombstones the engravers cut letters in relief and incision, but probably for the sake of clarity, as black-letter when

19 (left). *Detail of Hope from the Greenfield stone; (above, right) Billingshurst (Sussex), two Portland headstones to William and Sarah Green-field, 1793–1800, and Ann Worsfold, 1796, typical Sussex headstones of the Regency period; (below, right) Hadlow (Kent), Elizabeth Saxby, 1782: upper part of headstone with delicately cut half-lengths of girls busied in devotional reading.*

20 (above). *Sherington (Bucks.), John Campion, 1787: upper part of headstone, 26½ in. high, 14 in. wide, showing a scene derived from emblem-imagery—the death-chamber with the protagonists Death and Time; (below) St Margaret, Leicester, John and Elizabeth Ireland, 1776–1804: central panel of Swithland slate headstone 16¾ in. long, 12¾ in. wide, showing Death taunting the dying man with the pleasures of the world.*

21. *The Last Judgement:* (above) *East Dean (West Sussex), Richard Vallar, 1776: upper part
of Portland headstone, showing Christ the Judge with apocalyptic angels awakening the dead,
flanked by Death and Time;* (below) *Rothley (Leics.), William Hunt, 1794: panel from Swithland
slate headstone, 11 in. long, 9¾ in. wide, by Hind of Swithland. The resurrection of the dead is
envisaged as taking place in the carver's native churchyard.*

22. *Details of carving: (above) St Mary de Castro, Leicester, Samuel Bankart, 1799: oval panel from headstone, 13 in. long, 10 in. wide, by William Firmadge of Leicester representing Chronos or Father Time; (below, left) March (Lincs.), detail of panel 24 in. long, 18 in. wide, from chest-tomb of Marianne Ingersoll, 1816, showing two rustic deities, one holding ears of corn and a reaping-hook, the other a cornucopia of fruit and flowers; (below, right) St Mary de Castro, Leicester, Susanna Gamble, 1821: a fashion plate figure of Faith or Religion cut by a member of the Kirk family.*

unduly compressed reduced itself to illegibility, the stone-carvers introduced an archaic form of alphabet that was to remain as a transition
between Gothic and Roman until the general acceptance of the latter
in the seventeenth century. Such letter-forms can be seen on a slab to
Abbot Peter de Snape, 1436, at Jervaulx Abbey, whose origins refer
back to the Carolingian renaissance and can be recognized in the cross-
barred A, the looped C and D, and the W composed of overlapping
Vs. Such lettering was adaptable both to relief or incision and passed
through several variations. Its letter-bars were ornamented with spurs
or knots, or its extremities forked (following a precedent established as
early as the fourth century in the Damasian inscriptions cut by Filo-
calus). Such exuberances are to be found generally in the applied arts
during the Renaissance period both in metal, plaster and wood. Due
largely to the influence of this latter material, gravestone-cutters began
to thicken the bars of these quasi-Carolingian characters, expanding the
ends of limbs and adjusting their proportions so as to reduce to a minimum the background area, which after being sunk to the required
depth, gave the illusion of relief. Such inscriptions, mainly upon
ledgers, are fairly widely distributed both in the North and in the West
Country, where the more intractable magnesian limestones and granites
were especially adapted to such relief letters, as for instance, on Christopher Bligh's fine tomb at St Gennys, Cornwall, 1593. A similar effect
was obtained on the cast-iron slabs made from wooden moulds found
in the early smelting-areas of the Weald and Coalbrookdale.

The particular influence of a wood-carving technique on the work
of the stone-mason can be clearly seen in two groups of monuments,
c. 1670–1720, throughout the West Riding and the Vale of Belvoir
(Plate 29); and to a lesser extent in many ledgers of this period, which
retain the simple arched surround supported by pilasters, a common
motif on furniture design and ornamental woodwork. The first group
shows Dutch influence in its use of floriated initials and the palmette
motif, sprouting hearts and tulips, which is reminiscent of the designs
found on wooden chests and chair-backs of the Jacobean period. Even
when the carvers had relinquished relief for incision, this palmette
was imitated in calligraphic flourishes, as can be seen not only in the
West Riding, but on early slates such as those by the so-called "Bingham master" at Great Gonerby (Lincs.) 1731.[26]

FIG. 60. *Calligraphic devices from Swithland slate headstones, c. 1750–1780.*

The Vale of Belvoir headstones (a folk-art type, which may have originated from a workshop in the Hickling area) show the division of the surface into three parts for imagery, data and epitaph (Plate 29). They can be recognized by their characteristic angel-heads with triangular chip-carved wings accompanied by Latin tags and mortality emblems, with the genealogical data often cut in true relief. The tedium and time involved in the execution of such relievos soon led to the masons' reverting to incision. This unduly brief excursion into relief (and its short recrudescence in the Gothic Revival) prevented our native stone-masons from exploiting many of the decorative and symbolic possibilities of the technique, which can be seen in many excellent German memorials today.[27]

The majority of seventeenth century memorials are inscribed in Roman capitals, usually of fairly even strokes, with little emphasis on serifs and often noble in form and proportion; but in the early years of the eighteenth century carvers began to evolve wedge-shaped chisel-forms with rudimentary hair-lines, so that the component parts of the letters are almost separated in stencil-fashion. This technique, already obvious in the Vale of Belvoir, where both ascenders and descenders were projected into tight little curlicues, is an obvious feature both in Kent and in Cotswold, the latter area including initials in which the flourishes have an abrupt shading from thick to thin. This is a device inspired by calligraphy, where the pen can play such tricks of transition, and it marks the beginning of the influence of handwriting, which in the Midlands and Cornwall, where slate offered a medium capable of emulating engraving, was to flourish with unprecedented virtuosity, whereby the stone-mason imitated the work of contemporary penmen.

The revival of calligraphy that took place in Europe during the seventeenth and eighteenth centuries was related to the growth of diplomacy and commerce, with the scribe in the new guise of clerk. This tendency is evident in the albums of our own writing-masters, of whom many, like the admirable Cocker, were also teachers of arithmetic and included receipts, bills and invoices among their sample sheets. The opening-up of English trade in the late seventeenth century led to the production of the Roundhand which, when Britain became foremost in commerce, was recognized as the standard writing-style in Europe and America. From the technical point of view the interests of the copper-plate engravers and the penmen were mutually dependent, the same fluctuations from thick to thin being shared by the pressure-strokes of the burin and the pen.[28]

The desire of the gravestone-engravers to rival the efforts of calligraphers can be seen in the developing layout of the Swithland slate headstones. The first of these, from Thurcaston and Swithland itself, during the latter years of the seventeenth century, are small, crudely lettered in capitals, with text set out in lines of equal width, and the initial letter modestly flourished. Within thirty years, this first word of the superscription, usually in black-letter, is flourished with interlaced patterns

FIG. 61. *Incised swan on slate headstone by William Bonser (Cottesbrooke, Northants.).*

and sprays of flowers, and the tendency to add more flourishes or "strikings" increases, so that by 1750 it has been taken from its context and centralized into an elaborate heading, thus changing the text from being a page to a frontispiece. On this field, as in engraved book-illustration and on trade-cards, a full repertoire of different hands, Gothic, Roundhand, Italian or Chancery, was able to riot in exuberance. Such zest for engraving rather than cutting inscriptions spread to work on freestone, where its excess of sensibility has often been reduced by weathering to illegibility.

The skill attained by some of these gravestone engravers falls little short of metal-chasing; and Sparrow of Radcliff, William Charles of Wymeswold, Button of Crick, Bell of Leicester or Staveley of Melton were all remarkable exponents, yet apparently largely self-taught from the study of these writing-manuals. One would assume the existence of evidence to prove that gravestone-engravers of this calibre were also professional writers, but this is far from being the case. Apart from the well-known example of Baskerville, the typographer, who practised both arts in his youth, the writer can only introduce Jonathan Buckerfield of Leicester who produced slates at Kibworth Harcourt, 1744, and others as far afield as Simpson (Bucks.); and William Bonser of Burton Overy, members of whose family were prolific engravers.[29] Admittedly there were schoolmasters who would teach writing in the village schools such as John Newton or Henry Castledine of Syston, 1720-1800; or parish clerks like Robert Waddington of Clipston, 1717–91, and Thomas Allt of Breedon, 1770–1850, who together with the parson and the pedagogue made up the triumvirate of culture in the village.[30] For these men, gravestone-making was not their only source of livelihood, and their products were comparatively few. The modest output of Robert Waddington, for instance, seems to have been confined to his own parish and neighbouring villages, and yet his "command of hand" shown on the slate to John Wright, 1751, at Husbands Bosworth (Plate 30) is a worthy rival to the work of Cocker, whose initials seem to have been his source of inspiration.

It is difficult to identify precisely the individual writing-masters whose manuals were most often studied by the carvers, but it was probably George Bickham (whose compendium of contemporary work in *The Universal Penman*, 1743, was published in parts) who had as much influence as any.[31] Special books were also written for trade use, but these are now extremely rare, for it is understandable that the majority did not survive constant workshop use and finally disintegrated, the invariable fate of popular literature.

In the Cotswolds, particularly in the Stroud Valley, and in North Yorkshire, where fixing engraved brass plates to ledgers was customary, some masons were also metal-engravers; the West Country practitioners included such men as Hamlett, Freebury, Franklin and Cook of Gloucester, who was probably related to the family of statuaries in that city, and whose plate to John Sheppard, 1805, at Miserden is a characteristic example of his skill. Cornish slate engraving shows little calligraphic influence, although there is an interest in the imaginative free-play with letter-forms; at Hartland (Devon) for instance, letters are spurred and the verticals fantastically interwoven with rings. However, by the 1750s, they were producing magnificent Roman letter-forms similar to the type-face initiated by Caslon in 1722 (as on the stone to John Lark, 1754, St Endellion) and this continued to be the norm on freestones throughout the country until the characters of Bodoni, with their unbracketed serifs and greater variation between thicks and thins, led to an excessive neatness, which when combined with the severity of neo-classic ornament became Spartan to dullness.

Fig. 62. *Calligraphic device from headstone by Bell of Leicester, 1750 (Gilmorton, Leics.).*

In the early nineteenth century, after a century of experiment with the classical letter, typographers began to invent a series of display types in which not only its proportions were altered, but its components decorated. Certain of these experiments may well have been the pioneer work of contemporary sign-writers and engravers, for the latter were using patterned letters during the late eighteenth century, and later in the Victorian period both lithographers and commercial illustrators contributed to the vagaries of type-design. An ebullient creation of type-forms is a phenomenon of the Victorian era, and now that the purist reaction to many of its excesses has developed more sense of proportion, it has become possible to give it impartial and serious study (Plate 31). The Festival of Britain largely helped to effect this more impartial attitude, as its designers reintroduced certain of these type-faces during the Festival year, and these eventually passed into the printer's repertoire.

It is a curious fact that as soon as these experimental faces were introduced, they were imitated by both the slate-cutters of the Midlands and Cornwall; in fact, some of the slate-cut letters coincide in date with their fellows on the typographical sample-sheets, and this suggests a possible interchange of ideas between the two classes of craftsmen.[32] The first shadowed letters in type appeared in 1815, although three-dimensional lettering for architectural use on street-signs and fascia-boards had been current some years previously.[33] In type their use often

FIG. 63. *Lettering from slate headstone by Robert Oliver (Egloshayle, Cornwall).*

appears vulgar owing to the stridency of black and white; when cut in slate, however, the reverse effect of light sparkling from them on a drab background gives to even the wildest of these letter-forms a rich-ness of pattern and redeeming charm, linking them with the bravado of canal-boats and fair-booths in which the Victorian tradition is still perpetuated.

The carvers concentrated their main decoration and their ornate types on the superscription, as well as using a variety of type-faces in the text, seldom, however, equalling the typographer's excess in this respect, although George Wothers of Market Bosworth, at Hinckley, 1837, cut ten different faces in the inscription. Robert Oliver of St Minver used fern-like leaves in his floriated surrounds, and on the body of his letter-forms, along with bold shaded letters set within borders of delicate tendrils.

This galaxy of type—Fat-face, Egyptian, Tuscan, Italian, Clarendon, etc.—was largely superseded elsewhere in the 1850s by Black-letter and Versals, introduced through the Gothic Revival, although it still persisted in the West. Such Gothic lettering was used on cemetery memorials but was eventually replaced by the sans serif or block letter. Painted black against this dead white marble, or inset with pre-fabricated lead,[34] it plumbs the depth of the letter-cutter's art but lamentably remains in common and current use.

The influence of Art Nouveau which initiated both a semi-abstract treatment of lettering where the inscription was made into pattern, emulating a characteristic of certain oriental scripts, as well as serious attempts to invent new letter-forms appropriate to different materials, might well have given monumental lettering a new lease of life. Unfortunately its expressionist ideas, although effecting a revolution abroad, found little favour with our insular designers.[35]

On the other hand, largely inspired by Morris and the Art and Crafts Movement, Johnston's rediscovery of calligraphic principles, and Gill's advocacy of a stricter use of Roman chisel-cut forms, led to a purist introduction of the Trajan Column alphabet as the acceptable norm.

INSCRIPTIONS AND EPITAPHS

Books on epitaphs are legion, but many are incompletely recorded, repetitive and unreliable. The standard collections which deal mainly with medieval monuments and interior tombs are those of Stow (1598), Camden (1610), Weever (1631), Le Neve (1718–29), and Gough (1786–99), and they are now of considerable importance as they record many monuments which are no longer in existence. The most reliable sources for churchyard monuments are the various collections which have been printed in the transactions of local archaeological societies, or contributed in manuscript either to local archives or such an invaluable central source as the Society of Genealogists' library. Probably the two best attempts at a general review of epitaphial literature are Pettigrew's *Chronicles of the Tombs* (1857) and the Rev. T. E. Ravenshaw's *Antiente Epitaphes* (1878), but a critical examination of the material in relation to social history and literary sources yet remains to be done and would be a work of considerable value for the light it would inevitably shed on the many minutiae of contemporary existence.[36]

ROMAN

Roman inscriptions were factual and laconic; usually confined to recording the deceased's name, age, rank or occupation and, in a soldier's case, his years of service, concluding with the names of the heirs or individuals who paid for the monument. Such data is usually prefaced by the customary evocation to the Divine Shades (D.M. for *Diis Manibus*), concluding with the statement of burial (H.S.E. for *Hic situs est*). Christian converts replaced the classical formula by *Hic jacet* and, through a contempt for pagan precision which often recorded the exact months and days of life's term, added the phrase, *Plus minus* (more or less) after the years of age. The last colloquy of shade and mourner, *Ave salve* (Hail! Farewell!), and the address to the passer-by in the street of tombs, *Siste viator* (Pause, traveller), and also Martial's epigram *Sit tibi terra levis* (Light be the earth upon thee), were all used on post-Reformation monuments and gravestones with their particular anglicized variants.[37]

POST-ROMAN

Post-Roman texts in the areas of Celtic Christianity were often bilingual, inscribed both in Latin and Ogham characters, such as the stones from Fardell (Devon) and Trescastle (Brecons.) in the British Museum. The Latin of such hybrids is often ungrammatical, and minuscules are used indiscriminately with capitals. The longest inscription occurs on a purloined Roman pillar at Eliseg, near Llangollen.

ANGLO-SAXON AND DANISH

Pillow-stones from Lindisfarne and Hartlepool include the first use of *Requiescat in pace* (in post-Reformation times contracted to R.I.P.), the

Greek letters Alpha and Omega—a provincial use of a formula already outmoded on the continent—and *Orate*, the earliest Christian request for the prayers of the passer-by. Later Welsh crosses such as those at Llantwit and Margam (Glam.) of the tenth to eleventh centuries use the initial phrase, *In nomine Dei*. Scandinavian influence is shown by bilingual Latin and Runic inscriptions on the high crosses of Bewcastle and Ruthwell, the latter containing part of the North Anglian poem, *The Dream of the Rood*, where the cross seems to speak with a supernatural individuality concerning its fate and purpose. In Man nearly half the monuments have brief Runic inscriptions, engraved both on the edge and face of the slabs, the most famous being at Kirk Michael, commemorating Malbrigd, which asserts that "his kinsman Gaut made this and all in Man".[38]

Apart from these, the headstone to Frithburga at Whitchurch, and the well-cut inscription to Herebericht the priest at Monkwearmouth, most Anglo-Saxon and Danish memorials are uninscribed, and with few exceptions this is also the case with churchyard monuments of the medieval period.

MEDIEVAL

The language used on important epitaphs during this time shows the emergence of the vernacular for, whereas from the time of the Conquest Latin and Norman-French were general, the first English inscription occurs on the brass at Brighton Baldwin (Oxon.) 1370, characteristically enough to John le Smith; from this time it became customary to use English, though larded on occasion with those Latin concoctions dear to the heart of Dr Johnston, and reserved, even today, for the more pompous and official inscriptions.[39]

During the Middle Ages the general prayer addressed to God became particularized into an appeal to the living to pray for the departed soul, in the belief that its time in purgatory could thus be curtailed, with occasionally the added inducement of a personal indulgence for such piety.[40] Church-gifts were also mentioned, not only for motives of individual spiritual insurance, but to remind the reader of his share in such benefits.[41] Such public works as bridges were popular gifts and, of course, a great deal of the splendour of church-building is directly related to these prayer-factories established first by the monastic houses, and later by local patrons and land-owners in the form of private chantries, whose chapel became the family burial-place.[42]

POST REFORMATION

Towards the end of the Middle Ages elegies for men of importance, often of some length, and probably written by a member of their household, seem to have been displayed on scrolls or tablets placed near their tombs, thus supplementing its factual reticence with eulogy.[43] After the Reformation doctrinal changes which encouraged the cult of personality, coupled with a zest for literary gymnastics, combined in the epitaph the features of biography, moral and religious reflection as a self-contained unit. The majority of such epitaphs, belonging to the larger tombs of the sixteenth and seventeenth centuries, are outside our present scope; but apart from the few well known verses by famous poets actually engraved on tombs, a great deal of ingenious, and indeed, much fine second-rate verse was produced by unknown poetasters for the tombs of this period. Their customary puns, anagrams and acrostics are part and parcel of the emblematic imagery used by the carvers, who, in Hazlitt's words: "forced the image, whether learned or vulgar, into the services of the muses … if there was the most remote circumstance, however trifling and vague, for the pretended comparison to hinge on." In contrast, churchyard inscriptions for the most part are brief and factual, and it is not until the eighteenth and nineteenth centuries that verbose and vain-glorious epitaphs occur, along with those showing a range of expression from the sublime to the ridiculous, from tenderness to brutality, in epitome of the contradictions which form the complex English character.[44]

Officially, the College of Arms was responsible for the supervision of heraldry and epitaphs, but in the early years of the seventeenth century its authority was declining. With the breakdown of sumptuary laws and older class distinctions, Weever's definition of a monument, made in 1631, was already old-fashioned: "Sepulchres should be made according to the qualitie and degree of the person deceased, that by the tombe everyone might be discerned of what ranke hee was living"—a definition that fails to take into account the competitive snobbery of human nature. An epitaph, he declared, should consist of "the name, the age, the deserts, the dignities, the state, the praises both of body and minde, the good or bad fortunes in the life, and the manner and time of the death, of the person therein interred". His friend Camden, with rather warmer feelings, argued that in epitaphs "love was shown to the deceased, memorie was continued to posteritie, friends were comforted, and the Reader put in mind of human frailtie". Others, like Fuller, might assert that "the shortest, plainest and truest are the best", but reticence is hardly a typical feature of Georgian monuments, which in their worst verbosities contain ludicrous excesses of boasting and impeccable moral virtue. Even humbler gravestones reflect this taint, as if the voices of the people were passionately exerting their smaller claims on posterity, through the medium of their gradual emancipation to literacy and freedom of speech. As we have already seen, clerical reaction came in the nineteenth century, where one authority, in discussing epitaphs, asserted: "Their fulsomeness and utter want of truth while praising the departed, outdo anything of that kind in the pagan world itself, so that 'to lie like an epitaph' has grown into a saying; nay, downright pagan instead of Christian sentiments may be sometimes found inscribed on them." Although similar ideas are echoed by churchmen today, who are naturally anxious to prevent grief from expressing itself publicly in heterodox fashion, the historian, no less than the student of human nature is thankful for this bulk of inscriptions, recognizing its value as illuminant to many minutiae of life, which in the absence of documents would for ever remain unknown.

Up to the nineteenth century the greater part of epitaphial verse, no less than carving, was mainly concerned with the fact of mortality, and the levelling factor of Death as King of Terrors—often expressed in medieval mortality literature in dramatic form, where the skull, skeleton or dead man are made to speak with the living, in such themes as the Quick and the Dead, the Dance of Death and the Ars Morituri. It is probably no accident that such themes became prominent in the fourteenth century, when the Black Death took such a heavy toll of life, and the tomb-makers introduced below the effigy the ghastly corpse to point the moral expressed in that most prevalent of epitaphs:

> As you are now; so once was I;
> As I am now; so shall you be;
> Therefore prepare to follow me.[45]

The periodical outbreaks of plague, which only ceased after the mid-seventeenth century visitations, were succeeded by epidemics of small-pox and cholera, all of which, in the almost total absence of preventive measures for public health, swelled the mortality rate.[46] Inadequate diet also led to widespread tuberculosis, made painfully evident by the common epitaph:

> A pale consumption gave the final blow.
> The stroke was fatal, though th' effect came slow.[47]

and it is as an expression of genuine suffering rather than to hypochondria that we owe so many:

> Afflictions sore long time I bore
> Physicians were in vain
> 'Till God did please Death should me seize
> And ease me of my pain.

together with such variations as: "And fierce diseases wait around, to hurry mortals home", "In pain and sickness long I lay", "With patience to the last he did submit", "Worn out by sickness and disease", or the curious epitaph in which Christ is represented as a Doctor dispensing euthanasia:

> Pains were my Portion, Physick was my Food;
> Groans were my Devotion; Drugs did me no good;
> Christ was my Physician, knew which way was best,
> To release me from my Pain, and set my Soul at rest.

Death reaped a grim harvest from babes, for there was appalling infant mortality both in town and country; and, while Mrs Ann Clarke, midwife of Tiverton (Devon) d. 1733, might declare that during her last thirty-five years' practice she had helped five thousand children into the world, it may be unlikely that half of them lived. Indeed Jonas Hanway was proud of the fact that out of the 1,384 children to be taken into the Foundling Hospital during the first fifteen years of its existence up to 1756 only 724 died,—but this was admittedly in London where for more than half the eighteenth century the number of burials exceeded baptisms. Every churchyard yields some evidence of this appalling waste of life, so that two exceptional examples must serve as a grim reminder of the common lot of mothers in the past.[48]

Keighley (Yorks.); Rebecca Town, d. 1851, aged 44, of whose thirty children only one reached the age of three years, the rest dying in infancy.

Easton-in-Gordano (Somerset) Harriett Pains, d. 1850, aged 10, together with fourteen of her brothers and sisters who died in infancy.

Death in child-bed was naturally common; poor Patience Johnson, buried in St Paul's, Bedford, who "Laboured long and patiently in her vocation", succumbed in 1717 after bearing twelve sons and twelve daughters; while Ursule Claridge, died 1696, is shown on a pleasantly-carved tablet on the south wall exterior at Horley (Oxon.) in the act of suckling her child, Stone, who survived her by three days. The apathetic acceptance of such conditions is shown by the frequent use of an epitaph adapted from Prior:

> Happy the Babe who privileged by Fate
> To shorter Labour and a lighter Weight,
> Received but Yesterday the Gift of Breath,
> Order'd tomorrow to return to Death.[49]

These innocents were also commemorated under the simple bucolic images of lambs, doves, buds, flowers and fruits, a popular verse being extracted from Leigh Richmond's *Annals of the Poor*:

> This lovely bud so young and fair
> Called hence by early doom,
> Just came to show how sweet a flower,
> In paradise may bloom.[50]

Roses, violets and lilies are among the floral metaphors, while at Great Meeting Chapel, Leicester, William Lewis' death in 1768 is commemorated by the familiar image of the flower lopped by the reaper's blade, which here, unusually, is the poppy:

> So some tall Poppy that's o'ercharged with Rain,
> Droops its faint Head and sinks upon the plain.[51]

At Breedon-on-the-Hill (Leics.) 1680, and Michelney (Somerset) 1766, we find:

> Like birds of prey Death snatch'd away,
> This fair and harmless Dove ...

In contrast, some striking examples of longevity can be found, the palm going to Henry Jenkins, who at the age of 12 carried a horse-load of arrows for the Battle of Flodden, yet died in 1670 at the prodigious age of 169 and is buried in Bolton (Yorks.), although that "Old, Old, very Old Man" Thomas Parr of Great Willaston (Cheshire), who died in 1635 at the age of 152 and was buried in Westminster Abbey, is more popularly known. Others include: Isaac Ingall, butler of Battle Abbey (Sussex), d. 1798, aged 120; Henry and Sibil Clarke in Stoke-on-Trent churchyard, both dying in 1684, aged 112; William Billinge of Long-nor (Staffs.) "born in a cornfield" who served at Gibraltar and Ramillies, d. 1791, aged 112; Matthew Peat of Wirksworth (Derbys.) d. 1751, aged 109, whose epitaph asked: "few live so long, who lives well?"; the vital Sarah Jarvis of Corsham (Wilts.) d. 1753, aged 107, who some time before her death "had a third set of teeth"; Joseph Watson, park-keeper, buried at Disley (Cheshire), "the first that perfected the art of driving the stags", who, the year before his death in 1733 at 104, was reputed to have been present at the killing of a buck; agile Anne Abraham of Kilmersdon (Somerset) d. 1849, aged 104, whose epitaph related that up to two years before her death she regularly walked her mile and a half to work, "and with a laudable feeling of independence ... resolutely refused parochial relief", etc.

Among other exuberancies of nature one could note the quads born to John and Elizabeth Clark of Towcester, "all born and baptized the 13th and buried the 15th December, 1760"; the Moll Flanders example of Alice Burraway, d. 1729, and buried in Martham (Norfolk), pro-ducing a son by her own father, who eventually married her, the double incest, it is reported, not being discovered until twenty years after; the romantic lovers Rodger Wrighton and Martha Railton, buried in one grave, 1714–15, at Bowes (Yorks.);[52] or the redoubtable Phoebe Hessel, buried at St Nicholas, Brighton (Sussex), who served as a soldier to be near her lover, nursed him when wounded, married and outlived him to become a ginger-bread and apple woman up to her death in 1821, aged 108.

Life and energy burnt with a clear flame in others; such as Martha Blewitt, d. 1681, commemorated by a tablet in the tower of Birdbrook (Essex), with nine husbands, whose funeral sermon was preached on the text "Last of all the woman died also", and Robert Hogan of the same parish, who married his seventh wife in 1739; of Richard Tully, d. 1725, at St Catherine's, Gloucester, with nine wives; and Jeremiah Simpson of Welton churchyard near Hull, married eight times, and dying in 1719. There are curious coincidences, such as Francis and Mary Huntroods, at Whitby (Yorks.), both born, married and dying on the same day, September 19, at the age of eighty within five hours of each other in 1680; and Sarah Tomkin, of Boughton Monchelsea (Kent) 1865, who being blind for twelve years received back her sight on "Oculi Sunday, the Third Sunday in Lent".[53] There are unfortunate grotesques such as Sarah Biffin buried in St James cemetery, Liverpool, 1850, who, although born without arms or hands, progressed from a fair-ground freak to a miniature painter, marrying and receiving a pension from William IV; such Brobdingnags as Daniel Lambert of Leicester, buried in St Martin's, Stamford, 1809, who weighed over 52 stones; William Bradley of Market Weighton (Yorks.), d. 1820, 7 feet, 9 inches high and 33 stones in weight; and Jane Ridsdale of Hampsthwaite in the West Riding, d. 1828, just over two and a half feet in height.[54]

Accidental and violent deaths reveal contemporary occupational hazards, together with local crimes, of which such inscriptions are often the sole surviving records. Fatalities of shipwreck and deaths of excisemen and smugglers are numerous in the churchyards of coastal districts, testifying to the prevalence of smuggling; there are the inveterate country combats of poachers and gamekeepers; labourers' falls from horses, carts and trees, masons from buildings; of miners and quarrymen down pitshafts, of railway engineers scalded by exploding boilers, etc. Recorded fatalities such as deaths through asphyxiation by wellsinkers, or through having fires in bedrooms with tightly shut windows (the usual rustic habit), often bear practical advice on how to avoid them. At Marton (Yorks.), three men in 1812 lost their lives "by Venturing in to a Well at Marton when it was filled by Carbonic Acid gas, or fixed air. From this unhappy accident let others take warning, not to Venture in Wells Without first trying whether a Candle will burn in them. If the candle burns to the bottom they may be entered with safety: if it goes out, human life cannot be supported". Elizabeth Picket, 1781, was burnt to death through her clothes catching fire, and her stone at Stoke Newington (London) admonished: "Reader—if ever

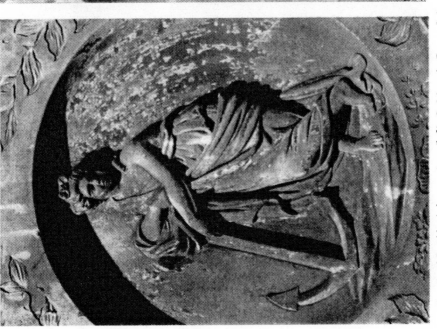

23. *Details of Swithland slate carving: (left) St Mary de Castro, Leicester, Ann and William Dowse, 1790: a robust figure of Hope with her customary emblem, the anchor; (right) Burton Lazars (Leics.), Mary Blower, 1781, by Christopher Staveley: the greatest of the Christian virtues personified as a mother nourishing her children.*

24. *Biblical scenes:* (above) *Soham (Cambs.), Jonas and Mary Clark, 1810: upper part of headstone showing the Sacrifice of Isaac. The carver has invested Abraham with Britannia's shield;* (centre) *Hadlow (Kent), Henry Kipping, 1784: upper part of headstone representing the Noli me Tangere theme, where the carver has emphasized Mary's mistaking Christ for the gardener by putting a spade in His hand;* (below) *East Peckham (Kent), William Martin, 1781: upper part of headstone representing The Good Samaritan, where the Samaritan is portrayed as a medieval page or squire, and the Levite in the habit of a contemporary parson.*

you should witness such an affecting scene; recollect that the only method to extinguish the flame is to stifle it by an immediate covering."

Such post-mortems show the value of gravestones as reading matter and sources of instruction, which also pandered to the appetite for horror and violence.[55] Immune from the laws of libel, the headstone to Sarah Smith at Wolstanton (Staffs.) 1763, brands her murderer and is reminiscent in its tone of the popular melodrama:

It was C......s B......w (*sic*)
That brought me to my end
Dear parents, mourn not for me
For God will stand my friend.
With half a Pint of Poyson
He came to visit me
Write this on my Grave
That all who read may see.

The brutal murder of Mary Ashford, buried at Sutton Coldfield (Warws.) 1817, after "having incautiously repaired to a scene of amusement" had unusual consequences. Abraham Thornton was tried for the crime but acquitted, whereupon the girl's brother sued for retrial and, as the law then provided that the issue could be decided either by wager-of-law or wager-of-battle, Thornton challenged Ashford to a duel, but as the brother cried off, he was declared legally innocent. Two years later an act was passed to nullify this ancient custom, so obviously open to abuse.

The literary equivalent of the emblems of trade or occupation carved on the memorials of craftsmen is that class of epitaph in which their products are metaphorically compared with the factors of life, decay and resurrection. Perhaps the palm must be given to this example from Lydford (Devon:)

Here lies, in horizontal position
the outside case of
GEORGE ROUTLEIGH, Watchmaker;
Whose abilities in that line were an honour
to his profession,
Integrity was the Mainspring, and prudence the
Regulator,
of all the actions of his life.

Humane, generous and liberal,
His Hand never stopped
till he had relieved distress.
So nicely regulated were all his motions,
that he never went wrong,
except when set a-going
by people
who did not know his Key;
even then he was easily
set right again.
He had the art of disposing his time so well,
that his hours glided away
in one continual round
of pleasure and delight,
Until an unlucky minute put a period to
his existence.
He departed this life
Nov. 14, 1802:
aged 57:
wound up,
In hopes of being taken in hand
by his Maker;
And of being thoroughly cleaned, repaired,
and set a-going
in the world to come.

The influence of emblem imagery is apparent well into the nineteenth century and witnessed by versatile metaphors.[56] As has already been noted, the influence of Quarles seems paramount, and perhaps its finest expression on a headstone is the bold eighteenth century carving at Swaffham Priors (Cambs.), which shows the Soul as Cupid, standing on Fortune's wheel exposed to the fickle winds of Fate, with its quatrain from the Ninth Emblem:

Nor length of days, nor solid strength of brain
Can find a place wherein to rest secure;
The world is various, and the earth is vain,
There's nothing certain here, there's nothing Sure.

226

At Stow-on-the-Wold (Glos.) *c.* 1700, there is a headstone with allusions to alchemy and surgery:

> By heaven dissected when ye unseen wound
> Search'd by my maker's probe was mortal found;
> Death's menstruum ye melted Element
> Within this urn lyes my Experiment;
> After a ferment in the Grave to rise
> An Elixir vitae into paradise;
> Or else (as metalls when transmuted prove)
> May be sublimed into a Lamp above.

Life was metaphorically compared with a pilgrimage; a gay stage, an empty tale, span, lighted taper, dream, vapour, bubble, bitter draught, or as grass, withering hay,[57] leaves, flowers or fruit, even as a lottery.[58]

A familiar figure with his dart or scythe (for he sometimes takes on the attributes of Time or Chronos) Death is personified as a grim reaper, assassin or wrestler, as well as a bird of prey, a frost, tide or overflowing stream, a whirlwind, a broom sweeping away the cobweb of Life, or Atropos clipping its Thread. Only gradually does the emphasis on mortality relax, and the euphemism of sleep or peace become adopted in its place.

The grave is described at Chipping Sodbury (Glos.) on a stone to Elizabeth Oldfield, 1642, as "The Wardrobe of my dusty clothes", reminiscent of Fuller's description of it as "a plain suit", but its common metaphor is a bed or "tenement of clay", such as Finedon (Northants.) 1709, "Here lyeth Richard Dent, in his last tenement", or at Folkestone (Kent), where Rebecca Rogers's last abode, 1688, is given advantages which would appeal to the contemporary tax-payer, "from chimney-money too this cell is free: To such a House as this who would not tenant be". Christ is given the role of a Shepherd (for infants), a Physician (for sufferers), a Bridegroom (for virgins), and an Admiral (for sailors).[59]

The persistence of certain medieval themes among Georgian epitaphs is not the least among their interesting features. Apart from the well-worn "As you are now ...", a quatrain founded on the *Earth upon*

Earth Middle English poem is found in various guises on tombstones, such as Gilmorton (Leics.) 1750:

> Earth walks on Earth like glittering Gold;
> Earth says to Earth, all's made of mould;
> Earth builds on Earth, Castle and Towers,
> Earth says to Earth, all shall be Ours.[60]

and as late as 1837 on a headstone to William White, bricklayer, formerly in the graveyard of Croydon parish church.

Among established poets Pope and Young were often quoted, but the bulk of Georgian epitaph verse was presumably the work of local rhymesters, such as parsons, school-masters or parish clerks, often derived from the ballads which were the stock-in-trade of pedlars or Running Patterers.[61] Among the inevitable murders, squibs and scandals of this catch-penny stuff, the vanities of the world and the imminence of death were perennial themes, and older verses were often revised to suit changes in taste and idiom. Their often complex origins can be illustrated by the curious epitaph:

> The World's a City full of crooked streets;
> And Death the Market-place where all men meet;
> If Death were merchandise that men could buy,
> The rich would always live, the poor must die.

where the confusion of ideas seems due to composite sources; the first two lines deriving from the old ballad of Death and the Lady, the last couplet from an epigram in Wootton's *Remaines*, and also *The Two Noble Kinsmen*.

What becomes obvious in any survey of gravestone epitaphs during the eighteenth century is the comparative absence of any Christian declaration, which, owing to the underlying fear of Popery or distaste for enthusiasm, led to the anomalous use of classical imagery. Nevertheless, towards the end of the century, the increasing use of Biblical texts (most of them significantly drawn from the Pauline Epistles) and a new emphasis upon salvation through faith become apparent, probably due to Methodist influence among the lower orders of society, and the educational value of the Sunday School movement.

Tractarian zeal castigated the pagan elements both in memorial design and sentiment, advocating a more precise orthodoxy, which led to a decline in emblematic modes of expression, and the increased use of extracts from psalms and contemporary hymnology. Kelke, in his *Churchyard Manual*, 1851, advocated that epitaphs should be natural and simple, should include a Biblical text, and avoid any prayer for the dead, or hint that Death was the final Judgment, so that they could "become an effective and a popular medium of conveying religious instruction and improvement". It would seem evident, from the point of view of common sense, that gravestones had more significance in the days of general illiteracy than they have today, and it is a reasonable assumption that many rustics may have gained from them some smattering of letters. However, with the spread of popular education, through Hone's tracts, the activities of the Society for the Diffusion of Popular Knowledge and the *Penny Cyclopoedia*, Victorian excesses of sentiment and bathos found unrestricted display in the new cemeteries. In conclusion, it is instructive to read the notes on epitaphs in *The Churchyards Handbook*, 1962, as representing the Church of England's current attitude towards gravestone inscriptions: "The object of an epitaph is to identify the resting-place of the mortal remains of a dead person. It should, therefore, record only such information as is reasonably necessary for that purpose, and perhaps some words which may console or instruct whoever reads it." Apart from simple genealogical data, it advises as a rule that texts be drawn from no other sources than that of the Bible or Book of Common Prayer, and that its tone should be "neither obtrusive nor presumptuous and, in particular, it must not be laudatory." In brief, the epitaph should record not the idiosyncrasies of an individual, but the fact of his burial, thus eschewing the cult of personality which is the link which binds the living and the dead.

The following are representative monuments with metaphorical epitaphs or carved emblems relating to the deceased's trade or occupation:

Auctioneer. Corby Glen (Lincs.), 1835, to Joseph Wright, a burly auctioneer of twenty stone, who fell over when driving his trap and was dragged along the ground:

Until grim Death, with visage queer,
Assumed Joe's trade of Auctioneer,
Made him the Lot to Practice on,
With "going, going" and anon,
He knocked him down to "Poor Joe's gone".

Barber. Broadway (Worcs.), 1786, to William Haslam; carved relief showing curling tongs, scissors, razor, and brush.

Bell-Ringer. Monuments with carvings of bells include, Closworth (Somerset), 1711, to Thomas Purdue, aged 90, first of a family of bell-founders, whose work occurs throughout Devon (*Western Antiquary*, 1882, vol. I, p. 159); Copdock (Suffolk.) *c.* 1780, headstone with oval relief of female figure holding book and reclining on a bell, derived from Bartolozzi's engraved heading for the "Oxford Youths"; Stoney Stanton (Leics.), 1853, to John Orton; Northmoor (Glos.), has a pleasant rustic tablet to Richard Lydall, 1721, which shows this rector in wig and bands, while on the gallery at the back of the church is cut "Richard Lydall gave a new Bell And built this bell loft free And then he said: before he dyed Let Ringers pray for me 1701". Epitaphs to veteran ringers include: Leeds (Kent), 1818, James Barham, aged 93, who during thirty years rang in Kent and elsewhere 112 peals of not less than 5,040 changes in each peal, and on April 7 and 8, 1761, assisted in ringing 40,320 Bob Majors on Leeds Bells in 27 hours. Bingley, (Yorks.), 1844, to Hezekiah Briggs, aged 80, sexton for 43 years said to have buried 7000 corpses, "Till Death called a Bob, which brought round the last change". The epitaph concludes with the pleasant lines:

Ring on, ring on, Sweet Sabbath bell,
Still kind to me thy matins swell,
And when from early things I part,
Sigh o'er my grave, and lull my heart.

Admonitory rules for ringers were often painted on boards, the earliest at Scotter (Lincs.); they are also to be found at Crosthwaite (Cumb.), St Minver (Cornwall), where the names of ringers and instruments of their trades are included.

Blacksmith. A common epitaph begins: "My Sledge and Hammer lie reclined, My Bellows too, have lost their wind; My Fire's extinct, my Forge decayed; And in the Dust my Vice is laid," etc. It occurs at

Nettlebed (Oxon.) 1746; Chiddingfold (Sussex), 1766; Gainford (Durham) 1777; Hexton (Herts.) 1795; Sutton (Surrey) 1812. Cromer (Norfolk), to William Howes, 1773, shows sledge and anvil; Holy Trinity, Wolverton (Bucks.), 1776, has farrier's tools.

Brewer. Newhaven (Sussex), 1785, to Thomas Tipper, the original brewer of Tipper's Ale, a popular drink of George IV at Brighton:

> Philosophy and History well he knew,
> Was rais'd in Physick and in Surgery too,
> The best old Stingo he both brewed and sold,
> Nor did one knavish act to get his Gold,
> He played through Life a varied comic part,
> And knew immortal Hudibras by heart. . . .

This headstone shows a carving of the old bridge at Newhaven.

Brickmaker. Farnham Royal (Bucks.), to Henry Dodd, "who began life as a ploughboy within a mile of St Pauls London, and after a fortunate and successful career as a brickmaker and contractor . . ." died 1881, aged 80. His brickfields were at Rotherfield in Sussex, and his London depot at Hay Wharf, New North Road. This gabled granite tomb, signed by A. Nicholson, 66 Mark Lane, London, bears two metal reliefs by F. Rocher; that on the north side showing a ploughman leaning over a three-horse plough, with blazing sun and ploughboy asleep under a tree, whip in hand, his head resting on a firkin; and on the south sailing barges and a paddle-steamer, with the inscription "Originator of Annual Sailing Barge Matches—the true School for the Navy". At Blakeney (Norfolk) 1798, the stone to Michael Jackson, bricklayer, shows level, dividers, square, ruler and trowel.

Builder. Sarnesfield (Herefs.) 1694, to John Abel:

> This craggy stone a covering is for an architector's bed;
> That lofty buildings raised high, yet now lyes low his head;
> His line and rule, so death concludes, are locked up in store;
> Build then who list,
> Or they who wist,
> For he can build no more.

The stone showed Abel and his two wives, and a rule, compasses and square. Colton (Staffs.), 1804, to James Heywood, aged 55, with square and compasses:

The Corner Stone I often times have dress'd,
In Christ, the corner-stone, I now find rest;
Though by the Builder he rejected were,
He is my God, my Rock, I build on here.

Chobham (Surrey), 1757, to John Alexander, aged sixty-seven:

Houses he built, with Brick, with Wood and stone;
But all his art coul'd not support his own;
Death push'd, he strove, vain was ye weak essay;
Down dropt at last his tenement of clay;
Flatt as himself his houses time will throw;
That JOHN e'er lived what mortal then will know;
Yes, for one fabric he consing'd (*sic*) to fame;
The lasting fabric of an honest name.

Butcher. Towcester (Northants.) 1820, to Samuel Wood; oval panel showing cleavers, steel and carving-knife.

Carpenter. Newent (Glos.) 1722, to Edward Taylor; stated to be "Head workman in contriving and rebuilding the roof of this Church in the year 1679". Taylor had worked in London, probably as apprentice to John Longland, master carpenter at St Paul's, before retiring to Newent. His part in the rebuilding of its church and roof is vividly described in a contemporary account (refer Colvin, under Taylor). St John sub Castro, Lewes (Sussex), 1747, to Mark Sharp: footstone carved with saw, jack-plane, augers, axe, mallet, gouges, square, bevel and compasses. Hanslope (Bucks.) 1759, to Joseph Cox senior, aged 92, showing arms of the Carpenters' Company and saw, auger, axe, chisel. His wife Elizabeth died in 1762, aged 101, "their descendants at their death were 10 children 62 Grandchildren and 102 Great Grandchildren, in all 174". Another headstone to a member of the same family shows a wider range of tools, including a drill and spokeshave, see S. Lewis, "A Family of Stone carvers, the Coxes of Northamptonshire", *Northamptonshire Past and Present*, 1953, vol. I, no. 6). Cobham (Kent) 1760, to Richard Gransden, also carved with various tools; Longnor (Staffs.), 1787, to Samuel Bagshaw, aged 71:

But Death who viewed his peaceful Lot,
His Tree of Life assail'd, His Grave was made upon this spot,
And his last Branch he nail'd.

Clock-maker. Berkeley (Glos.) 1665, Thomas Peirce, aged 77: "...who no man taught, Yet he in Iron, Brass and Silver wrought; He Jacks, and Clocks and Watches (with art) made, And mended too when other words did fade. When his own Watch ran Downe on the last Day, He that made Watches, has not made the Key To winde it Up, but Useless it must lie Until he Rise Againe no more to die". Uttoxeter (Staffs.) 1822, Joseph Slater, aged 49, whose epitaph concludes with Addison's lines, "the hand that made us is divine". Bolsover (Derbys.) 1836, Thomas Hinde, aged 19; the epitaph uses the concluding lines of George Routleigh's memorial at Lydford, which bring to mind Paley's use of the watch in his *Natural Theology* to prove the existence of God.

Coach-maker. Codicote (Herts.) 1773, Robert Nash, aged 60, and his son-in-law, John Fuller, died 1732, coach-carver. The carving shows a coach on its "horse" in process of construction.

Coffin-maker. Barnes (Surrey), 1724, Henry Mitchell, with carpenter's tools and coffin.

Cricketer. Petersfield (Hants.), John Small, 1737–1826:

> Here lies, bowled out by Death's unerring ball
> ... this last of Hambledonians, old John Small,
> Gave up his bat and ball,
> His leather, wax and all.

Sutton Valence (Kent), John Willes Gyrd, 1777–1852, reputed to be the first to introduce round-arm bowling. Sawston (Cambs.) 1875, Charles Sheldrick, with carving of bat and ball, pads and stumps. Lewknor (Oxon.) 1885, Thomas Smith, "who died suddenly", lunette showing ball breaking wicket. This same device, inscribed "Bowled at Last", occurs on Richard Barlow's memorial, 1919, in Blackpool cemetery, also to Lillywhite at Highgate, and Keeton at Wadsley (Yorks.).

Exciseman. Alresford (Hants.) 1750, Benjamin Brown:

> No Supervisor's Check he fears;
> Now no Commissioner obeys,
> He's free from cares, Intreaties, tears,
> And all the Heavenly Orb surveys.

Falconer. Great Livermere (Suffolk) 1689, William Sakings, "forkner" to three kings, Charles I, II, and James II.

Farmers. Headstones carved with various agricultural implements are numerous. A fine design showing plough, harrow, sickle, reaping-hook, rake, hay-fork, etc., grouped about a central sheaf, occurs in the Bucks.–Berks. area at Beaconsfield, Upton, Winkfield, Wooburn, *c.* 1770–86. There is another individual group, with implements around an angel's head in the vicinity of Olney (Bucks). Mock "arms" with implements on a shield at Redbourn (Herts.), to Jonathan Rose, 1817, show also a winnowing-sieve, seed-bag, flail and milking-stool. See also Beckenham, Frindsbury, Sutton-at-Hone (Kent); Sidlesham, Westbourne (Sussex); Stoke Poges (Bucks.); Durley, South Hayling (Hants.); Pebworth, Hardwicke, Standish (Glos.); Fladbury (Worcs.), etc.

Fencing Master. St Michael, Coventry, 1733, John Parkes, "a Gladiator by profession", who after fighting 350 duels in Europe, "At length quitted the stage, sheathed his sword, And with Christian resignation, Submitted to the Grand Victor".

Gamekeeper. Two delicate reliefs, showing the gamekeeper with his dog and gun, occur at Harefield (Middx.), 1744, to Thomas Mossendew, and Shrawley (Worcs.), 1814, where Hobday of Bretforton has shown the deceased firing at a covey, with epitaph:

> No more with willing dog and gun,
> To rise before the laggard sun;
> No more before the social can,
> Tomorrow's sport with joy to plan;
> Death took his aim, discharged his piece,
> And bade his sporting season cease;

Deene (Northants.), 1752, John York, "shot by accident", with gun and femur saltire-wise; Shrivenham (Berks.), 1839, John Place, gamekeeper to the Beckett estate, "accidentally killed by the discharge of his own gun" after being married only six weeks.

Gardener. Lambeth parish churchyard, London, the Tradescant tomb, *c.* 1662 (repaired 1773); here were buried the famous three Johns, of whom father and son were "gardeners to the Rose and Lily Queen ... who thence shall rise, And change this Garden for a Paradise". Their collection of rareties, which they "as Homer's Iliad in a nut, A World of Wonders in one Closet shut"—the so-called Tradescant

Ark—formed the nucleus of the Ashmolean Collection in 1657. Leeds suggested, in *Archaeology of the Anglo-Saxon Settlements*, p. 38, that an urn in this collection, still at Oxford, was one of the original pots from Walsingham which inspired Sir Thomas Browne's *Hydriotaphia*. The tomb, part of which is preserved in the Ashmolean, showed such curiosities as a crocodile, shells, Egyptian buildings and a hydra. Greenford (Middx.), 1863, William King, with device of straw beehive.

Horse Dealer. Kesgrave (Suffolk), 1851, John Chilcot, chest-tomb with horse-coper and buyer haggling over a horse; at Woodbridge nearby the same mason has carved a horse on the tomb to Abraham Easter, 1850.

Miller. Wiverton (Norfolk) 1725, to Thomas Smith, millwright, showing dividers, saw, axe, mill-stone and "thrift" (for sharpening mill-stones); Hildersham (Cambs.) 1778, to John Ashby, with carving of windmill (examples also at Denver, Norfolk, and Friskney, Lincs.). Windmills were a common feature of Fenland landscape during the eighteenth century and were used for drainage and pumping. Thomas Neale in 1748 described more than fifty mills in Whittlesey parish alone (where there is a headstone to a Fen waterman with punt-pole, anchor, spade and eel-trap). On Highdown Hill, near Ferring (Sussex), John Oliver built a pyramidal monument during his lifetime along with a former summerhouse from which he used to watch the prospect—leaving £20 to keep both in repair. The tomb was engraved with Scriptural texts, and carved with figures of Death and Time. He was an eccentric who spent his time in smuggling, reading the Bible, and making weather-vanes. He kept a coffin under his bed and latterly lived as an anchorite in the summer-house, which was painted with figures of prophets and verses of Scripture. At his funeral in 1793 ..." the coffin was borne by a number of young women dressed in white, one of whom read at the tomb a sermon which the miller had written for the occasion" (*Ward Lock Guide to Sussex*, p. 80).

Musician. Frampton (Glos.) 1795, to William Keyes, blacksmith, with music-albums, violin and bow, flageolet, French horn and bassoon—the work probably of John Pearce, whose tablet in the church to himself and his brothers Samuel and James ("Accomptant and Professor of Music") shows a cherub playing a lyre, and another holding a scroll of music on which is engraved a song "composed by J. Pearce".

John also made a tablet in Westbury church to Thomas Sinderby, 1812, showing a violin and music-album. Violins or kits also occur on a ledger in Spalding (Lincs.), and headstone at North Stoneham (Hants.). At Stamford St Mary, (Lincs.), David Alter, 1847, has a bow and album, carved by Hibbitt of Colsterworth; and at Old Weston (Hunts.), 1809, there is a fiddler in contemporary costume. The lyre is fairly common and occurs on a tablet at Boston (Lincs.) to Job Philips, 1850, with the musical score of Balfe's *Then you'll remember me*. Harps are to be found at Blakeney (Norfolk) 1822; Harvington (Worcs) 1830; and David playing the harp at Eastbourne (Sussex); Whitchurch (Middx.), has a tombstone erected in 1868, to William Powell, d. 1780, parish clerk when Handel was organist to the Duke of Chandos, and reputed to be the inspiration for his *Harmonious Blacksmith*. The opening bars of *I know that my Redeemer liveth* from *Messiah* are engraved on tombstones at Burton Overy, 1817, and Burbage (Leics.), to William Garner, 1881, organist at the latter church for twenty-four years. Model marble pipe-organs occur in Hampstead cemetery, and Kildwick (Yorks.) and a grand piano at Highgate.

Painter. St Nicholas, Ipswich (Suffolk), 1849, to George Groom, with easel, palette and brushes, maulstick and crayons.

Parish Clerk. Bakewell (Derbys.): two parish clerks are buried here—Samuel Row, d. 1792, and his son Philip, d. 1815:

> who now with Hallelujahs Sound,
> Like Him can make the Roofs rebound?

The Gentleman's Magazine, February 13, 1794, noted that the father united the offices of sexton, clerk, singing-master, will-maker, and school-master, and through his respect for antiquities protected the Vernon tombs, taking rubbings of the inscriptions; Crayford (Kent), 1811, Peter Isnell, clerk for thirty years, "and here, with three wives, he awaits till again, The trumpet shall rouse him to sing out Amen"; Bingham (Notts.), 1850, Thomas Hart, clerk for fifty-eight years, "... correct he read and sung so well; His words distinct, his verse so clear ... Death cut the brittle thread, and then, A period put to his Amen"; Wolverley (Worcs.), 1854, Thomas Worrall, clerk for forty-seven years, succeeding his father James, d. 1806, whose term was thirty years of service. Such posts were usually for life, and often hereditary, and this accounts for the local power of these officials, who could be pillars of strength or thorns in the flesh to their incumbents.

Policeman. Montgomery, 1903, William Davies, local constable, carved relief showing helmet, truncheon, bull's-eye lantern and belt, encircled by a laurel wreath.

Prize Fighter. St Mary, Nottingham, 1880, William Thompson, aged 69, known as "Bendigo", twice British champion and never defeated in the ring. His monument is a crouching marble lion holding a scroll inscribed:

> In life always brave, fighting like a Lion,
> In death like a Lamb, tranquil in Zion

(illustrated, *Country Life*, March 31, 1960, pp. 674, 675).

Railway Engineers. Bromsgrove (Worcs.), 1840, Thomas Scaife, an "engineer" or driver on the Birmingham and Gloucester Railway, who died through the explosion of an engine boiler. This headstone, like another to Joseph Rutherford, who died at the same time, has a carved relief of a locomotive. The epitaph is the often-quoted:

> My engine now is cold and still,
> No water does my boiler fill,
> My coke affords its flame no more
>
> ... my steam is now condens'd in death,
> Life's railway's over o'er, each Stations past,
> In death I'm stopp'd and rest at last.

Rat Catcher. Chipping Norton (Oxon.), 1763, to Phillis Humphreys,

> "who has Lodg'd in Many a Town and Travelled far and near,
> By age and Death Shee is struck down To her last Lodging here."

Road-Maker. Spofforth (Yorks.), 1810, John Metcalf, known as Blind Jack of Knaresborough, who built or remade some 180 miles of roadway. His headstone bears a poem composed by his admirer, Lord Dundas (*Country Life*, April 16, 1943, p. 713; *ibid.*, April 21, 1960, pp. 880–82).

Sailor. Carvings of ships and naval scenes are common in coastal districts, mute evidence of shipwrecks and smuggling fatalities. Fine examples occur in the Portsmouth area, such as Warblington and South Hayling. The monument in Portsea churchyard to Admiral Kempenfelt and the crew of the Royal George, 1783, was made by James Hay senior of Portsea "in a pyramidal form ornamented with marine trophies, arms and sculptured urns" (Gunnis). See also Bosham, 1750, Sidlesham, 1765, 1809 (Sussex); Sheringham, 1807, Wells, 1809, Yarmouth, 1780, 1790 (Norfolk); Walberswick, 1781 (Suffolk); Binstead, 1785 (I. of Wight); Saul, 1831 (Glos.). Scarborough has several headstones with anchors and rudders, such as Anthony Pearson and his brother, Governor of Scarborough, 1822. St Lawrence, Ramsgate (Kent), 1903: "This marks the wreck of Robert Woolward who sailed the seas for fifty-five years. When Resurrection gun fires, the wreck will be raised by the Angelic Salvage Co: surveyed and if found worthy, refitted and started on the voyage to Eternity".

Schoolboy. Coughton (Warws.) 1851, to Edward Jackson, who died aged 15, and whose chest tomb has an affecting epitaph. Its west end is carved with a horse, on the saddle of which is fixed a small mortarboard, also gun, cricket-bats, fishing-rod and creel; the east end shows a harbour moored with dinghy moored by a jetty, a three-masted schooner and other craft.

School-Master. Beckenham (Kent) 1750, to John Cade, "one skilful in his Profession", suggested by the various dog-eared books, terrestrial globe, geometrical and drawing instruments, trumpet and recorder, carved on the headstone. At Wateringbury in the same county, Edward Greensted's tablet bears the Sign of the Zodiac, 1797. Horley (Oxon.), two monuments to local school masters; John Edwards, d. 1776, and William Catchpole, d. 1895, who taught for forty-four and thirty years respectively in the village school.

Shepherd. Olney (Bucks.) 1779, to William Langley, "pasture keeper", now illegible, until recently showed a scene with sheep-fold and ricks, similar to Sheringham (Norfolk), 1820, with a hurdled flock guarded by a sheep-dog. St John-sub-Castro, Lewes, 1747, to John Ward, shepherd with flock and angel above. Church Honeybourne (Worcs.), shepherd catching sheep with crook, together with a sacrificial lamb—a fine relief, now illegible, by Samuel Hobday; Hothfield (Kent), 1868, to James Gaunt, with carved shears and crook.

Snake Catcher. Brockenhurst (Hants.), 1905, to Harry (Brusher) Mills, so-called because he used to brush the New Forest cricket ground and for a "long number of years followed the occupation of Snake Catcher in the New Forest, His pursuit and the primitive way In which he lived caused him to be An object of interest to many"—carved relief showing Mills, staff in hand, holding a snake by his hut of branches.

Soldier. Two of the most popularly known epitaphs to soldiers are at Winchester and Minster-in-Sheppey. The first commemorates Thomas Thetcher "who died of a violent fever contracted by drinking small beer when hot the 12th of May, 1764, aged 26 years", with the epitaph:

> Here sleeps in peace a Hampshire Grenadier,
> Who caught his death by drinking cold small beer;
> Soldiers, be wise from his untimely fall,
> And when ye're hot drink strong, or none at all.

The second is to Henry Worth, gunner, 1779, and shows two cannon.

> Deep in the earth his carcase lies entomb'd,
> Which Love and Grog for him had honeycomb'd,
> His match now burnt, expended all his priming,
> He left the World and us without ere whining,
> Jesting apart, Retired from wind and Weather,
> Virtue and WORTH are laid asleep together.

Squire. Swithland (Leics.), 1745, to Sir Joseph Danvers of Swithland Hall. This fine chest-tomb of slate by Henry Hind, bears two delightful panels cut in low relief. The south panel has the caption:

> Be Chearfull, O Man and labour to live,
> The mercifull God a blessing will give,

and shows a ploughman driving a three-horse team accompanied by a plough-boy, and a house in process of construction with two masons at work, one of whom is cutting ashlar at a banker. The north panel is headed:

> When young I sayl'd to India East and West,
> But aged in this port must lye at rest,

illustrated by a composite landscape where Swithland church is shown on a distant promontory with a domed and castellated fort in the foreground, and a three-masted ship in the harbour. Chalfont St Giles (Bucks.), 1728, to Timothy Lovett, another travelled man, whose footstone reads:

> Italy and Spain, Germany and France,
> Have been on Earth my weary Dance,
> So that I own ye Grave my Greatest Friend,
> That to my Travels all has put an End.

Stonemason. Country stonemasons usually appropriated the coat-of-arms of the Masons' Company as their generic emblem, i.e. three castles between a chevron charged with an open pair of compasses, as well as illustrating their monuments with various tools of their craft—the square, level, plumb-line, compasses, ruler, hammer, mell or mallet, trowel and chisels. Stones of this sort can be seen at Cleeve Prior (Worcs.) to Michael Campden, 1741, cut by John Laughton of Cleeve, d. 1754, whose own memorial is in South Littleton; Belton (Rutland), 1787; and at Oundle (Northants.) to John Mansfield and Charles Braddock, which include a "drag" (used to comb or mark the surface of stone) and a "lewis" (to grip ashlar when being hoisted). William Sanderson's epitaph at Yarwell in the same county has the moving lines:

> Tread lightly on his ashes ye men of genius
> For he was your kinsman,
> Weed his grave clear ye men of goodness,
> For he was your brother,
> But alas! alas! he is gone his genius is fled.
> To the stars from whence it came,
> And that warm heart with all its
> Generous and open vessels are
> Comprised in a clod of the valley.

Waggoner. Palgrave (Suffolk), 1787, to John Catchpole, showing a waggon drawn by six horses in pairs, and epitaph:

> My horses have done Running, my Waggon is decay'd,
> And now in the Dust my Body is lay'd;
> My whip is worn out and my work It is done,
> And now I'm brought here to my last home.

25. (above) *Holy Trinity, Wolverton (Bucks.), Mark Elmes, 1797: upper part of Hornton headstone, 30 in. long, 14½ in. wide; passion emblems, including a pelican in her piety nestling on the cross. In the early years of the present century, the stone showed traces of brilliant colour;* (centre) *St Margaret, Leicester, Robert Denshire, 1761: upper part of Swithland slate headstone, 33 in. long, 14½ in. wide, by Robert Kinnes of Leicester; the Blasted Tree and Burning Bush combined with mortality and passion emblems to signify Death and Resurrection;* (below) *Lowdham (Notts.), Ann Leak, 1820: upper part of Swithland slate headstone by Thomas Wood of Bingham; apocalyptic angel rousing the dead from their tombs.*

26. *Details of angels from headstones:* (above) *Burton Lazars (Leics.), 1737, calligraphic angel by Stephen Staveley (reproduced from full-size rubbing); (centre) Weston-sub-Edge (Glos.), 1741; (below) Michaelstow (Cornwall), 1776 (reproduced from rubbing).*

Bisbrooke (Rutland), 1813, to Nathaniel Clarke, with a wagon drawn by four horses in single file with church tower behind, and farming implements flanking the scene (*Country Life*, May 26, 1934, p. 551; April 28, p. 442). Stonemasons dispatched their headstones by these carriers when water transport was not available.

Notes

1. Published anonymously in *Monumental Journal*, October and November 1961. J. C. Loudon, *On the Laying out, planting, and Managing of Cemeteries; and on the improvement of Churchyards*, 1843. This great horticulturist considered the churchyard had an educational value. "To the resident poor, uncultivated by reading, the churchyard is their book of history, their biography, their instructor in architecture and sculpture, their model of taste, and an important source of moral improvement . . . how far then does the appearance of our churchyards answer the important educational ends they are calculated to effect?" p. 74.

2. This allegorical theme was spread by auxiliary cavalry stationed in the Rhine area from which part of the invading British force was drawn in A.D. 43. In Christian times it became related to the combat of Good and Evil, such as St George and the Dragon. The cult of St George was strong in east Europe, where in Bulgaria alone 1,200 reliefs of this type have been recorded (G. Kazarow, "The Thracian Rider and St George", *Antiquity*, 1938, vol. 12, p. 47. Haverfield, "Sepulchral Banquet on Roman tombstone", *Arch. Journal*, vol. 56, pp. 326–31).

3. For fircones and symbolism (see *Antiq. Journal*, vol. 19, p. 194; *Proc. Soc. Antiq.*, vol. 32, 58–62).

4. Apart from provincial classical carving, an element of indigenous Celtic design is sometimes conspicuous in Roman–British work. Pervica's headstone at Newcastle; the *Sol Invictus* at Corbridge; or the slab to the fountain-goddess, Coventina, found at Chesters., where she floats upon a water-lily holding a goblet and a water-plant, show a folk-art quality independent of time or place. Many of the naïve angels on later tombstones seem to be nature-sprites, evoked from the subconscious by the chisel.

5. A fragmentary example from the Calf of Man, shows a similar treatment to the mid-eighth century Athlone crucifix. Manx slabs are decorated with cavaliers and various domestic and game animals suggesting hunting scenes similar to Scottish work. For the latter see Mowbray, "Eastern influence on the Carvings at St Andrews and Nigg", *Antiquity*, vol. 10, pp. 428–40. The St Andrews chest-tomb is the finest in Great Britain of this period and shows David and the Lion in a hunting scene, similar to headstones from Nigg and Aberlemno. Known as the Shrine of St Rule, its original gabled shape can be seen reconstructed in the Cathedral.

6. W. Bonser, "Survival of Paganism in Anglo-Saxon England", *Birming. Archael. Soc. Trans.*, 1932, vol. 56; M. A. Murray, "Female Fertility Figures", *Journal Roy. Anthrop. Inst.*, 1934, vol. 64, etc.

7. The Good *v*. Evil combat was personified in ancient Egyptian mythology by Ra or Horus striking down the great Serpent Apepi or Set, head of the powers of Darkness, and transmitted to Coptic art where Christ thrusts a spear into the jaws of a crocodile. On the Thracian reliefs the cavalier is shown spearing a snake. The effigies of Anglo-Norman prelates were shown thrusting the pastoral staff into a dragon's jaws; and this device assumed for the later cabbalists an alchemical significance. The original sixteenth century statue of St Marcellus on the doorway of Notre Dame Paris, shown in this stance, was replaced in the nineteenth century by a statue in which the staff was curtailed, thus destroying its esoteric significance.

8. Over forty examples of the Tree of Life theme have been recorded. Wyverns are found in coffin-slabs at Iona and Sligo Abbey as late as 1489 and 1566.

9. For such geometric pattern (see P. M. Johnston, "Romanesque Ornament in England", *Journ. Brit. Arch. Ass.*, 1924, vol. 30, p. 91).

10. The earliest source for the Legend of the Cross (as related in *The Golden Legend* of 1270) was probably the apocryphal *Gospel of Nicodemus* or *The Acts of Pilate*, fourth century. The intention of such legends was to relate the Tree of Knowledge, associated with Adam's Fall, to Christ's Cross, as the Instrument of Redemption (see M. R. James, *The Apocryphal New Testament*, 1924). An enigmatic remark of Christ in Luke 21 : 31, which may have related to a Jewish allegory, was expanded in the Middle Ages into the Legend of the Green Tree and The Dry (see M. R. Bennett in *Arch. Journal*, 1929, vol. 83, p. 21), while the contrast of green and blasted trees to signify Life and Death had also an alchemical significance and was adopted in the emblem books.

11. This design was repeated by Roubiliac in stucco in the Gothic temple at Pains-hill, near Cobham, Charles Hamilton's estate, which included most of the fashionable picturesque "antics" of the time, including the famous hermit. In another part of the grounds, in a gloomy wood were two paintings by Hayman, "one representing the unbelieving Christian dismayed and full of horror at the approach of Time, who exhibits an hourglass; the other the dying Christian, meeting the dart with pious resignation" (*The Gentleman's Magazine*, 1781).

12. M. Praz, *Studies in 17th century Imagery*; R. Freeman, *English Emblem Books.*

13. Sundials made of Delabole slate are numerous in Devon and Cornwall. Most remarkable is the Tawstock dial, with lines cut to indicate meridian at cities in both Europe and the Middle East, made by John Berry of Barnstaple, 1757, who, assisted by his son Thomas, also signs dials at Marwood, 1762, Pilton, 1780. Other examples: Ermington, 1766, by J. Doleman; Kenn, 1783, by John Peagum; Saltash Town Hall, 1727, by Edward Stephens. The gnomon at Lelant has a figure of Death, similar to

tombstone carvings at St Breock, 1761, and Joan Mullis, 1744 at Linkinhorne, cut by Daniel Gumb, an eccentric mason who lived in a hut-dwelling near the Cheese Wring (*The Reliquary*, January 1898, pp. 42–46).

14. The type of angel used in the early Victorian period is a compound of Italian and Teutonic sources. The work of Moritz Retsch (introduced into England through the engravings of Henry Moses, protege of Thomas Hope of Deepdene) helped to establish it. Retsch's fame was established by his illustrations to Faust, *c.* 1828; and his outlines and fondness for sixteenth century German costume set the style for the illustrations fostered by the Art Union's albums of poetry.

15. The presence of God is usually denoted by the Triangle amidst a blaze of light, with or without the Divine Name; or by the Eye in radiance, signifying His omniscience. Christ was later symbolized in similar fashion by the monogram IHS inscribed within a glory.

16. The custom of hanging up in church artificial garlands to commemorate the death of "maiden" persons, usually girls, is referred to in *Hamlet*: "Yet here she is allowed her virgin crants ..." Paper gloves invariably attached to the garland symbolize the gage thrown down to a calumniator of the deceased's reputation. Early examples were often elaborate, made of wire (such as those found at Bromley, Kent, 1733) or wood, ornamented with paper, silk and horn. The custom seems to have been general, dying out in the London area, *c.* 1750, and surviving longest in Derbyshire until end of nineteenth century, where several churches still retain specimens. At Abbotts Ann, Dorset, the custom is still observed, and the church contains 40 specimens, the oldest *c.* 1716 (see photograph in *The Field*; September 17, 1959). Walsham-le-Willows (Suffolk) has an example to Mary Boyce, 1685; and maid's gloves are kept in vestry of Flamborough (Yorks.). Also Chamber's *Book of Days*, vol. 1, p. 271; Brand's *Popular Antiquities*, vol. 2, p. 305; C. Hole, *English Custom and Usage*, 1950.

17. For shells on graves see: J. Jackson, *Shells as evidence of Migrations of Early Culture*, 1917; *Antiquity*, September 1937; *Antiq. Journal*, July 1931, vol. 2, p. 253. The custom of throwing stones on the body is referred to in *Hamlet*, where the priest at Ophelia's burial says "For charitable prayers, shards, flints and pebbles should be thrown on her" (Johnson, *Byways in British Archaeology*, pp. 285–289. The quality of whiteness seems to have a curious funerary significance. The great barrow of New Grange was originally covered with white quartz pebbles, and these stones are to be found associated with both prehistoric and more recent interments. Headstones were periodically refreshed with white colouring, and the tradition of "whited sepulchre", as a latent folk-memory, may account for the popularity of white marble memorials today.

18. Mrs Esdaile, in *English Monumental Sculpture*, pp. 32, 33, considered John Bacon largely responsible for establishing the Mourner and the Urn through his work as a designer for the Coade factory. He was an ardent Methodist, and the friend of such Evangelical divines as John Newton and John Romaine. There is reason to believe that many stonemasons were Nonconformists. The Dunicliffe and Bagnall families of Melbourne (Derbys.) were notable examples.

19. An early example, again by Roubiliac, is his figure of Religion holding a cross on the cenotaph to Edward Holdsworth, Gopsall (Leics.) 1758, of which Madame Soyer's large statue of Faith at Kensal Green, 1843, and Joseph Edward's statue of Religion for Mrs Vaughan at Highgate, 1866, are variations.

20. Only two crucifixes on headstones are known to the writer: Coningsby (Lincs.), 1772; Edburton (Sussex), 1791. In Ireland a remarkable series of eighteenth and nineteenth century crucifixion scenes on headstones has been recorded by Mrs Ada Leask; their iconography, although essentially Romanesque, shows the personages of the drama in contemporary dress (*Journal Roy. Soc. Ant. Ireland*, vols. 73–78, 84, 85).

21. The pelican in piety occurs at Hendon (Middx.) and Spalding (Lincs.), where a mother also holds her child before a cross. The phoenix is found at Fen Stanton (Hunts.) 1800; parrots nibbling flowers at Islip (Northants.) 1778, by Samuel Turner and at Humberstone (Leics.) 1780, by William Kirk; chained swans at St Mary Arden, Market Harborough; a bird mourning its fledgling at Minsterworth (Glos.); a falcon on wrist, together with Hope and anchor, at Highworth (Wilts.) 1816; a fine eagle at Fladbury (Worcs.) 1799, by Thomas Laughton.

22. See also Dom Ethelbert Horne, "Wings, Sword and Heart Badge", *Antiq. Journal*, vol. II, p. 287. The heart emitting a sprig or shoot had an alchemical significance. St George's, Stamford (Lincs.) 1786, has a heart sprouting a palm branch, implying Victory through Love. Some of the simpler designs belong to folk-art, such as sun, moon, stars, hearts, diamonds, fleurs-de-lis, etc., found also on horse-brasses and the pole-heads of Friendly Societies, including the nineteenth century Burial Clubs to which so many of the poorer classes contributed. At Speldhurst (Kent) 1741, are figures of Death and Time with inverted moons above stars; Catsfield (Sussex) 1751, has inverted crescent moons with human faces; suns in splendour are also common.

23. In medieval art the psychostasis, or weighing of souls, was performed by St Michael. The idea also occurs at Hathern (Leics.) 1785, where a hand emerges from clouds holding scales, the lower pan labelled Eternity, at Quorndon (Leics.) 1787, and Long Sutton (Lincs.). At Mid-Littleton (Worcs.) a figure of Justice holds sword and scales.

24. Minor puzzles are the sources of such imagery as the angel and the Magi, cut by John Harrison of Pateley Bridge, 1795–1862, to his wife Jane, where the kings are

dressed in Sumerian skirts accompanied by urns bearing crouching lions, and the head-stone has an oriental cresting; or Hobday's hydras on Sarah Ford's headstone at Bretforton, 1797, curiously reminiscent of Anglo-Norman design. Among other *curiosa* could be mentioned satyrs at West Peckham (Kent) and Badby (Northants.); a Medusa head at Wrentham (Suffolk) 1843, in cast iron; swastika at Thame (Oxon.) 1817; and figures of Hope (as Britannia) at Diss (Suffolk) 1802, and Eastbourne (Sussex) 1801.

25.   William Howitt, writing in 1838, lists the books that might be found in the possession of an average pious yeoman "where they know little of what was going on in the world, and where yet you were sure to find, in some crypt-like hole in the wall, or in a little fire-side window, about half-a-dozen books; the Bible; Hervey's *Meditations among the Tombs*; Baxter's *Saints Everlasting Rest*; Romaine's *Life of Faith* or *A Drop of Honey from the Rock Christ;* Macgowan's *Life of Christ;* or Drelin-court *On Death*—or such like volumes."

26.   So described by Mr M. W. Barley in his brief analysis of early Nottinghamshire slate-carvers in *Thoroton Soc. Trans.*, vol. 52, 69–86.

27.   German and Swiss monumental slabs on which this tradition is based show extraordinary virtuosity. See eighteenth century examples from Schleswig-Holstein in Gegering, *Die Schrift Atlas*, 1952, plates 204, 205.

28.   *The English Writing Masters and their Copy Books*, 1931; and *London Tradesmen's Cards of the 18th Century*, 1925, by Sir Ambrose Heal, are standard works on this sub-ject.

29.   Baskerville's original plaque advertising himself as a gravestone-cutter is built into the wall of Birmingham Central Library. No existing monuments can be proved to be his.

30.   The Cornish tombstone-engraver William Westaway was the village school-master at Bradworthy and renowned for his copper-plate handwriting. He worked at his tombstones in the schoolroom while teaching. His son Thomas, of Bradworthy, was a metal-engraver and dealer in stone, while another son, Jeremiah of St. Endellion, made gravestones (information from Mr Thomas Westaway, great-grandson of the above William). Mr Smith of Burton Overy, aged 90, could recall as a boy Arthur Neale of Burton (1787–1856), a cripple, who kept a small school and, when class was dismissed, worked on gravestones which he kept in a sort of sliding-tray beneath his table-top. Walter Gale of Mayfield was its schoolmaster from 1750–51. According to his diary (*Sussex Arch. Soc. Trans.*, vol. 9, pp. 182–207) he was a surveyor, mathemati-cian, tombstone engraver, sign-painter and designer of needlework.

31. A re-print of *The Universal Penman* was issued by Dover Publications, New York, 1941. Books showing rule and compass methods for letter-construction include: Joseph Moxon's *Regulae trium ordinum literarum typographicarum, etc.*, 1676; George Bickham's *Geometrical construction to form the twenty-four* (sic) *letters of the alphabet, c.* 1765; William Hollins's *The British standard of the capital letters contained in the Roman alphabet"*, 1813; B. P. Wilme's *Manual of writing and printing characters*, 1845 (information from Mr James Mosley of St Bride's Printing Library).

32. E. Brown, "The Cornish Engraver", *Architectural Review*, April 1944, pp. 98–105, is the only published account of this work.

33. J. Jaques who, as already noticed, published a catalogue of metallic ornaments for decorating gravestones, *c.* 1820, claimed in this "puff" to be the inventor of the stereographic or projecting letters "in Composition, Wood, or Brass, for Shop Fronts and Window Tablets. ..."

34. According to an advertisement of his, E. J. Physick the statuary, first introduced "imperishable inscriptions in solid lead" upon English monuments in 1853.

35. The architect Mackintosh's interest in lettering was shown in a few designs for tombstones, such as an example at Kilmalcolm, illustrated, p. 177, in N. Gray, *Lettering on Buildings*, 1960. This book, and its author's previous *Nineteenth Century Ornamental Types and Title Pages*, 1938, are the only scholarly works available which deal with Victorian and architectural lettering.

36. See also *Memorials of the Dead*, the Journal for the Society for preserving the Memorials of the Dead in the Churches and Churchyards of Great Britain, Norwich, 1883, and English Monumental Inscription Society, founded 1909. A member of the Society of Antiquaries had proposed making a corpus of English inscriptions following the model of Gruter's *Inscriptiones Antiquae*, but unfortunately this was not adopted (see Gough, *Sepulchral Monuments*, vol. 2, p. ccxxxiii, etc.). Pettigrew's work was intended to form part of a new edition of Gough.

37. Such inscriptions aroused Tractarian wrath. Rock, in *Church of our Fathers*, 1852, condemned the use by a Norfolk rector of the Latin phrase *Quem Dii amant, adolescens moritur*, adapted to Christian use for children's memorials as "their time was short, the longer is their rest; God called them hence, because He saw it best".

38. Apart from Latin tags, multi-lingual inscriptions on churchyard monuments are rarities. Beneath the formal Latin text on Regina's headstone at South Shields is a line of Palmyrean script. Greek and Hebrew occasionally occur; as on the stone to Mary Stokes, 1711, at Eye (Suffolk) in Latin, Greek and English; Eleanor Best, 1782, Kirk Leavington (Yorks.) with "Our Life remains but as smoke and shadow" in Greek, Hebrew and Latin; Charles Warstell, 1781, Romaldkirk (Yorks.) and John

Chessell, 1763, at Brading (I. of Wight), both in Hebrew. Robert Chambers, the statuary, 1710–1784, was a Hebrew scholar, who, according to Mr Gunnis, "had almost a mania for the language", using it on his monuments, and on the fine tomb to Lt.-Gen. William Evelyn, 1783, at Send (Surrey) in his signature.

On a tablet to Jane Delamotte, 1761, in St Mary's Sculcoates, Kingston upon Hull, is an inscription in Byrom shorthand; in the Lansdowne cemetery, Bath, there is a memorial to Jane Pitman, 1857, wife of the famous Isaac, "Fonetik Printer of this Siti". St Paul, near Mousehole (Cornwall) has a stone to Dolly Pentreath, 1772, reputedly the last speaker of Cornish, with a text from Exodus in the old language; while at Penderyn (Brecons.) is an inscription in old Bardic.

39. Latin tags are common on slate headstones in the Midlands, often minutely engraved on scrolls amid the imagery, and no other churchyard carvers used them to the same extent. *Memento mori; Mors janua vitae; Cum incerta sit hora vigiliae,* are common—more rarely couplets appear, as on Christopher Staveley's magnificent headstone to James Rubins, 1761, at Grantham (Lincs.) headed:

> *Tu memor humanae Sortis qui tollit eosdem*
> *Et premit, incertas ipse verere vices.*

40. An inscription in Clapton church (Glos.) thirteenth century, promises a thousand days of pardon for prayers (*Antiq. Journal,* vol. 31, p. 338). A slab at Lichfield, to Richard the Merchant, asserts that, in return for his gifts to the church on earth, he is appointed merchant to St Michael in heaven. Strype, in *Ecclesiastical Memorials,* vol. 2, p. 293, recording sixteenth century desecration, mentions "caskets full of pardons" being found within graves. An exorcism in cipher was found on a paper inserted under a brass plate on a ledger in a Lancashire churchyard (place and date unrecorded) in *The Reliquary,* vol. 10, p. 134, pl. 17, probably an anti-witch device, reminding one of the Pendle witch-covens, and Dr Dee's attempt to raise the dead in Walton-le-Dale churchyard (Weever, *Ancient Funerall Monuments,* pp. 45, 46).

An essential feature of the hearth on the older cottages of North Yorkshire and Lancashire was a rowan-tree post intended to avert witchcraft. Cp. "Witch Posts", M. Nattrass, *Gwerin,* vol. 3, no. 5, pp. 254–67; also *Some Reminiscences and Folklore of Danby Parish and District,* by Joseph Ford (stonemason of Danby), Whitby, 1953.

41. The brass to Henry Nottingham and his wife at Holme-by-the-Sea (Norfolk) 1400, records their donation to the church of its steeple, choir, vestments and bells. In Wainfleet (Lincs.) a tablet to Edward Barkham, 1735, records his gifts to the church, including the altarpiece, and for the communion table "a very rich crimson velvet carpet, a cushion of the same, and a beautiful Common Prayer-book; Likewise with two large Flagons, a chalice with a cover, together with a paten, All of silver plate", as well as a perpetual endowment of £35 per annum for a sermon and prayers every Sunday.

Charitable bequests or Doles were a later development, e.g. Daglingworth (Glos.)

on a brass in the porch, 1638: "The Dissection & Distribution of Giles Handcox who Earth bequeathed to Earth, to Heaven, his Soule, to Friends his Love, to the poore a five pound dole, to remaine for ever & be employed for their best advantage & releefe". His descendant, Jeremiah, left £100 in 1730 for religious instruction of the poor in Daglingworth.

42. In some parts of Wales the custom of praying for the dead over their graves in the eighteenth century led to the making of head and footstones cut with notches for the mourner's knees (Elias Owen, *Old Stone Crosses of the Vale of Clwydd*, pp. 22, 23).

43. Among such elegies were *The Lament of the Soul of Edward IV* and one on Jasper, Duke of Bedford, d. 1495, both attributed to Skelton. Puttenham refers to the custom in his *Art of English Poesie*: "for they make long and tedious discourses, and write them in large tables to be hanged up in Churches and Chauncells over the tombes of great men, and others". Shakespeare refers to this in *Much Ado about Nothing*, Act 4, Scene 1: "And on your family's old monument, Hang mournful epitaphs." Such painted boards exist at Kingswick, 1590; Holmer, 1652; Breinton (Herefs.) 1685; North Ockendon, 1594; Elmstead (Essex) 1664; Clymping (Sussex) 1633; Boston (Lincs.) 1626, with the interesting epitaph: "My corps with kings and monarchs sleeps in bedd ..." etc.

44. Pope's comment "the burthen of church walls, and the shame as well as derision of all honest men" could apply to such specimens as John Grace, 1780, in Stoke (Cheshire) who "possessed by Temper every moral virtue, By Religion every Christian Grace. ... In a word few have ever passed a more useful Or more blameless Life." Perhaps the greatest gift to the genealogist is the Beaver monument in Wokingham churchyard (Surrey) which gives a history of the family from the time of Charles I.

45. On the north wall of the tower, Ashwell (Herts.), there is a medieval graffito describing the great wind which marked the cessation of the Black Death. The earliest English corpse monument is Bishop Fleming, Lincoln Cathedral, 1430, but the theme was first used at Laon, 1393. See E. C. Williams, "Dance of Death in Painting and Sculpture in the Middle Ages", *Journal Brit. Archaeol. Instit.*, vol. 1, 3rd series, and for later examples the Messenger of Mortality broadsides in the Douce Collection. For the antiquity of this epitaph, and its relation to medieval laments such as "Farewell This World is but a Cherry Fair", see "A Middle English Epitaph", *Notes and Queries*, April 1961, pp. 132–35. Another version of the phrase is the Latin *Quid eram nescitis; quid sum nescitis; ubi abii, nescitis, Valete!* found in English versions such as the rag-pickers' epitaph at Wymondham (Leics.) 1809; and West Down (Devon) 1797, thus:

> Reader, pass on, nor waste your precious time
> On bad biography and murdered rhyme;
> What I was before's well known to my neighbours
> What I am now is no concern of yours.

46. At Worth Matravers (Dorset) is buried Benjamin Jesty of Downshay, d. 1816, age 79, born at Yetminster and "particularly noted for having been the first Person (known) that introduced the Cow Pox by Inoculation, and who from his great strength of mind made the Experiment from the (cow) on his wife and two sons in the year 1774". The adjoining gravestone to his wife, d. 1824, shows she survived. Jenner introduced cow pox vaccination in 1776. Cholera victims were often buried in collective graves, covered with a mound (Hutton Rudby, Yorks., c. 1840), or in separate plots. In Paulton churchyard (Somerset) two such plots are marked with tablets. The first records the death of 23 men, 23 women and 26 children "from the dreadful scourge of Asiatic cholera" in less than a fortnight in 1832; the second, another visitation from October 1849 to January 1850, when the death-roll involved 62 individuals.

47. One of the most famous quacks of his day was John St John Long, son of a Limerick basket-maker, the painter John Martin's only pupil. He turned from painting to medicine, "having discovered an original method of treating consumption, rheumatism and other diseases by the application of corrosive liniments and friction". By 1828, he was a Harley Street physician of renown, but two years later, owing to a patient's death, he was tried for manslaughter, found guilty and fined. He resumed practice but died four years later from consumption, which he refused to treat by his own methods, and left £1,000 for his monument in Kensal Green (T. Balston, *John Martin*, p. 71). His epitaph justifies his checkered career. At Godalming (Surrey), Nathaniel Godbold, 1799, advertised himself on his gravestone as "Inventor and Proprietor of that excellent Medecine The Vegetable Balsam for the Cure of Consumption and Asthmas."

48. At Shipton (Yorks.) it was the custom to bury at midnight any woman who died at the birth of her first child, the coffin being carried under a white sheet held by four women. In Lancashire, when a mother died within a month of childbirth, the baby was held over the grave at the funeral (W. Andrews, *Curious Church Customs*, p. 142).

At Bingham (Notts.), a headstone of 1812, by Wood, includes these lines from Young's *Night Thoughts*: "Each Child snatch'd from us, is a Plume, Pluck'd from the Wing of Human Vanity". The Nurse epitaph is fairly common; it occurs early on the tomb in Richmond (Yorks.) to Sir Timothy Hulton and family, 1629, along with the Life as an Inn metaphor: see painted board in Elmstead, (Essex) 1664:

> As Nurses strive their Babes in Bed to lay
> When they too liberally the Wanton play;
> So, to prevent his future grievous crimes,
> Nature, his Nurse, got him to Bed betimes.

The origin of the popular Life as an Inn epitaph may be a phrase in Bishop Henshaw's *Horae Succisivae*, 1631, expanded by Quarles in *Divine Fancies*, 1633.

49. Equally popular was John Wesley's verse, from one of the several epitaphs he wrote:

> When the Archangel's Trump shall blow
> And Souls to bodies join;
> Millions will wish their lives below
> Had been as short as mine.

At Altarnun the tomb of Diggory Isbell, granite mason, records the fact that he was the first to entertain John Wesley on his Cornish visit in 1744.

50. Carvings of children on headstones have already been mentioned. Dead children were signified by their holding a skull, as on the magnificent tomb to Arthur Knowles at Elmore (Glos.) 1707. Richmond, as a clergyman, deplored the custom of "trifling, licentious travellers, wandering about the churchyards of the different places through which they pass, in search of rude, ungrammatical, ill-spelt and absurd verses among the gravestone" and suggested clerical supervision of epitaphs.

51. See head and footstones in Waterstock (Oxon.) 1652 … "So are ye an as I am so shal ye bee, Thy Life a floure thy breth a blaste". Penshurst (Kent) has several fine slates, c. 1830–45, whose imagery includes the sickle and cut rose, the broken lily, and serpent with poppies. As the classical emblem of sleep, the use of the latter was deplored by the Tractarians; but for a fine example, see the headstone to Matthew Moy, Epsom (Surrey) 1817, with cherub-heads above a large poppy plant (the soul arising from sleep), with two angels kneeling at each side, and fine anthemion scrolls above.

52. "He died in a fever, and upon tolling his passing bell, she cry'd out, my heart is broke, and in a few hours expired, purely thro' love. …" Mallett made them the subject of his ballad, *Edward and Emma* and their monument was erected in 1848.

53. Oculi Sunday: so-called because the Sarum Mass for that day began with Psalm 25: "Mine eyes are ever looking unto the Lord. …"

54. Also John Middleton, 1578–1623, the "Child of Hale", 9 feet, 3 inches tall, buried in Hale (Cheshire); Benjamin Idle, 1826, buried at Calverley (Yorks.) in a coffin 8 feet long; Richard Joy, 1742, the "Kentish Samson", in St Peter's, Thanet, with the appropriate epitaph, "And the same Judgment doth befall; Goliath Great or David small." Foreigners include Rasselas Belfield, an Abyssinian, buried 1822, at Windermere (Westmd.): "A slave by birth, I left my native Land; and found my freedom on Britannia's Strand; Blest Isle, Thou Glory of the Wise and Free, thy touch alone unbinds the Chains of Slavery." Scipio Africanus, negro servant of the Earl of Suffolk, was buried, 1720, at Henbury near Bristol: "I who was born a PAGAN and a SLAVE, Now sweetly sleep a CHRISTIAN in my GRAVE; What though my hue was dark my SAVIOUR's sight, shall change this darkness into radiant light. …" The

cherubs on his headstone are appropriately painted black. Maria Sophia Rose, native of Bengal, buried Ifield (Sussex) 1847, was a servant to the Capper family for seventy years. John Panis, a Red Indian child, died at Hayes (Middx.) 1763.

55.   But at Windle Abbey (Lancs.) a headstone as late as 1874 bears the superscription: "O Reader, if thou canst read, look down upon this stone ... etc." Unusual fatalities were Simon Gilker, "Killed by means of a Rockett", November 5, 1696 (headstone at Milton Regis, Kent) and Judith Eyre, "in Consequence of having accidentally swallow'd a Pin", 1747–48 (interior tablet, Dedham, Essex).

56.   In Ely Cathedral a ledger to William Pickering and Richard Edgar, who both died on Christmas Eve, 1845, has a remarkable metaphorical epitaph which shows the persistence of such imagery. Entitled *The Spiritual Railway*, it reads:

> The Line to Heaven by Christ was made,
> With heavenly truth the Rails were laid,
> From Earth to Heaven the Line extends,
> To Life Eternal where it ends.
> Repentance is the Station then,
> Where Passengers are taken in,
> No FEE for them is there to pay,
> For Jesus is himself the way.
> God's Word is the First Engineer,
> It points the way to Heaven so dear.
> Through tunnels dark and dreary here,
> It does the way to Glory steer.
> God's Love the Fire, his Truth the Steam,
> Which drives the Engine and the Train.
> All you who would to Glory ride,
> Must come to Christ, in him abide.
> In First, and Second, and Third Class,
> Repentance, Faith and Holiness,
> You must the way to Glory gain,
> Or you with Christ will not remain.
> Come then, poor Sinners, now's the time,
> At any station on the Line,
> If you'll repent and turn from sin,
> The Train will stop and take you in.

57.   It was a common annual custom in the past to strew church floors with hay or rushes for warmth, some particular meadow being reserved for this purpose. Rushes are still strewn in St Mary Redcliffe, Bristol, and on graves at Tarvin (Cheshire), and the Rush Bearing ceremony is kept up at Grasmere. Reeds are laid down at Barrowden (Rutland), hay at Shenington, and Wingrave near Aylesbury (C. Hole, *English Custom and Usage*, 1950, 3rd edition, p. 81.

58. The Bubble-Span theme occurs in Francis Bacon's *The World*, a paraphrase of a Greek epigram by Posidippus. Compare the synopsis of metaphors in the epitaph to William Brough, 1815, Heanor (Derbys.):

> What is Life? a Breath; a Dream;
> A Bubble in a rapid Stream; `
> A lurid Shade, with scarce a ray;
> A Short and Stormy Winter's day;
> A falling Star; a morning Flower;
> A passing Cloud, an Autumn Shower.
> A flying Shuttle, nay a Span;
> So short and frail's the Life of Man.

A sermon on the theme "Human life is but a bubble" is still preached annually at Hendon to members of the Stationers' Company, who afterwards inspect the grave of Richard Johnson, founder of the custom in 1795 (C. Hole, *ibid.*, p. 143).

George Withers, in his *Collection of Emblemes Ancient and Modern*, 1635, introduced a lottery in the form of a numbered wheel, which with the aid of a pointer referred the reader to the appropriate page of his "fortune". Another device represented the four winds, with a pointer to direct the reader to the four books, each of fifty emblems, into which the work was divided. A tomb in Zennor (Cornwall) 1790, shows the latter device, with the epitaph:

> Hope, Fear, False joy and trouble,
> Are those four winds which daily toss this bubble,
> His breath's a vapour and his Life's a span,
> 'Tis glorious Misery to be born a Man.

At Broughton Giffard (Wilts.) the epitaph to Robert Longe, 1620, puns on the name: "The life of man is a true Lottery, where venturous Death draws forth lots short and long", etc.

59. Such as one at Whatton (Notts.), to William Innocent, 1811, showing a child and two lambs (by Wood), and "Suffer little children ..."; and the evocative phrases on headstones to Ann and Thomas Dowsing, 1795 and 1808, Little Glemham (Suffolk): "the Shepherdess is gone, and the flock is straying", and "the Shepherd is gone in hopes of the flock returning to the Lord". The usual sailor's epitaph is:

> Though Boreas' blasts, and Neptune's wave
> Did toss me to and fro,
> In spite of both, by God's decree,
> I harbour here below;
> And here I do at anchor ride
> With many of our fleet,
> Yet once again I must set sail,
> Our Admiral Christ to meet.

60.   Included in Carleton-Brown *English Lyrics of the Thirteenth Century*. Compare with John Edwards's epitaph (St Ives (Hunts.) 1822): "A crumb of Jacob's dust lies here below, Richer than all the mines of Mexico. ..."

61.   For extracts from Pope see: Great Meeting chapel-yard, Leicester, 1754 (from *Verses to the Memory of an Unfortunate Lady*); Sapcote (Leics.) 1791 (from *An Essay on Man*); Wymeswold (Leics.) 1796 (from his translation of the Iliad). All Saints, Aldwinkle (Northants.) 1815, and Lutterworth (Leics.) 1773, contain extracts from *Night Thoughts*. The common "O cruel death, how could you be so unkind, To take him before and leave me behind", seems to be adapted from Waller, similar to the phrase "He's seldom old that will not be a child" from his *Epitaph on Lord Andover's Son*. William Hayley was an inveterate writer of epitaphs, and two examples of his verse commemorate parish clerks, Henry Hammond and William Bryant, 1779, at Eartham (Sussex). The typical blacksmith's epitaph "My sledge and hammer lie reclined ..." has been attributed to him, although it occurs as early as 1746 at Nettlebed (Oxon.).

4

Technique

TRAINING; QUARRIES;
TRANSPORT; WAGES AND PRICES

IN ENGLISH villages and country towns the texture and colour of the stones used in their buildings and monuments create a visual harmony as individual as local landscape, dialect or custom. They are chastened to hues as subtle as the weather which is both their scourge and comfort, gravestones especially being exposed to its frosts, winds and flurries of sun and rain, so that to choose stone that will bear such testing demands a sense that only long association with its winning and cutting can develop, and which cannot be got by book-learning. Perhaps more markedly than any other, the mason's craft has always tended to run in families, and there are many of its workers alive today whose heritage can span the centuries. From this multitude one could quote as typical the Cornish Menhinnicks of St Mabyn with thirteen masons in five generations since 1700; the Pittaways of Taynton with seven generations of stone-cutters, including their modern representative who is master-mason to Liverpool Cathedral; the Rudkins of Mountsorrel and Groby who had forty members of the family as craftsmen in stone, brick and plaster from the seventeenth to nineteenth centuries, or those families in the Ketton area such as Belton, Betts, Croft, Crowson, Dickens,[1] Gilbert, Halliday, Hibbins, Hubbard and Ireson. In such districts where stone has been immemorially quarried, these men laboured with little expectation of fame other than some local repute, and content for the most part with modest gains. Stubborn in upholding tradition, independent in outlook, their common bond was that integrity and pride in skill which distinguishes the craftsman in any place or time.

It is impossible to do them adequate justice within the space available for the following notes. All that can be done here, apart from sketching in the historical development of traditional practice, is to give details of the working conditions of a few representatives among these post-Reformation craftsmen who are still strangers to the general public, and whose merits it is one of the purposes of this book to introduce.

Companies of craftsmen were in existence during the Roman-British period, when each craft had its *collegium*, but it was not until the Middle Ages that its equivalent, the guild, was introduced. Rules for masons in London were first drawn up in 1356, and by the fifteenth century a general fellowship existed which maintained standards of careful workmanship and just prices by a direct link between maker and buyer without the inflating artifice of middlemen. With the rise of capitalism during the later medieval period Merchant Guilds assumed control of towns and borough, so that, although equal in theory, Craft Guilds could only function through their tacit consent. The various Livery Companies by a strict control of membership and payment of dues effected for their members an enjoyment of the local trade which they were zealous to preserve. The London Masons' Company (whose initial charter was granted in 1677) did not recognize a member of a provincial guild as entitled to practise in the City, unless he applied for admittance as a "foreigner" to their own body. In the seventeenth century it was still instituting "searches" for bad workmanship, but the dearth of building craftsmen after the Great Fire and the Parliamentary permission granted for the admittance of foreign workmen weakened its power and prestige, as by this act such men were allowed after a residence of seven years the same liberties as native freemen. In this way, ironically enough, the large influx of Low Country immigrants eventually led to their virtual capture of the City tomb trade.

Even as early as the thirteenth century "imagers" or tomb-makers were recognized as a separate branch of stonemasons, and the variety of monumental styles during the Gothic period argues the maintenance of local quarry-workshops or centres of production which, in the declining years of the alabaster trade at least, became a monopoly in the control of a few families. The increasing demands of the merchant class for ambitious memorials made tomb-making a lucrative branch of masonry, which under seventeenth century trade expansion and

27. *Details from slate headstones in Nottinghamshire by Thomas Wood of Bingham:* (above) *Bingham, Thomas and Mary Hind, 1820; lunette in low relief with pastoral scene, 14 in. long, 5¼ in. high;* (centre) *Lowdham, George East, 1826; upper part of stone with engraved pineapple and acanthus scrolls;* (below) *Whatton, Mary Hall, 1810; portion of pastoral scene similar to that from Bingham (16 in. long, 8 in. wide).*

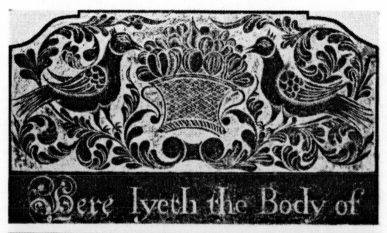

28. *Treatment of superscriptions:* (above) *Salford Priors* (Warws.), *John Haines, 1760: upper part of Forest of Dean headstone, 26½ in. long, 15 in. wide, by Laughton;* (centre) *typical heading of Swithland slate headstone, 23½ in. long, 15 in. wide, first half of eighteenth century, with calligraphic angels in spandrils, Gothic script and "strikings";* (below) *Leadenham* (Lincs.), *Thomas Hale, 1815: upper part of Swithland slate headstone, 27¾ in. long, 13½ in. wide, by Wood of Bingham (all reproduced from full-size rubbings). The Salford example shows the ancient symbol of birds pecking fruit; Wood has changed the conventional doves bearing olive-sprays into pheasants, curving their tails into a convenient arched label for the lettering.*

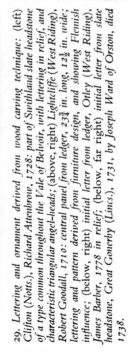

29. Lettering and ornament derived from wood carving technique: (left) Clifton (Notts.), Richard Attenbrow, 1728: part of Swithland slate headstone of a type common throughout the Vale of Belvoir, with lettering in relief, and characteristic triangular angel-heads; (above, right) Lightcliffe (West Riding), Robert Goodall, 1710: central panel from ledger, 23¾ in. long, 12½ in. wide; lettering and pattern derived from furniture design, and showing Flemish influence; (below, right) initial letter from ledger, Otley (West Riding), James Barber, 1778 in relief; (below, far right) initial letter from slate headstone, Great Gonerby (Lincs.), 1731, by Joseph Ward of Orston, died 1738.

30. *Calligraphic influence on Swithland slate headstones in Leicestershire:* (left) Syston, 1747, lettering by James Sparrow; (above, right) Husbands Bosworth, John Wright, 1751, by Robert Waddington of Clipston (actual size of detail shown 13 in. square); (below, right) Burton Overy, William Weston, 1734 (actual size of detail shown in rubbing 20½ in. long, 8 in. wide). Within a generation this simple type of heading was superseded by elaborate "strikings".

town development enabled men to set up both town and country practices as "statuaries" or monumental masons.

Apart from such specialists, the class of master-masons continued the medieval habit of combining building with carving, typified by the magnificent series of tombs made by members of the Masons' Company well into the eighteenth century, until the rise of the architect deprived them of their function as designers and reduced them to the status of builders in the modern sense. About this time in the 1750s the "men of taste" began to break down the homogeneity of the craft of stone by using the terms mechanic and stonemason in a derogatory sense, thus establishing that snobbish difference which Morris tried to overcome in the Victorian period, but which we maintain today by making a distinction between carving and sculpture. In the country, however, such differences were less marked, and the methods of working practice show a variety stemming from medieval times and often continued into living memory.

Owing to the durable nature of the material, and the post-1750 custom of signing work, it has been possible to examine the Swithland slate industry in the Midlands with a degree of proof that, with the one exception of Cornwall, is absent elsewhere.[2] In these counties, where the material could be easily distributed by river, and later by canal-transport, the negligible freight-charges enabled a large number of craftsmen to operate—at first in villages scattered throughout the area, and later in towns which encouraged larger firms to flourish. We can thus distinguish the following types of craftsmen as producing monumental carving:

(*a*) The town statuary whose repertoire consisted of interior tombs and tablets, mantel-pieces and other decorative carving.

(*b*) The village craftsman whose main trade was churchyard head-stones and monuments, such as Wood of Bingham, Charles of Wimeswold or Sparrow of Radcliff.

(*c*) The master-mason, such as Stretton of Nottingham,[3] Staveley or Firmadge, who was not only a builder and surveyor, but a minor statuary.

(*d*) The quarry-owner, such as the Hind family, who exercised control over the Swithland pits and also made monuments.

(e) The family-contractors, such as Bell, Bettoney and Dones, whose various sons were engaged in some building-craft, as painters, plasterers, bricklayers, carpenters, etc., and could pool their labour when needed.

(f) Firms and partnerships, apart from these family groups, which maintained more than one workshop and became in effect general contractors and employers of labour.

(g) Casual work on the part of schoolmasters, parish clerks, sign-writers or other craftsmen, who engraved a few tombstones mainly for pocket-money or recreation.[4]

TRAINING

Training involved an apprenticeship of seven years to a recognized master; sons, however, became their father's apprentices without the usual need for indentures. An apprentice could be transferred to another master or buy out the remainder of his term. At the end of this period, if he had sufficient funds, he could set up as master, but many men who could not afford to do so, or who had not served their full time, became journeymen or day workers. In the Middle Ages, at any rate, these free-lance workmen, often formed their own clubs or yeomen guilds. Mainly peripatetic, they were from the employer's point of view, an independent and irresponsible type of employee, although in later times they often settled down as regularly employed workmen of a master or firm.

It is easy to sentimentalize over the apprenticeship system; its unruly and scapegrace element has been emphasized enough in literature, but it obviously depended upon the mutual give-and-take of personality. Thomas Burman's treatment of John Bushnell, by trapping him into marriage with the servant he had himself seduced, and Bushnell's revenge in embezzling from his master and escaping to Rome, were exceptional, yet the conflict between youth and experience, which often put the apprentice in the position of a neophyte undergoing all the rigours of initiation is perhaps an inevitable feature of the system, which could be argued indifferently to be either its strength or weakness.[5] In similar fashion the wandering mason was by no means confined to the Middle Ages, for during the last century, since the time when the brothers O'Shea were chiselling their "parrots and owls" on

Ruskin's Oxford Museum,[6] Irish skilled or semi-skilled labour has always sought out employment wherever there is building activity. English masons who were not lucky enough to step into their father's shoes often wandered about the country seeking work until they had gained enough experience or capital to settle down.

George Witcombe, for instance, born at Compton Dundon (Somerset) 1831, was the son of a small builder and quarry-owner who was also the landlord of the local inn. At the age of 8 he started work minding pigs; then with some smattering of school, he worked as a "rough-mason" for his father and other local builders, until at the age of 22 he was reckoned an "A-1 mason" earning 16s. a week. He then left home and for the next three years tramped about, first to London, without success, then back to Newport (Mon.) working on jobs of a few days' or weeks' duration. His worst six months involved a perambulation through thirty-four counties, during which his working time was only three weeks, an interesting sidelight on this troubled period of depression when the last Chartist struggle was in progress. He became a member of the Stonemasons' Society, whose members could stay at local "club-houses" and claim bed and breakfast plus sixpence for the road, and won his experience hard. He eventually arrived in Maidstone, where his earnings were then 4s. a day, worked on church building in the district and eventually founded a small monumental business in the town in 1856, in which two of his sons, Henry and George, joined, and which still flourishes in the hands of his descendants today.[7] While it was usual for the eldest son at least to follow his father's trade, the master's apprentices, usually limited to two at a time, often married into the family. Indeed, to maintain quarry-rights and continuity of tradition, the almost rabid conservatism which is characteristic of the craft was encouraged not only by intermarriage between mason families, but fostered by the inevitable diehard reaction of the hand-worker opposed to industrial conditions. The large-scale investment of capital in the Italian marble industry which followed the setting-up of cemeteries during the nineteenth century had an adverse effect on the prosperity of our native quarries, which began to enjoy a brief period of recovery during World War II, when an embargo was laid on such imports of foreign stone, but have since had a relapse owing to re-entry of foreign stone into the country.

England in relation to its size contains a rich variety of stone suitable for building and carving, and many of its quarries have been worked since early times. The flint-knapping of Brandon (Suffolk) which is mainly in the hands of the Snare family, continues a tradition that extends back to the prehistoric period. The remains of Roman-British buildings and statuary show the use of native oolites such as Barnack stone, and Purbeck for wall-slabs; while along the line of Hadrian's Wall the quarries from which its stone was taken can sometimes be identified by inscriptions left by workmen. In the Middle Ages the different virtues of local stone were well understood, and vast quantities were extracted from Barnack, Weldon, Ketton, and Ancaster in the Midlands; Taynton in Cotswold, Bath stone near Box; Portland, Reigate and Maidstone rag in the south; granites in the West, as well as roofing slates from Delabole, Colly Weston and Horsham, and our native marbles Purbeck and alabaster from Corfe, Derbyshire and Yorkshire.[8]

Quarriers' rates of pay were similar to those of ordinary labourers, while women, at the cheapest rate of all, were sometimes used for stone haulage. The raw material was cut into ashlar, as well as pre-fabricated architectural units such as voussoirs, newel-pieces, mouldings etc. but, apart from this building stuff, it is fairly evident that carvers' workshops nearby were turning out sepulchral monuments. Apart from these larger sources of freestone and hardstone, innumerable smaller quarries were widely distributed from which were dug walling stones of smaller size suitable for the coursed or random rubble masonry, which have given their several characteristics to the stone-built houses, barns and dry-stone walls found throughout the length and breadth of England.

It was obviously to the interest of a master-mason to own or have an investment in a quarry. Notable examples during the Middle Ages were the Canons of Corfe, and later, Wren's master-masons, the Strongs and Kempsters, who owned the quarries at Taynton and Burford from which came much of the stone for the City churches and St Paul's. Among lesser quarry owners during the nineteenth century, some of whom were also gravestone-makers, one could instance

Nathaniel Smart of Attleborough; Thomas Siddons and Stephen Swinnerton of Duffield; William Bingham, Richard Bromhead, Anthony Buckles, William Catley and Charles Lindley at Mansfield; Samuel Marples at Melbourne, Samuel Musgrave of Nether Seal, and George Pickard digging Hopton Wood stone at Bonsall; Jesse Rutherford of Wingerworth and Samuel Freeman of Halifax; William Smart of Arundel the local statuary with his quarry at Codmore Hill near Pulborough; John Jackson,[9] Samuel Wilson and the Rudkins of Mountsorrel and Groby, who worked the latter slate after the better quality at Swithland had become exhausted.

The seven water-filled chasms can still be seen in Swithland woods from which issued the multitude of slabs which were cut into tombstones and widely distributed throughout Leicestershire and the adjoining counties. The Leicester historian Nichols has fortunately left a description of the industry as it existed in the early years of the nineteenth century. The slate was drilled and blasted and drawn up to the surface in pieces varying from a hundredweight to a ton and a half. "Various are the uses to which the blocks are converted, some into common slates, and others into slabs for curriers to dress their skins upon—also into sink stones, salting stones, mill stones, cheese presses, chimney pieces and tombstones". Some of the huge curriers' slabs measured 9 by 4 feet; roofing slates varied from 6d. to 3s. per score; and chimney-pieces cost 2s. 6d. per foot with an extra charge for fine polishing. The older slabs for gravestones were polished on one face; later specimens which are thinner have both surfaces smoothed. They were usually about 6 feet long and charged according to width, 20d. per foot at width of 20 inches, rising by 1d. per inch up to 30 inches wide; at 3 feet or over, 2s. 9d. per foot. The labourers were paid from 2s. 3d. to 2s. 6d. per day during the summer, with a winter rate of 2s. daily, sawyers working on a piece-rate of 10d. per foot sawn. When Nichols wrote in 1804, the quarries were owned by the Hon. Butler-Danvers, the Earl of Stamford and Robert Hind, "a gentleman well-known from his ingenious devices on these slate stones". Hind rented from the Earl and thus had a working control of the industry. The Hinds were domiciled originally at Swithland, where Thomas Hind, labourer, was churchwarden in 1633. The earliest slate-cutter was John, apprenticed to William Heafford of Leicester in 1718, for several years

261

both Warden and Steward of the local Slaters, Plasterers and Tallow chandlers' Guild, dying some time previous to 1768. His brother was presumably Henry of Swithland, 1691–1773, buried at Woodhouse Eaves, whose two sons, Henry, 1726–1801, and Robert of Whetstone, 1735–1812, were both slate-cutters. Other members of the family, as yet unrecorded, must have produced gravestones, for there are comparatively few churchyards in the county which do not contain at least one specimen of their work. Their earliest signed headstone is at Whetstone, 1728, and one of the last was signed by a Hind of Groby, which suggests they had an interest in these neighbouring pits. About 1800 the Hinds retired to Whetstone, where they built a house with slate portico now known as Whetstone Pastures, before which stands a rough-hewn slate obelisk $17\frac{1}{2}$ feet high, reputedly the largest crag blasted from the quarries.

Slate for interior tablets was used much earlier in Cornwall than in the Midlands, and the gravestones seldom achieved the sophistication of the Swithland style. Delabole quarries were larger than Swithland and are still worked, the best slate being found at the lower levels, which are over 400 feet deep. Slate was also available on the borders of the county, and during the rising prosperity of Devonport and Plymouth in the early years of the nineteenth century there was a considerable settlement of statuaries and gravestone-makers exploiting the Cross Hill slate quarry, and setting up yards along the road between it and the new cemetery, from which their products were also dispatched by water up the Tamar and its tributaries.

TRANSPORT

Our most remarkable example of stone-transport must have been the carriage of the Blue Stones, each weighing upwards of four tons, from the Prescelly mountains to Stonehenge, a distance of 135 miles as the crow flies. It is now thought that this feat was effected by floating the stone on rafts along the South Wales coast up the Bristol Avon to Frome, and thence overland to the River Wylye at Warminster and downstream to Amesbury. The Romans, while possessing the advantage of good roads, also used water-ways for stone-carriage, their major achievement being the cutting of the Car Dike between the Witham and intervening water-courses to the Nene, along which they quarried from Wansford to near Oundle.

The great area of the Fens before the time of Vermuyden's drainage consisted of marsh, mere and broad, and the navigation of these intricate channels lay in the hands of the local Fenmen who by raft and wherry conducted its traffic, which in later days consisted of imports of coal and Baltic timber, with stone and wool dispatched downstream. It is for this reason that such apparently inaccessible parishes on their island-hards as Wisbech, Long Sutton, Holbeach etc., are full of magnificent headstones originating from the Midland inferior oolites.

The Fenland abbeys of Peterborough, Ramsey, Crowland, Bury St Edmunds and Sawtry all possessed quarries at Barnack, and in the twelfth century the Sawtry monks made a canal to carry their stone through Whittlesea mere. The strategic position of the quarries at a point where only a five mile gap separates the Nene and Welland gave them easy access to both river systems and accounts for their long-standing importance.

The three main river arteries were the Trent, Severn and Thames. In the first two cases, packhorse routes converged on their heads of navigation at Welshpool and Willington, while the Thames was navigable up to Oxford. The traditional route for Teynton stone[10] was overland to Eynsham, and then by water to Hythe Bridge in Oxford; but in Kempster's day Cotswold stone was shipped at Radcot Bridge, near Faringdon, and despatched downstream to the City.

Stone of tested repute with hard weathering qualities obviously justified the high initial cost of lengthy transport that may have been necessary. Caen stone for Norwich Cathedral in 1287 was shipped to Yarmouth and taken by barge to the Norwich wharf at a freight charge double the cost of the material. From the famous medieval quarries at Holywell (near the modern Clipsham pits in Rutland) stone for Windsor Castle, 1363–68, was taken by water down the River Glenn to Surfleet, and then shipped from Kings Lynn. Stone supplied in 1367 for Rochester Castle came from such a variety of sources as Caen, Beer, Stapleton in Yorkshire, Reigate, Fairlight near Hastings and Maidstone. Suitable local stone was used wherever possible, and a quarry dug especially for a new building project. Excavations in 1955 in Wakefield city centre revealed the site of the old "Goody Bower" quarry which supplied the stone for All Saints Church (the present Cathedral), erected a stone's throw away.

Road transport, even over short distances, was relatively more expensive. In 1314 stone from Winshull quarry for Tutbury Castle cost £11 7s. 8d. and its haulage over a mere 6 miles £15 19s. 2d.; and to give a more humble example: a load of stone for which John Litchfield received 1s. was taken from Duston pits to Hardingstone (5 miles) at a cost of 7s. 6d. in 1774 (Hardingstone parish records).

The problem was the same for tomb-makers sending their finished work over a distance. Gerard Johnson in 1591 was paid £200 for his two tombs to the Earls of Rutland made for Bottesford. These were shipped to Boston and there loaded by 17 workmen into 15 carts for the 30 mile journey overland, which alone cost £12 5s. It was natural therefore for carvers to set up their shops in places accessible to wharves or establish their own in towns on some navigable river. Thus we find the City carvers at Southwark and concentrations of statuaries at Bristol, York and Norwich,[11] as well as lesser-known individuals such as Joseph Hewson and Richard Ward at Lincoln; William Charlton of Kings Lynn; William Larke at Yarmouth; Benjamin Plows at York; Robert Ragg and George Evans at Gloucester; and Morris and Parsons at Lewes. Other firms found it good business to establish both a wharf and more central depot. In this respect documentary evidence, previously unpublished, sheds interesting light on stone transport in the early nineteenth century in the case of John de Carle and his son Benjamin, who had shops at Bury St Edmunds and Ballingdon near Sudbury. It is here quoted in some detail, as being typical of many country master-masons' practice, whose output consisted of both building and sepulchral monuments.

These master-masons used three types of stone: York, Ketton and Portland. The first, chiefly for paving and gravestones, was obtained from Samuel Freeman of Cromwell Bottom, near Halifax. It was loaded at Selby, sent by sea to Mistley in Essex, and then delivered by coal barges to Ballingdon near Sudbury, where the De Carles had a branch. Freight was charged at 7s. per ton. Another Yorkshire firm, Dobson & Whitehead of Woodlesford, near Leeds, supplied ready made sink stones and troughs.

Ketton stone, obtained from John Wade, was taken by lighter and barge from Wansford, by the Nene and Fenland water-ways to Lynn, and thence to Bury down the Ouse and its tributary, the Lark. Freightage for the first stage was reckoned at 17s. per ton. Portland stone was shipped from the yard of Messrs. Steward at Westminster to Ipswich at the cost of 15s. per ton. Grindstones were obtained from Richard Kell, at Newcastle, being sent by sea to Lynn, and thence by river to Bury. Orders were usually dispatched in early spring, quarrying and delivery taking two months.

The arrangement for transport was usually made by the De Carles with watermen and freighter captains. Only one vessel, the *Lively* (captain, George Jary) was a regular trader between Newcastle and Lynn, but there were many other coal barges by which the stone could travel. For the most part the same conveyancers were dealt with, the barge owners, Messrs. Stockdale of Lynn, and the local watermen, Francis Browne of Isleham and Joseph Mann of Reach. The general use of water-traffic for the conveyance of stone is brought out clearly in this correspondence; and it becomes obvious why York stone was so widely used, being delivered along with coal, at a freightage-cost under half that of the Midland and Southern traffic.

The De Carles seem to have ordered about sixty or seventy tons of Portland, and about half that quantity of Ketton and York, on a yearly average. As business men they were honest, yet shrewd, dealing with the same suppliers over many years, making prompt payment, and exacting their rightful discount. From 1783 to 1787 they were carrying out building work on four country houses in Norfolk and Suffolk which had been designed by Soane, and from 1824 to 1838 worked on church restoration at Waldingfield and Fornham, at Sible Hedingham rectory and Horringer Hall.

In 1826 they were commissioned to construct a portico at Ickworth House, near Bury, which Francis Sandys had designed for that remarkable prelate, Frederick Hervey, Earl of Bristol and Bishop of Derry. It was to consist of four Ionic columns 27 feet high, which the De Carles intended to make in three drums apiece, and for which they accordingly ordered about a hundred tons of best West Cliff Portland stone. They had been previously working on the basement of the house and now began to lay the brick base for the portico while waiting

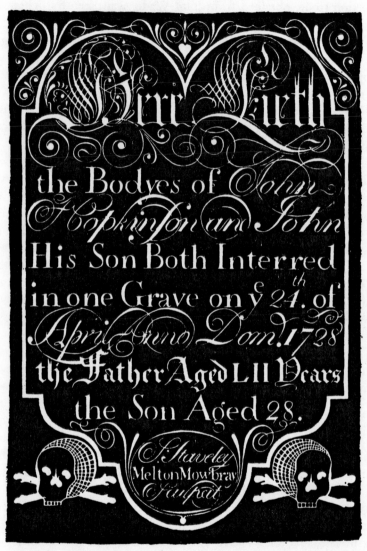

FIG. 64. *Slate headstone (Hickling, Notts.), 1728, by Stephen Staveley.*
FIG. 65 (right). *Slate headstone (Grantham, Lincs.), 1761, by Christopher Staveley.*

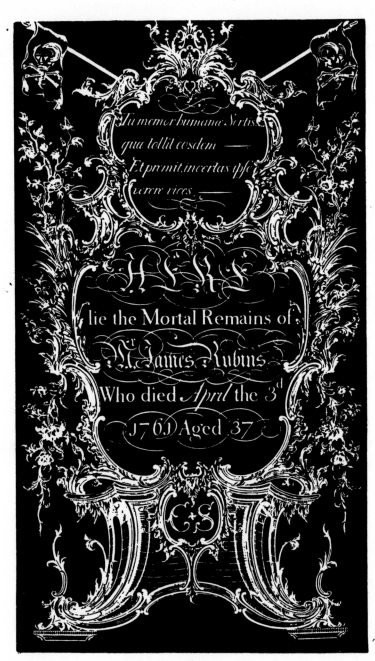

for the stone to arrive so that their task would be complete by August as specified. In spite of several urgent letters to Stewards, the stone merchants, it was not until the end of June, that their ship (appropriately named *The Meanwell*) landed a cargo of stone at Ipswich. Benjamin went down to see it and remarked, "Probably we shall be able to get our caps and bases complete, but was very sorry to observe some blocks of the very hard and objectionable sort intermixed. . . ." A quantity of inferior stone had been offered to them at a reduced price, but "we cannot use the bad stone, it becomes a dead stock with us and causes such confusion and trouble between our sawyers on account of hardness, so we are disappointed in finding that the Column shaft pieces are not yet ready." Their patience began to wear thin—a letter of July 10 is peremptory: "We write to be informed *decidedly* whether we are to be furnished with the Portland Blocks for Columns—and *when*. We are already brought into serious *dilemma* through your long delay, considerable sacrifice already awaits us, and unless you *immediately* freight a vessel we shall be prevented the *execution* of our *engagement.*"

Steward's agent, Mr Searle, made a visit to Portland Isle towards the end of July and promised some personal expedition of the elusive columns. De Carle reported at the end of August that Mr Lake's stucco "has not shown any more defects" but he had yet to complete the underpart of the parapet.[12]

Stewards delivered another load of stone in August to Tovell's wharf in Ipswich. It seems probable that the latter, who had visited the De Carles at Bury, had been asked to take over the columns, for during September they were beginning work on the architrave. "Four or five long Blocks we have sawed with an expectation to form a great part of the Architrave but each has proved so venty or coarse as by no means to become introduced for that purpose. I have not yet been able to realise more than one piece." They did not expect to be able to use more than 12 feet or so of this stone, owing to its quality, and needed about 70 to 80 feet for the portico. "We do hope that the two long pieces ordered originally with a view to the Columns will assist us a little providing you should not require them for ... the shafts." Should their own stone fail, perhaps Tovell could help them from his own stock? "If every other resource should fail us we must adopt the plan of working part in two scantlings."

A further payment of £120 was made to Steward in September, three cargoes that year totalling 176 tons having been delivered, together with a request for two blocks for the column shafts. The work was carried on through the winter, for on February 26, 1827, another urgent letter to Steward requests the "three blocks for the finish of the Architrave." An acrimonious letter to Tovell on June 12, 1827, relating to alleged over-charges mentions the cartage of two pieces of column, apparently worked by the Ipswich firm. The portico seems to have been finished in 1827 or early 1828, for on March 11 of the latter year the De Carles wrote to the Rev. Mr. Hall at St Peter's College, Cambridge: "According to Lord Jeremy's desire I have repeatedly examined the Portico at Ickworth. I saw it again on Friday last—the work appears very substantial and secure." In this letter the contract for Ickworth is mentioned; £150 had been paid in October, 1827, and a bill for a further £715 17s. 9½d. was included. In July John De Carle died, aged 78.

The pattern of stone distribution was easily altered by new methods of transport. When Ralph Allen laid down his iron tramway in 1731 to bring down Bath stone from the quarries at Combe Down to the Avon, it began to compete with the use of Portland; and in the early nineteenth century owing to the growth of canals, this stone, which could be taken by barge at 1d. per ton per mile to Oxford, led to the virtual replacement of the Cotswold and Midland freestones on the college fabrics. Similarly the Midland canals accelerated the trade in slate memorials and led to their wider distribution outside the county.[13]

In 1785 William Firmadge of Leicester made a survey for a canal to link the Soar and Trent with the Erewash and Grand Trunk canals, and in 1791 Christopher Staveley of Loughborough (1759–1827), the eldest son of the Melton Mowbray master-mason, was appointed surveyor to the Leicestershire Navigation Company at a salary of £200 per annum. The Company's work under the hands of the contractor Pinkerton had not been going well and, when his contract ended, Staveley took charge both of canal construction and the railway, The Forest Line that was part of the project. In March, 1793, work was progressing, and the line was ready to receive its permanent way. Staveley was then told to press on with the canal from Loughborough to Leicester, which was opened in 1794. The contract of the engineer,

Jessop, expired that year, and Staveley was accordingly appointed Superintendent of Works at a salary of £70. The Company was short of money, and bad luck dogged Staveley, the bricks supplied were bad and expensive, and the timber contractor sent unsound wood. He finished the Blackbrook Reservoir in 1796, but it unfortunately burst three years later after a thaw following a hard winter and caused considerable flood damage which cost the Company £2,025 in compensation. Work came to a halt in 1797, but enough had been done to facilitate the transport into south Leicestershire of coal from Derby and of Welsh and Swithland slate. Christopher's son, Edward, 1795–1872, worked with his father at the architectural practice he had in Leicester and in 1825 was appointed jointly with him as Surveyor and Engineer to the Leicester Navigation Company which had begun to start operations afresh. While negotiations were going on in 1833, Edward fled to America after embezzling nearly £1,700 of company funds. Apparently his brother Christopher was involved in this scandal for he seems to have committed suicide the same year at the age of 35. Edward's career in the New World appears to have been prosperous. He first worked in Baltimore where he made a survey for the City water supply, and another for the Delaware Rail Road. In 1842 he left for Canada, worked on the Welland Canal near Niagara Falls, then moved to Kingston, Ontario, Montreal, and finally settled in Quebec about 1845, where he opened offices and, among other work, made an excellent map of Canada which was re-printed in several editions.[14]

A branch of Staveley's canal stretched to Market Harborough, and the effect of transport on sepulchral monuments is clearly shown here, where within the space of less than a mile were concentrated a number of stonemasons' shops near the old burial-grounds of St Mary Arden and Little Bowden, with river, canal and railway a mere stone's throw apart. In St Mary Arden the older stones of the early eighteenth century were conveyed from the quarries by river, to be later replaced by slate brought by canal-barge, while at Little Bowden, in addition, are foreign white marble monuments of the nineteenth century carried by rail.

Cheaper transport led to competition and the growth of monopoly firms which destroyed the economy of the old village workshops. The firm of Shenton, Hull, and Pollard is a typical example, for its partners, apart from being the most prolific minor statuaries in Leicestershire during the nineteenth century, were also builders, dealers in Roman cement, salt, lime, timber, and makers of school slates.[15] In similar fashion the Broadbents, starting as statuaries and slaters, had become slating and tiling contractors by the end of the nineteenth century, with their main office in Leicester, and branches at London, Liverpool, Cardiff, Worcester and Hull.

WAGES AND PRICES

Any adequate idea of the value of wages can only be obtained by using the contemporary cost of living as a yard stick and relating payments for skilled and unskilled labour. Conditions varied more widely in different parts of the country than they do today; in the North for instance, agricultural wages and living-standards were more frugal than those of the South. The tragedy of the Black Death caused labour shortage, although building seems to have been less interrupted than might be supposed. With the decline of the open-field system the husbandmen and yeomen farmers prospered but began to disappear as a class when the effects of enclosure made themselves felt. There was trade expansion during the Tudor period, and the changing fortunes of the wool trade were related to that of stone-working through the patronage of the wool merchants.[16] Factory growth caused a displacement of population but, while bringing prosperity to the North, took away from the labourer the cottage industries which had augmented his scanty wages, so that gradually the older country crafts, gravestone carving among them, lost face and meaning.

The medieval mason, in common with other craftsmen, had a smaller working year than is customary today owing to the various holy days that were observed, but his average day's work was from sunrise to sunset, and he was subject to fines for quarrelling, loss of tools and lateness. Payment was either in wages, which were less in winter than summer and could include a food and drink allowance, or by piece-rate, in which case he cut his banker-mark on worked stone, so that his production-rate could be checked. Items of clothing were sometimes provided, such as aprons, or gloves for handling stone, or straw hats for hot weather, while tools seem to have been supplied by the lodge.

Drink allowances were often given and here the pleasant ceremony of Closinghale, the drinking at the completion of a building, should not be forgotten.

The payment of the master-craftsman varied greatly and largely depended on his standard of education and native ability. His status was probably higher during the medieval period, for the City mason who succeeded him after the Reformation assumed the class of prosperous merchant from which his clientele was drawn, and it seems the exception rather than the rule for the noble Augustan patron to have received his statuary on equal terms.

"The maximum yearly earnings of a fully qualified craftsman were about £5 12s. 6d. up to 1350; £7 10s. from 1350 to 1500; and £8 15s. from 1500 to 1550",[17] but provincial rates of pay were generally lower. Similar variations of payment within the craft are to be found up to the middle of the nineteenth century; so that the following daily payments for the grade of craftsman mentioned above must be taken only as the roughest average.

> 1200–1500: 4d. to 12d. per day
> 1500–1700: gradually rising to 2s. 6d. per day
> 1700–1800: from 2s. 6d. to 3s. per day
> 1800–1850: from 3s. to 5s. per day

A working week usually consisted of 5½ days; averaging 9 hours daily. A a general rule, these rates can be reckoned as more than treble the usual pay of agricultural workers.

Graded payment was made to masons in the same firm, probably according to age and experience. In 1801 the master, Latter Parsons of Lewes, reckoned his time at 3s. 6d. per day, his workmen receiving the following rates: William Emery 3s. 4d., Floyd, Pearpoint and Ticehurst 3s., William Bedy 2s. 6d., Thomas Hatterall 2s. 4d., Gudger 2s. 2d. and H. Spelf, the boy, 9d. Part of a man's wage was sometimes kept back, e.g. David Lewis, employed by Rees Jenkins of Bridgend, 1857, paid in 3d. weekly towards the cost of his own headstone from his wage of 13s. per week. Sawyers could be paid by the day or on piece-rate. Latter Parsons' sawyer Tim Emmery, got 2s. 2d. per day, while Smart was paid £2 13s. for a month's work involving the sawing of 180 feet of Portland. At this time (1794) setting a saw was expensive,

31. *Effects of classical influence and typography on country headstones: (left) Harlaxton (Leics.), Charles Plowright, 1846, by Green of Denton, calligraphic influence replaced by that of typography; (centre) Great Ayton (Yorks.), Ann Jackson, 1853, a bold North Country treatment of classical motifs; (right) Lamport (Northants.), George Jenkinson, 1907: an imitation of an Attic stela, its effect spoilt by an insensitive treatment of the text.*

32. *Contrast in contemporary memorials:* (left) *headstone by Eric Gill (reproduced by courtesy of Sculpture Memorials);* (centre) *headstone, 4 ft. 6 in. long, 2 ft. 2 in. wide, Buxton cemetery, by A. J. Ayres. These headstones are representative of the school of thought amongst contemporary craftsmen which advocates the use of native stones, traditional design and Roman lettering, and is opposed to the manufacture of monuments in foreign marble, such as this three-dimensional angel* (right), *whose fellows can be seen, rank on rank, in contemporary churchyards.*

costing 10s. Steam-powered saws had been used by Richard Brown of Derby, although Henry Watson (1714–86) is often credited with the invention of the water-powered multiple-stone saw working at Ashford in 1748. The old hand-sawyers often spent their lives in this tedious occupation, as for instance John De Carle's man at Bury St Edmunds, Daniel Head (1744–1829), who had worked for thirty-eight years in their yard since the age of 11.

A good master attracted loyal service; when Latter Parsons died in 1848 he was carried to the grave by his ten workmen, whose average length of service was over thirty-three years apiece.

Little data can be presented as to the price of churchyard monuments before the end of the eighteenth century, as the average patron seldom had enough property to entail making a will and, while account-books of later date must often still remain in the possession of mason-families, their value as records is too little appreciated.

The diary of Richard Stapley of Twineham records a payment of £5 in 1729 to William Hazlegrove, stone-cutter of Shoreham for a stone laid on the grave to the wife of Anthony Stapley. Other details of this family, who were also carpenters, and apparently of some reputation in the county at this time, are mentioned by Sussex diarists. In 1714 Thomas Marchant relates how he went with a friend to Shoreham and "agreed while there with James Hazelgrove for the tombstone for my father, at 3s. per foot, and 7s. 6d. for squaring it and working the edges, and 1d. per letter for the inscription." In 1727 he "Dined at W. Hazelgrove's, and cheapened a tombstone"; (this was his mother's, who had been buried twelve days before). "He asked me 3s. 6d. per foot when cleans'd, and a 1d. a letter for the inscription. But R. Smith offered me some much cheaper, I think, at about 2s. 2d. per foot, the inscription the same."[18]

Representative prices from account-books of firms include:—

c. 1800. May and Parsons, Lewes.[19] The average price for the typical Sussex head and footstone linked by a stone grave rail, usually made in three different qualities of Portland, cost from £4 to £5, and chest-tombs of the simple sort about £15.

c. 1827. Gilliam's, Dorking. Head and footstones from £4 to £6.

c. 1824–32. De Carle and Son, Bury St Edmunds. Their characteristic monuments, similar to those made by their contemporaries in Bury, the Steggles, had head and footstones linked by a gabled ridge-stone costing £10 10s. A square pedestal tomb at Woolpit, 1832, with iron palisade was £28 15s.; without the rail £23.

c. 1840–55. Jenkins's, Bridgend. Prices of head and footstones usually with a bodystone varied from £2 to £7, or more.

Kelke's *Churchyard Manual*, 1851, contains various designs with their prices by the architects Giles Gilbert Scott and W. Slater. These show carved headstone crosses from £2 to £6; coped stones of £10 to £12 "if not elaborately ornamented"; and chest-tombs, "the most costly of churchyard monuments", from £20 to £50.

The various items were listed in the bills submitted to clients, of which the following are characteristic:

Gilliam, Dorking.

	£	s.	d.
1827. October 17. Mr Reynolds, Mickleham			
To head and foot stone in Mickleham Churchyard	4	3	0
12 dozen and 10 letters to Do. @ 1s. 6d.		19	3
Cartage and Fixing Do.		6	0
	£5	8	3

	£	s.	d.
1827. Mr Randall Vigo			
To taking up, cleaning and painting in White Color a Head and footstone in Dorking churchyard		9	0
A new footstone to Do.		13	0
8 dozen and 9 old letters painted @ 1s.		8	9
5 dozen and 0 new Do. @ 1s. 6d.		7	6
To fixing Do.		3	6
	£2	1	9

Jenkins, Bridgend.

1855. May 25. Mrs David, Newcastle

To a new headstone, plinth and gravestone in the solid, fixed at Newton churchyard	6	10	0
Scripture verse 3 dozen 5 letters @ 1s. 3d. per dozen. Cutting and painting	4		3¼
Fixing tombstone, Lime etc.		7	6
Painting Do. 2 coats @ 4s. per Coat		8	0
	£7	9	9¼

During the eighteenth century the usual charge for cutting letters was 1d. per letter. Painting the stone and lettering, usually black on a white surface, was a usual practice, considered a preservative.[20] Brand noted in 1804 the Glamorganshire custom of painting headstones with lime three times a year, at Easter, Whitsun and Christmas; while a writer in *Blackwood's Edinburgh Magazine*, 1820, remarked on the "frightful fashion of black tombstones" prevalent in Warwickshire and the neighbouring counties which had gilt lettering. The fashion for painting in polychrome, which was generally applied to stones other than marble during the Middle Ages and indeed on tombs up to the seventeenth century, seems to have shown its last vestiges on churchyard monuments. Paget in his *Tract upon Tombstones*, 1843, mentions painted angels on headstones, with pink and white faces, red cheeks, and gilt hair and wings, and examples found certainly suggest it as a widespread practice.[21]

Stone costs varied considerably, foreign marble being the most expensive, although it seems to have become cheaper during the years 1790–1830. Characteristic prices were: Portland stone 2s. to 4s. a foot; Purbeck 5s. 6d. to 7s. a foot; Black marble 10s. a foot; Statuary marble 2s. 9d. a foot; Surrey marble 3s. 6d. a foot. Mantelpieces in Portland 14s. to £1 12s.; in Statuary marble £13 13s.; in Sicilian marble £5 5s.; in Dore marble £1 8s. to £3; in Charlwood marble £4 10s. Slates (per hundred): Ladies 8s.; Countesses 13s.; Duchesses 23s. Six foot grindstones £1 1s. each; three foot grindstones 5s. 6d.

The ornamental marbles and spars of Derbyshire led to an industry in the eighteenth and nineteenth centuries that was as highly organized as the elaborate trade in the same locality during the Middle Ages. Its centre was Ashford-in-the-Water, where black marble (often inlaid with other coloured stone in the form known as *pietra dura* or under its local name of "bauble work") was used for chimney-pieces, table-tops, vases, flooring and statuary. Henry Watson (1714–86), belonging to the well-known family of masons working at Chatsworth House, was among the first to practice such inlay and was a pioneer of the "Blue John" trade, having his own mine at Castleton in 1756. After his death John Platt of Rotherham, 1728–1810, retained the sole marble-mining rights in the late eighteenth century, but in a few years owing to the growth of popular health spas the trade flourished and supplied the numerous "petrification warehouses" and lapidaries of Matlock, Bakewell, Buxton and Castleton. Several Ashford craftsmen, including the well-known Thomas Woodruffe, gained prizes at the Great Exhibition of 1851, but the trade dwindled and the works finally closed down in 1905.[22]

Apart from gravestones, some idea of the variety of work undertaken by master-masons can be obtained from the following items:

May and Parsons, Lewes.

Plaster and stucco ornaments supplied to Inigo Thomas's billiard-room at Ratton Place for £25, 1800; Glynde Place, ornamental frames, 1801. The firm also did a great deal of slating, the material being shipped to Newhaven, such as Thomas Tilt's ballroom at Brighton, 5,500 feet of Welsh slate,[23] £124 17s. 6d.

Gilliam, Dorking.

The Gilliam family had been functioning since 1714, when John Gilliam of Castleford (Yorks.) was apprenticed to James Wilson of Bramley, free-mason. John and William settled in Dorking in the early nineteenth century, where their practice was mainly grave-stones and building, continued up to a few years ago. They were employed a good deal by Thomas Hope, the rich connoisseur, on his mansion, The Deepdene in Dorking, and unpacked, mounted and set in place his unique collection of antique marbles which was eventually sold at Christies in 1917. During 1822 they were un-packing and cleaning columns and figures and preparing the "new building"; next year the Sculpture Gallery and new Library were got ready, and statuary removed from the entrance hall (which it seems was full to overflowing) to the Picture and Sculpture galleries. In 1824 the vase collection was unpacked and set up in the picture gallery, along with several figures in the Theatre. In 1825 pedestals were fixed in the Conservatory, bronzes assembled, as well as figure groups in the New Gallery. Next year work continued in arranging figures on plinths; and in 1827 marbles were moved to the front of the house, and vases to the Conservatory. Their more humdrum work during this period comprised the paving of Dorking town, the Quaker meeting house in 1823, and in 1825 the churchyard with York stone at 1s. 5d. per foot, for £11 12s. 7½d. From spring to autumn of 1823 they carried out restoration on Mickleham church, the wage bill being £23 14s. 5d. Examples of their simple headstones have been identified locally through their mention in these accounts; being unsigned they would otherwise have escaped notice.[24]

Jenkins of Bridgend and Maesteg, 1837–56.

This Welsh firm made gravestones and tombs, but like the Gilliams were not statuaries. Early accounts show sign-writing jobs, such as painted coffin-plates, costing about 1s. or 1s. 6d.; a ship's sign, 1830, 6s.; a "sine for the wagin", 1833, 2s. 3d.; six "toleboards" for Bridgend in 1840 (fifty-one dozen letters at 10d. a dozen, total £12 15s.).[25] Building work included four Gothic windows at £3 5s. and £4 5s. apiece for Newcastle Bridgend church, 1841; window-sills for Zoar Chapel, Maesteg the same year, £6 13s. In 1852 they supplied Gothic gate-pieces at Penllyn Castle for £21; an entire freestone front for a house in Bridgend, 1854, at £47 2s. 11d.; and work on the Octagon Tower of Dunland Castle, 1856, for £17 19s. 10d. Considerable patrons were the Earl and Countess of Dunraven, and in the same year the Jenkins made an arched doorway and new extensions to the Castle.

Their local stone cost from 3s. to 3s. 6d. a foot; walling stone 1s. a cartload; slates 2s. a load; Forest of Dean flags 3s. per yard. Plaster-of-Paris, Roman and Bath cements were all 1d. per pound; and Portland cement 12s. 6d. a cask.

Masons often traded between themselves, sometimes for stone supplies, or else some particular product for which they had a local reputation.[26] We find, for instance, Thomas Knowles of Oxford supplying William Godfrey, statuary of Milton near Abingdon between 1793 and 1801, with gravestones, a marble table and pedestal, and a complete marble monument for £9 9s. Thomas Knowles had worked for the Townesends, the great Oxford masons and in 1799 set up a yard in Holywell to produce monumental carving. He took his son Edward Nichols Knowles as partner in 1816, when living at Headington. The firm still flourishes in Oxford. Knowles produced a good many inscribed "mitchells" (square paving stones) and invariably gilt the lettering on his headstones. In 1800 May and Parsons supplied Portland slabs or "scants" to Jonathan Harmer of Heathfield, soon after returning from America to his native village.[27]

Jonathan senior (son of Joseph, churchwarden and parish bookkeeper) had two sons, John and his namesake born in 1762. He lived in a house called Stonecutters and was a mason, plasterer and bricklayer, leaving his sons hand-surveying books and tools. John, the younger of the two brothers, had gone out to America in 1793, working in New York as a bricklayer at 5s. 3d. sterling a day. As he informed his brother that a stonemason's lowest wage was 6s. (more than double the English rate) Jonathan joined him in 1795 with his family. He worked at first as a journeyman, and then as a painter, but lost three children through the prevalent scourge of yellow fever, and returned with his former Republican sympathies rather dashed, as can be seen in several letters which he wrote home. Back in Heathfield, he made an attractive series of some twelve designs for inexpensive terracotta plaques to be fixed to headstones including a basket of flowers (8s.); Charity (8s.); various urns (10s.); Faith and Hope (£1 12s.) etc. of which the original moulds are in Barbican House Museum, Lewes.[28] Some fifty of these plaques, which have been found on headstones in East Sussex (together with many headstones having now empty sockets), show their local popularity. Jonathan's son Edwin was a stonemason, and the old Republican sympathies were reflected in the names of his children—Lavinia, Washington, Cordelia, Augustus, Xenophon and Volney. His youngest son Sylvan (1803–84) was also a land-surveyor, who confirmed his father's discovery of lignite in the locality and compiled the parish survey and notes on which Percival Lucas' attractive book *Heathfield Memorials*, 1910, was based.

In 1853 Nathaniel Hawthorne was appointed United States Consul in Liverpool and described in his *English Notebook* a ramble he took with his family in The Wirral soon after their arrival in England. They found in the village of Bebington a derelict house built like a mock castle, with bristling cannon, carved wooden life-size figures of a dog in its kennel and a man sitting in an arbour, and enigmatic inscriptions upon its walls.[29] Unwittingly he had described the former residence of Thomas Francis, an eccentric stonemason who lived in the village from 1764 to 1850. Thomas restored the spire of the local parish church in 1806 for £100, the scaffolding alone costing £32 10s. 6d., and made heavy ledgers from the Storeton quarries, less than a mile from the churchyard, which had been worked since Roman times. His eccentricities seem to have developed in middle age and took two forms, an egomania centred on a consciousness of himself as being one of the last of the old local families, driving him to assume the role of local squire and benefactor, and an obsession with death.[30] His castellated house, ornamented with a fine figure of Britannia, was the result of his patriotic fervour at the time of the threatened Napoleonic invasion. A large relief, showing himself in frock-coat, like Moses striking the rock, with representations of his house and Bebington Ferry, commemorates his sinking a well in the village and is inscribed: "When the people of Bebington thirsted for want of water I cut the rock, and God gave them plenty." He ordered lead coffins for himself and his wife, which were kept in the dining-room and used for linen, except on birthdays, when Thomas and Ann lay in them in meditation. Thomas dug his own grave in the churchyard and smoked a peaceful pipe stretched out in it each Saturday night. He cut his own tombstone, which bears a draped urn, and the legend, *Labor vincit Omnia*.

His passion for ciphers and puzzles was expressed by the three wall-puzzles cut outside his house, of which Hawthorne could make no sense. The reader may care to try his prowess:

Subtract 45 from 45
That 45 May Remain.

My name And sign
is Thirty Shillings just
And he that will tell
My Name Shall
have a Quart on Trust
For why is not Five the Fourth
Part of Twenty the same in
All Cases?

AR

UBB

I

.

NGS

TO   NEF

ORAS

SE

S

While there were many of these Englishmen who could well say like Michelangelo that they took in their trade with their mother's milk, others discovered in themselves a natural talent which they had the enterprise to develop as truly self-made men. I can best conclude this brief account of stonemasons with the epitaph of such a craftsman, born in my own native county of spires and squires, whose villages, churches and great houses are still living witnesses to stone and those who love and live by it—the type of man on whom Gray mused that evening at Stoke Poges when he framed his testament to them with "short and simple annals".[31]

In Memory of Samuel Turner, Painter, Who was Born at a lone House in the Parish of Harrington in the County of Northampton. His occupation a Shepherd. His amusements were the beautiful scenes of Nature, His retirements the Study of Surveying, Dialing, Engraving &c. In the 35th Year of his Age, he removed to Market Harboro', and changed the Cottage for the Shop, and the Crook for the Pencil. His Works, that are left, will shew his Abilities. He travelled through a rough, and rugged Road of affliction, and Died in hopes of a Happy Eternity, the 13th Day of Febry 1784 Aged 67.

Notes

1. On Keysoe spire (Beds.) a tablet records the miraculous escape from death in 1718 of William Dickins who fell "From the Rige of the Middel Window in the Spier Over the South West Pinackel he Dropt upon the Batelment and their Broack his Leg and Foot and Drove down 2 Long Copein Stones and so Fell to the Ground with his Neck upon one Standard of his Chear. When the Other End took the Ground which was the Nearest of Killing him yet when he See he was Faling Cride Out to his Brother Lord Daniel Wots the matter Lord Heve mercy upon me Christ have mercy upon me Lord Jesus Christ Help me But Now Almost to the Ground." He lived, however, until November 29, 1759, aged 73. In 1735, when mending the spire of Market Harborough (Leics.) Jackson, the "steeple-mender" slipped from a broken crocket and was luckily caught by a scaffold.

Spires attracted acrobats, the best-known being Robert Cadman, buried in St Mary, Shrewsbury, where he replaced the weather-cock but was killed when attempting in public to slide down a rope fixed from the spire to the further bank of the Severn. Several well-known steeple-menders lived in Warwickshire, including John Chesshire, Henry Ulm or Home, and the Newcombe family.

2. Rare medieval signatures include: Llanveynoe (Hereford), ninth-tenth century— "Haedur made this cross"; twelfth century examples on Bridekirk font—Richard; Romsey Abbey choir capital—Robertus; Rollestone cross-shaft—Radulphus. On later work; Brenchley (Kent) headstone of 1670—"Don by Robert Diamond son of Matthew Diamond Ano Domi 1676"; Ingleby Arncliffe and East Harlesey (Yorks.), 1715, 1717—William Thopson; Carcolston (Notts.) 1720—James Sparrow; Breedon-on-the-Hill (Leics.), signed with unusual precision, "May 23, 1733"—George Dexter of Coleorton; Market Harborough (Leics.), 1743—George Person; Callington (Cornwall), 1753—John Burt; Deal (Kent), headstone to Esther Baker, 1764, by John Peach, signed "JP" with rebus of peach. Neville Northey Burnard of Altarnun, who afterwards worked for Chantrey, made several slate headstones when a youth. He carved the memorial to his grandparents at Altarnun with a bird and sprig of rose-mary, signed with his age, 14.

3. A typical "puff" is William Stretton's in *The Nottingham Journal*, 1778, who in his Marble and Petrifaction works had "a curious Assortment of Marble from most parts of the known World, Chimney Pieces etc. executed in the most elegant Taste; Marble Sideboards, Mortars, India Ink Stands etc. Mansfield Stone and Swithland Slate Tombs or Headstones executed in a superior manner." G. C. Robertson, *The Stretton Manuscripts*, 1910, describes his work. He was the first to introduce Welsh slates into Notts., 1790; his children were called Stella, Sempronius, Severus, Salacia, Sabina.

4. Schoolmasters who cut gravestones include John Newton, Thomas Eldridge of Lubenham and Henry Castledine of Syston who was also the parish clerk; Jeremiah

Goodman of Kibworth Harcourt 1765–1836, who was also Curate of Cranoe. Those who were parish clerks as well as gravestone-cutters were William Tunnicliff of Brailsford and Ilkeston, 1777–1843; Robert Waddington of Clipston; John Wootton of Wimeswold. William Norris of Brackley, fl. 1841, was a painter, gravestone-cutter and bird-preserver. Walter Gale, schoolmaster of Mayfield (Sussex) according to his diary, 1750–58, made maps, painted signs, designed embroidery and cut headstones, charging £1 10s., £1 13s. and £1 17s. 6d. for three examples in 1751.

5. See Eric Benfield, *Purbeck Shop: a stone worker's story of stone*; a unique book by a member of a family belonging to The Company of Marblers and Stone Cutters of the Isle of Purbeck, which was incorporated into the London Masons' Company in 1858 and still holds its Court at Corfe every Shrove Tuesday, when apprentices are admitted, and a football kicked along the old road to Poole to maintain the right-of-way of the old haulage route to the harbour. The stone-firms gave the Marblers credit for their output, which today is mainly bird-baths for the suburban garden. Compare this practice with the medieval payment by food and cash, which continued until later times, e.g. the Rev. Giles Moore of Horsted Keynes agreeing with John Blackiston, mason, that he and his son and boy gave him one day's work for 1s. and food, 1657 (*Sussex Arch. Trans.*, vol. 1, pp. 65–127). The ornate character of many memorials, which obviously involved many man-hours in production, may well have been part-paid by barter.

6. K. Clark, *The Gothic Revival*, pp. 272–74.

7. I am indebted to Mr Witcombe of Maidstone for this information.

8. For quarries and local stones refer to *Victoria County Histories* under their appropriate counties: J. Howe, *The Geology of Building Stone*, 1910; W. J. Arkell, *Oxford Stone*, 1946 (the latter book, similar to D. Hartley, *Made in England*, 2nd edition, pp. 107–38, gives drawings of tools and technical terms used by stone-workers). L. F. Salzmann, *English Medieval Industries*, has an informative chapter on Gothic stone-masonry; Joseph Moxon, *Mechanick Exercises, or the Doctrine of Handyworks*, 1678, describes later tools and working practice.

9. Jackson, anticipating Macadam, used broken fragments in road construction in the way adopted by the "Colossus of Roads". Over a thousand labourers, many of them imported from Scotland, were working at the Mountsorrel quarries at this time (T. R. Potter, *Rambles round Loughborough*, 1868).

10. Old quarry roads are usually sunken, owing to the weight of such traffic as the monolithic mash tun made of Taynton stone for Sir Compton Read of Shipton-under-Wychwood, which held sixty-five bushels and needed twenty-one horses for haulage (R. Plot, *Natural History of Oxfordshire*, 1705 edition, p. 77.)

11. At Norwich, 1548–1713, when the city was second in importance to London, a total of 254 masons and rough-masons were made freemen (Millican, *Freemen of Norwich*).

12. The De Carle accounts mention Lake, the plasterer, on several occasions. August 31, 1826: "The stucco work at Ickworth has not shewn any more defects since your man Pulham left." The latter craftsman may have been James Pulham, buried at Woodbridge (Suffolk) 1765-1830, who worked for William Lockwood, a local builder and plasterer at the latter craft. About 1816 Lockwood invented an artificial stone, Portland Stone Cement, and Pulham, along with his brother Obadiah, continued to work for him, later inventing a compound of his own which he named Pulhamite (see Lockwood, *Woodbridge in the Olden Times*, 1889). Identical plaques representing Christ and the Samaritan woman discovered by the writer and his wife in Doric Place, Woodbridge, and on a headstone at Wrentham (Suffolk) are probably Pulhamite, practically indistinguishable from Portland stone.

13. Easier transport probably accounts for the presence of work signed by Wray of Lincoln, Joseph Thompson of Nuneaton, and Sprawson of Warwick so far afield as Harefield (Middx.). An unusual stray is the slate to Mrs Ann Bonner, 1763, St Nicholas, Deptford, by William Charles of Wimeswold.

14. See A. T. Patterson, "The Making of the Leicestershire Canals", *Leics. Arch. Soc. Trans.*, vol. 27, pp. 66-99, and R. Abbott, "The Railways of the Leicester Navigation Company", *ibid.*, vol. 31, pp. 51-61. For other documentary evidence concerning the Staveley family in Canada I wish to thank Mr W. J. Hamilton of Dayton, Ohio.

15. Evidence suggests that Pollard and Shenton were the original partners, joined by Hull; then the Shentons dropped out and Hull and Pollard worked together until *c.* 1835, after which Samuel Hull continued by himself. The firm also built St George's Church, Leicester, 1826, designed by William Parsons (apprenticed to William Firmadge 1809) and the Obelisk on Naseby Field. Benjamin Broadbent was in partnership for a time with Hawley of Melton Mowbray. Nottingham firms included Hawley and Burton *c.* 1822, and Hawley and Cox *c.* 1830.

16. Decline of the wool trade in the seventeenth century led to an Act being passed in 1666 requiring woollen shrouds; this was amended by statute in 1680 and 1687 to require affidavits to this effect or a fine of £5. The Act was only repealed in 1814 and was unpopular with the upper classes. It was satirized by Pope in *Moral Essays* in the often-quoted lines:

> "Odious! In woollen! 'twould a Saint provoke!"
> Were the last words that poor Narcissa spoke.

Narcissa was probably intended for Anne Oldfield, the actress, who insisted on being rouged and dressed in her best when laid out. The printed affidavits varied from crude wood-cuts to fine engravings on vellum (see illustrations in *Sussex Arch. Soc. Trans.*, vol. 18, p. 190; *Country Life*, July 3, 1942, p. 35).

17. Harvey, *English Medieval Architects*, p. 324, which includes mention of the following monuments to master-masons and carvers: William de Wermington

d. *c.* 1350, Crowland Abbey; Richard of Gainsborough, fl. 1300–1350, Lincoln Cloisters; William Stubbard, d. *c.* 1430, St Albans Abbey transept; Thomas, John and Richard Wolvey d. *c.* 1428, 1461, 1491, all at St Michael, St Albans; Robert Spilsbury, d. 1462, York Minster nave; Henry Redman, fl. 1495–1528, brass in Brentford church.

18. In 1668–69 the rector of Horsted Keynes paid J. Wood, mason, and his servant 6s. for two days' work, "hee raysing mee 4d. a day on what I formely gave himselfe and man". As the London daily rate for a qualified mason was 2s. 6d., Wood did well out of the bargain.

19. A characteristic firm of master-masons and statuaries which has occupied the same site in Lewes since the sixteenth century. One of its earliest members, John Morris, who worked at Glynde House and built the chapel for £2,300, is recorded as re-cutting tombstone inscriptions there. The firm continued by absorbing apprentices and partners such as Edward May, John Latter Parsons, Charles Parsons, and various members of the Bridgman family, in whose hands it still flourishes. Preserved in the yard is a stock headstone of May and Parsons, *c.* 1800, with carved lunette of Hope, left blank for lettering. Masons cut these stock-blanks during the winter, when building was impossible. I wish to thank Messrs. Bridgman for their loan of personal documents.

20. When first cut from the quarry, stone is "green" and full of "quarry sap", but it hardens upon exposure to the air. Local stones have their own peculiarities and expectations of life. Whereas, for instance, slate seems eternal, many of the Forest of Dean headstones set up about the 1800s are beginning to shale. No attempt has been made to preserve them, although their virtues were recognized by Canon Blake in *Birmingham Arch. Soc. Trans.*, vol. 51, 1926. Stone is susceptible to frost, wind currents, salt air and air pollution. Soot, for instance, has reduced most tombstones in London and industrial districts to illegibility (see R. J. Schaffer, "The Weathering of Natural Building Stones", *Building Research Report*, no. 18, 1932).

21. Brightly coloured tablets are to be found throughout North Monmouthshire and Hereford, the work of the Brute family of Llanbedr near Crickhowell. The colours mainly red, yellow, green and blue, are said to have been made from vegetable dyes and lichens according to a recipe lost about 1840 (Harthan and Wight, "Brute Fecit", *Architectural Review*, 1947).

22. T. D. Ford, "Ashford Black Marble", *Liverpool and Manchester Geological Journal*, vol. 2, part 1, 1958. "Sussex marble" (used from Roman times) and quarried near North Chapel and Kirdford was another local stone often used for monuments.

23. Welsh roofing slates began to replace local varieties such as Horsham and Swithland about the end of the eighteenth century. The ancient quarries of Colly-weston (Northants.) however, still operate and have been mainly run by the Close

family during the last two hundred years. Stonesfield quarries (Oxon.) closed down about the 1900s, when wages were still about 2s. 6d. per day and slates £2 per thousand, as in 1820—prices being kept down by competitive undercutting. Slating, like other branches of stone-masonry, has its own language (Arkell, *Oxfordstone*, pp. 134–150).

24.   An interesting mason who enjoyed the company of a great poet was James Andrews of Olney, whose local headstones derived from Quarles have previously been mentioned. In the spring of 1780 he gave lessons in drawing to William Cowper, who called him "his Michelangelo", and produced "mountains, valleys, woods and streams and ducks and dabchicks". The diary of Samuel Theedon, 1791–94, the Olney schoolmaster (kept in Cowper's house at Olney) shows the poet's relations with the local townspeople. Andrews made a pedestal for a bust of Homer which Johnson presented to the poet in 1793 (see "Country Masons: a field of biographical research" by the present writer, *Genealogist's Magazine*, vol. 11, no. 8, pp. 274–280, where detailed references are given to many stonemasons of whom space prohibits mention here).

25.   William Charles of Wimeswold made a tablet for the local school in 1737, for 17s., its eight score of letters cut for 1s. per score. In 1741 William Chapman cut the sundial on Stoke Albany church for 10s. Above it is a carved wooden board, made by William Adkins, carpenter for £2 8s. in 1806, requesting men to remove hats and women their pattens before entering church. The latter admonition, together with an actual pair of pattens, is found in Walpole St Peter porch (Norfolk), *Country Life*, May 11, 1961, p. 1099; also at Wanborough (Wilts.). James Law of Lutterworth (1807–73) brother of George Law, the slate-cutter, 1798–1870, built All Saints, Gilmorton (Leics.) in 1861, of Ancaster and Attleborough Stone. Its porch and lychgate were made in 1897–98 by King and Ridley, of Lutterworth, in Attleborough and Weldon stone, and Stoney Stanton granite.

26.   Joshua Lepper, mason of Paulerspury (Northants.), in his will dated January 8, 1762, asked that a pair of gravestones, about three guineas, should be set up on his grave by Henry Cox of Northampton, if living, or, if dead, by some other good carver. Those existing on this grave bear inscriptions but no carving (information from Miss Dorothy Warren).

27.   John Stevens of Thame, 1647–1736, migrated to the New World, and set up a mason's yard at Newport, Rhode Island, in 1705. Members of the family continued to produce gravestones until the last of them, Edwin, died *c.* 1900, when the business was taken over by John Howard Benson, one of the foremost letter-cutters in America, who died recently. H. M. Forbes, *The Gravestones of Early New England*, Boston, Mass., 1927, gives an account of the interesting notebooks kept by the Stevens and illustrates the richly ornate folk-art of these memorials, which shows little affinity with our English work.

28. Memorials from the Coade factory of artificial stone at Lambeth, which functioned from 1769–1836, are sometimes found in churchyards, pleasantly designed and in excellent condition. The composition of this Lithodipyra was analysed by the L.C.C. research department in 1949 (S. B. Hamilton, "Coade Stone", *Architectural Review*, November 1954, pp. 295–301).

Richard Brettingham De Carle, d. 1791 (eldest son of Robert De Carle of Norwich, 1724–76), whose sister Ann was the first wife of James Sowerby, the botanist, himself married Ann Davy at St George's, Hanover Square, in 1774. He worked for the Coades, two specimens of signed work being the font at Debden (Essex), and a lunette applied to a headstone at Yoxford (Suffolk) commemorating Ann Davy, 1786, presumably a relation of his wife. Among later imitations of Coade stone were commonplace headstones by Thomas Grimsley of Oxford. In Lingfield church (Surrey) there is a sixteenth century tablet of glazed tiles in the style of encised effigial slabs; at Wolstanton (Staffs.) a headstone of sagger marl, 1737; and another terracotta at St Mary, Nottingham, of similar date, to the daughters of William Sefton, a local maker of clay pipes and earthenwares.

29. John Watson of Peckforton (Cheshire) who worked on Peckforton Hall, set up in his garden a large stone elephant with castellated howdah on its back. Josiah Lane, "the celebrated constructor of Rockwork", specialized in the making of those grottoes which were considered essential to an Augustan estate. He made that at Wardour, 1792, the Cascade at Bowood, and probably the celebrated examples at Pains Hill and Oatlands Park (both destroyed), the latter costing £40,000. Certain stones on Skiddaw are sonorous, and this fact was exploited by Joseph Richardson when, after thirteen years' experiment, he made a sort of xylophone, which under the name of "The Rock Band" toured Europe in the nineteenth century.

30. As an example of an old village family, the Buttons of Kimcote showed a decline of fortune over the years. In 1524 John Button was taxed at 21s., being the richest man in the village; in hearth-tax returns of 1670 Benjamin Button's five hearths show him to have had the largest house. By the end of the eighteenth century his namesake was paying a rent of £3 per annum and practising as a stonemason making slate headstones of considerable elegance. Thomas Sumsion, 1672–1744, buried at Colerne (Wilts.) left goods worth £329, including tools and a writing-desk. Members of the family worked as masons at Colerne up to World War II (Colvin). At Stanford-in-the-Vale (Berks.) tombstones were being produced as late as 1866 by members of the Strongs, probably related to the more famous family at Taynton who worked for Wren (L. G. Maine, *A Berkshire Village, its History and Antiquities*, 1866).

31. Masons' houses, dated, exist at Burford (Oxon.), built by Christopher Kempster, 1698; Swerford (Oxon.) by John Powell, 1836; in the main street, Weldon (Northants.), by Arthur Grumbold, 1654; Haunt Hill House, Weldon, by Humphrey Frisbey, 1643. The Grumbolds and Frisbeys were local quarry-owners during the sixteenth and seventeenth centuries.

Index of Monumental Stone Carvers

THE following list has been compiled from the evidence provided by signed work and personal memorials. Monumental masons whose names were published in directories but whose products have not been identified are not included. Where several masons of the same name are known to have worked in an area but no work has been identified, the names are given thus: ALCOTT Joseph/William/Edward, of Rugby and Coventry; fl. 1798–1880. An asterisk indicates the place of burial. The inclusion of more than one place-name, e.g. Bagnall of Castle Donington and Melbourne, implies that the craftsman had more than one workshop or moved his residence. Where a signature occurs without the habitat being named, the locality in which work has been found is given in italics; e.g. ASKEW Charles, fl. 1851; *Grantham*.

ALCOTT Joseph / William / Edward, of Rugby and Coventry; fl. 1798–1880

ALLT Thomas, of Breedon-on-the-Hill*; 1811–61

ALMOND T., of Heckington; fl. 1840

AMBROSE William, of Sleaford; fl. 1791

ANDREWS James, of Olney*; 1735–1817

ANDREWS Samuel, of Wisbech; fl. 1797–1841

ANDREWS, of Devonport and Morice Town; fl. 1810–78

ARBUTHNOT J., *Thirsk*; fl. 1729

ARCHER Thomas, of Gotham; 1789–1849

ARTHUR J., *Egloshayle*; fl. 1820

ASKEW Charles, *Grantham*; fl. 1851

ATKINS John, of Great Bowden; Islington*; 1745–1803

ATTEWELL, of Maidenhead; fl. 1830

BABB Samuel, of St Dominic; fl. 1849–59

BADCOCK John, of Kibworth Harcourt*; 1791–1838

BAGNALL Samuel, of Castle Donington and Melbourne; fl. 1809–70

BALLARD Francis, of South Littleton*; 1751–1811

BALLARD of Thurcaston; fl. 1772

BALLS Charles, of Yoxford*; 1822–70

BARACLOUGH William/John/Albert, of Nuneaton; fl. 1823–76

BARKER, of York; fl. 1820

BARNES William, of Long Clawson; fl. 1772–94

BARNWELL Joseph, of Attleborough; fl. 1844–53

BASS James, of Hinckley*; 1796–1837

BATES William, of Stoke Goldington*; 1738–90

BATT Joseph, of Epsom*; 1708–63

BAYLISS Nathaniel, of Woburn*; 1724–68

BEARCOCK John, of Chatteris*; 1682–1745

BEARDSLEY William, of Shipley; Kirk Hallam*; 1799–1849

BELL Joshua, of Strensham*; 1804–36

BELL William, of Melsonby*; 1713–30

BELL, of Leicester; fl. 1750–95

BELTON, of Metheringham; fl. 1850–62

BELTON, of Northampton; fl. 1866

BENNETT Thomas, of Frampton*; 1808–83

BENNISON M. D., of Sleaford; fl. 1842–52

BERRY John, *Devon*; fl. 1757–80

BERROWS G., of Much Marcle; fl. 1832
BETTONEY John, of Oadby*; 1790–1841
BIDMEAD Joseph and John, *Hereford*; fl. 1831
BIGGLESTONE James, of Hereford; fl. 1822–32
BILLYELD James, *Enderby*; fl. 1754
BIRCHALL, of Rugby; fl. 1851–75
BIRKENHEAD George, of Ashby-de-la-Zouch; fl. 1827–44
BIRKS J., *Lincs.*; fl. 1762–67
BIRTCHNELL Joseph, of Leicester; Kirby Muxloe*; 1801–55
BLACKSHAW, of Navenby; fl. 1848
BLAND William, of Maidwell*; 1658–1703
BLIZARD Andrew, of Pershore*; 1710–66
BONE, of Liskeard; fl. 1840
BONEHILL, of Warwick; fl. 1829–87
BONEY Caleb, of Padstow*; 1747–1826
BONNISON John, *Stokesley*; fl. 1755
BONSER William, of Clipston; fl. 1789–1857
BOULDEN T., *Illogan*; fl. 1866
BOYER, of Croyland; fl. 1792
BRABYN W., of Withiel; fl. 1837
BRADDOW George, of West Hallam; fl. 1774–1833
BRAMLEY, of Swithland; fl. 1817–42
BRAY S., of Roscare; fl. 1819–40
BREWER John, of Beccles*; 1712–96
BREWER Richard, of Grantham; fl. 1805–42
BREWIN John, of Grantham*; 1737–91
BREWSTER John, of Grantham*; 1727–97
BROADBENT Benjamin, of Leicester; fl. 1842–62
BROUGHTON George, of Gilmorton and Walton; fl. 1795–1839
BROUGHTON William, of High Wycombe; fl. 1842–49
BROWN H., of Nottingham; fl. 1827–68
BROWN H., of Sleaford; fl. 1817–39
BROWN R., of Whatton; fl. 1774–89
BROWN W., of Callington; fl. 1853–95
BRUNT Thomas, *Derbys.*; fl. 1757–68
BRUTE Aaron, of Llanbedr; fl. 1754–83

BRUTE John, of Llanbedr; fl. 1773–1840
BRUTE Thomas, of Llanbedr; fl. 1721–82
BRYAN John, of Painswick*; 1716–87
BUCKERFIELD Jonathan, of Leicester; fl. 1734–43
BULL Thomas, of Market Harborough*; 1824–66
BULL William, of Leicester; fl. 1763–95
BUNNY Benjamin, of Walton; fl. 1860–89
BURGISS John, of Uxbridge*; d. 183?, aged 59
BURROWS Richard, of East Leake; fl. 1845–71
BURTON John, of Somerby; fl. 1784–1827
BUSSELL William, of Gloucester; fl. 1843–50
BUTERIS John, of Burton Overy; fl. 1859–62
BUTTON Benjamin, of Crick; fl. 1771–1835

CAKEBREAD C., of Towcester; fl. 1872–89
CAKEBREAD Samuel, of Warwick; fl. 1825–41
CALAH Francis, of Shelford; fl. 1761–68
CALVER William, of Yoxford*; 1797–1854
CAMPDEN Michael, of Cleeve Prior*; 1689–1741
CARRINGTON John, of Loughborough; fl. 1828–35
CARRINGTON William, of Loughborough; fl. 1825–49
CARRINGTON William, of Birmingham; fl. 1857–64
CARTER George, of Epsom*; 1704–73
CARTWRIGHT Joseph, of Castle Donington; fl. 1816–76
CARVER, *Horncastle*; fl. 1730
CARVER, *Loughborough*; fl. 1751–97
CASTLEDINE Henry, of Syston*; 1739–1818
CATT John, of Sedlescombe*; 1817–91
CHALLANDS, of Grantham; fl. 1815–62
CHALLIS John, of Braintree; fl. 1790–1820

CHAMBERLAIN Robert, of Newark*; 1797–1850

CHAMBERS, of Stow-on-the-Wold; fl. 1867

CHANDLE Anthony, *Whaddon*; fl. 1673

CHANLER, of Hinckley; fl. 1838–59

CHAPMAN William, *Stoke Albany*; fl. 1741

CHAPPELL C., of Devonport; fl. 1866–75

CHARLES William, of Wimeswold*; 1708–64

CHARLTON William, of Wisbech*; 1726–62

CHECKETTS William, of Leamington; fl. 1841–80

CLARKE Edward, of Market Harborough*; 1800–40

CLARKE John, of Liddington*; 1767–1841

CLARKE John, of Market Harborough*; 1738–92

CLARKE Joseph, of Liddington*; 1766–1843

CLARKE Robert, of Liddington*; 1788–1871

CLARKE Robert, of Liddington*; 1813–57

CLARKE Samuel, of Market Harborough*; 1800–68

CLARKE William, of Market Harborough*; 1755–1831

CLAY Henry, of Leicester (St Mary's)*; 1765–1826

CLAY John, of Leicester (St Martin's)*; d. 1755

CLAYTON, *Darley Dale*; fl. 1822

CLIFFORD James, of Stow-on-the-Wold*; 1789–1851

CLIFFORD John, of Stow-on-the-Wold*; 1721–48

CLIFFORD Joseph, of Stow-on-the-Wold; *Nether Swell*; fl. 1846

CLIFFORD Richard, of Stow-on-the-Wold*; 1732–97

CLIFFORD Richard William, of Stow-on-the-Wold; fl. 1829–40

CLIFFORD William, of Stow-on-the-Wold*; 1658–1724

CLIFFORD William, of Stow-on-the-Wold; *Swerford*; fl. 1746

COCKSHAW Isaac, of Leicester; fl. 1829

COCKSHAW John, of Leicester; fl. 1781–1808

COLECOM James, of Merstham*; 1772–1822

COLECOM James, of Merstham*; 1802–70

COLES James, of Thrapston; Islip*; 1791–1834

COLES John, of Thrapston; Islip*; 1736–1816

COLLINGWOOD James Henry, of Grantham*; 1806–59

COLLINGWOOD William, of Grantham*; 1741–1805

COLLINGWOOD William, of Grantham*; 1779–1847

COLLINS J., of Devonport; fl. 1821–63

COOK Charles, of Rothwell*; 1743–1809

COOK George, of Rothwell*; 1787–1846

COOK William, of Rothwell*; 1810–59

COOPER Charles, of Ashby-de-la-Zouch; fl. 1809–56

COOPER S., of Haseley; fl. 1817–60

CORNEY Philip, of Bodmin; fl. 1812

COULSON Nathaniel, of Derby; fl. 1812–49

COULSON Thomas, of Barwell; fl. 1726–60

COWLES, of Aylesbury; fl. 1876

COX William, of Market Harborough*; 1804–53

COX, of Bidford-on-Avon; fl. 1861–76

CRADDOCK H., *St. Endellion*; fl. 1821

CRAGG Thomas, of Foston; fl. 1794

CRISP Thomas, of Badsey; fl. 1755–59

CROSS William, *Long Sutton*; fl. 1763

CROSSMAN W. H., of Newton Abbot; fl. 1864

CULLEN John, of Sleaford; fl. 1804–55

CURTIS J., *Chatteris*; fl. 1844

CUTTER Joseph, of Newcastle (St John*); 1790–1836

DAFT Robert, of Nottingham and Castle Donington; fl. 1803–16

DALTON J., *Brompton*; fl. 1859

DAMS Richard, of Kettering, Wilbarston, Market Harborough; fl. 1797–1807

DAVEY, of St Tudy; fl. 1843–46

DAVIS C., of Bidford and Pershore; fl. 1820–70

DAVIS Thomas, of Upton-on-Severn*; 1814–53

DAWKINS George, of Rothwell*; 1731–91

DAWKINS William, of Rothwell*; 1773–1800

DAWSON William Coldham, of Great Wilbraham*; 1806–35

DEACON, of Launceston; *Cornwall*; fl. 1850

DE CARLE Benjamin, of Bury St Edmunds*; 1788–1864

DE CARLE Charles William, of Bury St Edmunds*; 1782–1822

DE CARLE James, of Ipswich (St Matthew's*); 1775–1825

DE CARLE John, of Norwich and Bury St Edmunds*; 1750–1828

DE CARLE John Parkerson, of Bury St Edmunds*; 1773–1829

DEEVE Thomas, of Bury St Edmunds; fl. 1674–1716

DEXTER George and John, *Leics.*; fl. 1732–87

DOLMAN Joseph, *Melbourne*; fl. 1801–15

DOLEMAN J., *Ermington*; fl. 1776

DONES Charles, of Lutterworth*; 1795–1863

DOUGHTY H., of Yarm; fl. 1832

DREW Charles, of Bedford (St Paul's*); d. 1826

DUKE Giles, *Herefs.*; fl. 1781–99

DUNICLIFF Thomas, of Melbourne (Melbourne Baptist Chapel); 1781–1832

DURANCE James and Joseph, of Lincoln; fl. 1826–50

EADS J., *Thursley*; fl. 1786

EAST Peter, of Wisbech*; 1649–1713

EDKINS John, of Bidford-on-Avon; fl. 1792–1850

EDWARDS John, of Abergavenny; fl. 1804–33

EDWARDS Joseph, of Rye*; 1775–1807

EGLINTON Samuel, of Ashbourne; fl. 1766–80

ELDRED John, of Holbeach; fl. 1801–35

ELDRIDGE Thomas, of Lubenham; fl. 1820–35

ELLERY Thomas, of Wadebridge and St Breock; fl. 1830–42

ELLIOTT Joseph, of Market Harborough*; 1798–1840

ELLIOTT Thomas, of Peatling*; 1759–1842

ELLIOTT William, of Peatling*; 1787–1847

EVANS John, of Stroud*; 1762–1837

EVARARD John, of Attleborough, Nuneaton*; 1766–1839

FANSON R., of Stretton; fl. 1823

FERRIMAN David Beale, of Wimeswold*; 1788–1829

FERRIMAN Zaccheus, of Wimeswold*; 1812–61

FINNEY William, of Delabole; fl. 1795–98

FIRMADGE William, of Scraptoft*; 1726–90

FIRMADGE William, of Leicester, Scraptoft*; 1755–1836

FIRN John, of Leicester; fl. 1834–75

FISHER George and Stephen, of Newark; fl. 1843–51

FISHER James, of Loughborough*; 1791–1831

FLETCHER Thomas, of Longridge*; 1786–1821

FOSTER Thomas, of Lincoln; fl. 1822–38

FRANKLIN Joseph, of Stroud; fl. 1789–1812

FRANKLIN William, of Stroud; fl. 1805–60

FREEBURY James, of Stroud; fl. 1830–68

FREWER John, of Ipswich; fl. 1849–90

FRY James, of Great Berkhamstead*; 1816–46

FULLALOVE R., of Belton; fl. 1753

GARDINER, of Pershore; fl. 1863–92

GIBBS Timothy and Lemuel, of Shutford; fl. 1762–1870

HUTCHINSON J., *North Yorks.*; fl. 1762–1812

HUTCHINSON Samuel, of Colchester; fl. 1816–37

ILES Charles, of Burleigh and Hampton, *near Stroud and Cirencester*; fl. 1828–50

ISBELL Diggory, of Altarnun*; 1718–95

ISBELL James, of Plymouth; fl. 1814–30

ISBELL Richard, of Stonehouse; fl. 1794–1830

JACKSON Henry, of Lincoln; fl. 1804–49

JACKSON Robert, of Torpoint; fl. 1823–30

JACKSON Thomas, of Banbury*; d. 1670

JEFFS John, Towcester*; 1791–1867

JELLEY George, of Kenilworth; fl. 1816–58

JENKIN E., of Tremain; fl. 1805–45

JEPHCOTT, of Braunstone; fl. 1829

JOANES Ralph, of Horsham; fl. 1756–1801

JOHNSON George/John/Thomas, of Welford; fl. 1819–74

JOHNSON James Henry, of Leicester; fl. 1840–78

JOHNSON J. W., of Melton Mowbray; fl. 1838–57

JOHNSON Valentine, of Nottingham; fl. 1803–48

JOHNSON, of Bitteswell; fl. 1851–67

JOHNSON, of Gilmorton; fl. 1815–92

JONES Ebenezer, of Mountsorrel; fl. 1754–99

JONES John, of Bingham*; 1772–1837

KIDDEY John, of Sandiacre*; 1800–69

KIDDEY Thomas, of Sandiacre*; 1802–59

KILPACK James, of Lutterworth*; 1814–68

KINNES Robert, of Leicester; fl. 1741–61

KIRK William, of Leicester (St Mary's*); 1748–1821

KIRK William, of Sleaford; fl. 1791–1842

KIRK William and Charles, of Leicester; fl. 1839–51

KITELEY William, of Scaldwell; fl. 1791–1846

KNIGHT, of Bulwell; fl. 1809–43

LAMB Francis, of Bottesford*; 1738–1817

LAMB George, of Bottesford*; 1743–70

LANE R., of Chipping Campden; fl. 1739–1831

LANGTON William, of Gilmorton; fl. 1779–1821

LAUGHTON John, of Cleeve Prior*; 1711–54

LAUGHTON Thomas, of Cleeve Prior*; 1738–1824

LAUGHTON Thomas, of Cleeve Prior*; 1790–1852

LAW George, of Leire, Lutterworth*; 1798–1870

LAW Richard, of Leire, Lutterworth*; 1819–85

LEE J., of Bedworth; fl. 1857–80

LEEMING Robert, of Yarm*; 1785–1809

LEWIN John, of Evington; fl. 1749–75

LEWIN William, of Leicester; fl. 1831–43

LONGDIN John, of Darley Dale*; d. 1767

LORD, of Burbage; fl. 1847–1901

LOVELOCK William, of Beckenham*; 1840–97

LUFKIN George, of Colchester*; 1828–1913

LUFKIN Henry, of Colchester*; 1764–1823

MABBOTT, of Bingham; fl. 1840–43

MACY Philip, of Chilmark*; 1666–1711

MANDER R., of Banbury; fl. 1848–52

MARGETTS T., of Rushden; fl. 1825–53

MARPLES Samuel, of Melbourne; fl. 1808–38

MARSHALL Richard, of Belper; fl. 1806–17.

MARSHALL John, of Petworth; fl. 1876–89

MASKREY, of Derby; fl. 1827–32

MASON John, of Kibworth Harcourt; fl. 1854–80

MATSON John, of Bridlington*; 1760–1826

MATTHEWS Samuel, of Great Wigston*; 1816–66

MATTHEWS, of Plymouth; fl. 1849–60

MCCRACKEN William, of Leicester; fl. 1820–61

PROWSE William, of Devonport; fl. 1830–54

PRYOR Joseph, of St Budeaux*; d. 1864

PULFORD William, of Market Harborough*; 1761–1845

PULFORD William, of Market Harborough*; 1792–1831

PULFORD John, of Belton*; 1752–87

PULFORD Samuel, of Belton*; 1781–1854

PULHAM James, of Woodbridge*; 1765–1830

QUICK William of Plymouth; fl. 1814–55

RADCLIFF Joseph, of Nottingham; fl. 1758–78

READ William, of Stratford-on-Avon; fl. 1835–60

REDFERN John, of Derby; fl. 1834–50

RILEY Charles, of Louth; fl. 1815–46

RILEY Thomas, of Leicester; fl. 1766–1829

RING James, of Reading; fl. 1751–66

RIPPINER Samuel and John, of Oundle; fl. 1841–60

ROBERTS Matthew, of Whetstone; fl. 1813–53

ROBINSON Edward, of Belper; fl. 1835–58

ROBINSON J. B., of Derby; fl. 1826–83

RODERICK Rees, of Margam; 1780–1854

ROWLAND Samuel/Benjamin/Charles/Henry, of Horsham; fl. 1839–1913

ROWLAND Stephen, of Horsham; 1738–89

ROWLEY Henry, of Nuneaton; fl. 1851–82

ROWORTH Joseph, of Wimeswold*; 1747–1807

RUDKIN Thomas, of Groby, Ratby*; 1762–1844

SAMSON Giles, of Westbury; fl. 1755–60

SANDERS, of Plymouth; fl. 1831–48

SANDERSON William, of Yarwell*; 1763–1803

SCOTT Thomas, of Market Harborough*; 1765–1850

SEAGER William, of Coventry; fl. 1822–71

SEAGRAVE Henry, of Frisby*; 1739–79

SEAGRAVE John, of Frisby; fl. 1760–80

SEARCY George, of Nottingham; fl. 1818–54

SHEASBY John, of Wroxton*; 1705–58

SHEPPARD William and George, of Newark; fl. 1805–54

SHIMWELL Isaac, of Youlgreave*; d. 1812

SILLS Joseph, of Grantham; 1819–68

SIMPKIN John, of Bottesford*; 1749–1816

SIMPSON John, of Cottingham*; 1827–1900

SIMPSON William, of Cottingham*; 1804–87

SIMS Thomas, of Leicester; fl. 1777–95

SIMS, of Derby; fl. 1828–49

SLATER Thomas, of Shepshed*; 1779–1831

SLEEP J., of Landrake; fl. 1821–42

SMART Nathaniel, of Attleborough*; 1791–1860

SMITH Henry, of Elton; fl. 1854–65

SMITH Thomas and John, of Grantham; fl. 1764–1836

SMITH Thomas and John, of Kegworth; fl. 1812–28

SMITH Thomas and Richard, of Belgrave; fl. 1857–90

SMYTH James, of Woodbridge; 1771–1833

SMYTH Robert, of Ufford*; 1763–1837

SNARE Thomas, of Brandon*; 1794–1849

SPARROW George, of Grantham and Stamford; fl. 1757–1817

SPARROW James, of Radcliff-on-Trent; fl. 1716–87

SPENCER William, of Lutterworth; fl. 1832–72

SPITTLE William, of Hungerton; fl. 1828–68

SPRAWSON Richard, of Warwick; fl. 1847–75

SQUIRES George, of Cropwell; fl. 1857–69

STAFFORD T., of Whissendine; fl. 1858–80

STANLEY Joseph, of Norwich; fl. 1834–61

STANYON John, of Market Harborough; fl. 1825–75

WADE Richard, of Ketton*; 1805–72

WADGE E., of Linkinhorne; fl. 1833–44

WADDINGTON Robert, of Clipston*; 1717–91

WALKER John, of Market Harborough*; 1750–88

WALKER John, of Frisby*; 1792–1840

WALKER John and Samuel, of Nottingham; fl. 1793–1854

WALKER Richard, of Sherington*; 1691–1748

WALKER William, of Market Harborough*; 1716–93

WALKERDINE David, of Derby; fl. 1835–48

WALL J., of Stroud; fl. 1851–59

WALLIS James, of Newark*; 1747–1824

WALPOLE Robert, of Market Harborough; fl. 1846–69

WALPOLE William, of Loughborough; fl. 1822–31

WARD Edward, of Oadby; fl. 1836–63

WARD John, of Gotham; fl. 1851–63

WARD Richard, of Lincoln; fl. 1790–1849

WARD T. H., *Rayleigh, Essex*; fl. 1769–91

WARD William, of Coventry (Holy Trinity*); 1811–44

WARD, of Croyland; fl. 1829–37

WARMINGTON Thomas, of Leamington; fl. 1835–50

WEAVER, of Melton Mowbray; fl. 1829–86

WEBB John, of Linton*; 1697–1767

WEBSTER, of Loughborough; fl. 1734–79

WEBSTER John, of Wirksworth; fl. 1835–45

WESTAWAY Jeremiah/John/William, of Delabole and West Putford; fl. 1823–73

WESTON Thomas, of Hugglescote; fl. 1812–67

WESTON Richard, of North Kilworth*; 1825–87

WHEELER Frederick, of South Littleton*; 1797–1845

WHEELER John, of Reading and Faringdon; fl. 1827–63

WHEELER William, of South Littleton*; 1774–1833

WHITEHEAD John Fryer, of Beccles*; 1786–1850

WILCOX George, of Grantham; fl. 1830–47

WILKES Job/John/Joseph/Paul/Solomon, of Bidford-on-Avon; fl. 1792–1863

WILKINS Thomas, of Middleton Cheney*; 1741–69

WILLIAMS, of Plymouth; fl. 1814–21

WILLIAMSON Francis, of Esher*; 1833–1920

WILLS James, of Totnes; fl. 1811–50

WILSON John, of Newcastle (St John)*; 1732–92

WILSON Samuel, of Groby Quarry, Newton Linford*; 1823–79

WINFIELD John, of Wimeswold*; 1742–1809

WINFIELD John, of Wimeswold*; 1769–1815

WINFIELD William, of Wimeswold*; 1763–1832

WINN George, of Bury St Edmunds*; 1789–1847

WINN George, of Bottesford; fl. 1825–56

WOOD John, of Derby; fl. 1819–35

WOOD Thomas, of Bingham*; 1760–1841

WOOD W., of Barlestone; fl. 1819–72

WOODCOCK Thomas, of Hinckley; fl. 1756–72

WOODWARD, of Bakewell; fl. 1812–56

WOOLERTON Royle, of Rearsby; fl. 1817–62

WOOTTON William, of Kegworth*; 1736–1819

WOOTTON Benjamin, *Leics.*; fl. 1794–1802

WOTHERS Samuel, of Market Bosworth; fl. 1832–53

WRAY Benjamin, of Lincoln; fl. 1828–66

WRIGHT John, of Hickling*; 1771–1829

YATES Joseph, of Leicester; fl. 1828–72

YATES T., of Market Harborough; fl. 1842–47

YELLAND, of Devonport; fl. 1842–73

Glossary

ACANTHUS: thistle-like leaf which, with its flower resembling the honeysuckle or anthemion (q.v.), was the main plant motif used in classical ornament.

ACROTERION: pedestal or decorative finial placed on apex and lower part of pediment in classical building.

AEDICULE: pedimented surround to a niche, similar to the treatment of an exedra (q.v.).

ALTO RELIEF: high relief carving, as opposed to low, or bas-relief.

AMORINI: cupids, babies or cherubs, often combined with arabesques in classical and post-Reformation ornament.

ANTEFIX: classical ornament covering end of a rafter, usually in the shape of an anthemion.

ANTHEMION: ornament based on the acanthus flower, resembling honeysuckle.

ARABESQUES: light, rhythmic tendrils interspersed with animal motifs.

ARCA: classical form of sarcophagus (q.v.), in the shape of a truncated pyramid, often supported on lion feet.

ARCHITRAVE: lower part of the entablature (q.v.) in classical building.

ARRIS: sharp edge between moulded surfaces.

ASHLAR: regularly laid stone blocks with squared edges and smooth faces.

BALE-TOMB: Cotswold type of chest-tomb with semi-cylindrical or grooved top.

BANKER: stonemason's bench for cutting stone.

BANKER-MARK: personal device cut on wrought stones by the mason to identify work for quality and output (sometimes called a Mason's mark).

BARROW or tumulus: earth heaped above a prehistoric grave.

BASE-BEDDED: stones laid with natural strata horizontal.

BED-HEAD: see grave-board.

BODYSTONE: stone in the form of a ledger, coffin or corpse, placed horizontally between head and footstones.

BRACKET: support to a horizontal or vertical surface, its classical form usually an S or C-shaped scroll (see console, truss).

BRASS, MONUMENTAL: engraved plate of brass or latten (q.v.).

BUCRANIA: carved ox-heads or skulls combined with garlands, representing sacrificial victims in classical ornament.

CADUCEUS: winged wand, bound with snakes.

CAIRN: heap of rough stones or boulders.

CANOPY: ornamental covering or roof, flat or three-dimensional; when repeated in Gothic tracery it is known as canopy-work.

CAPITAL: head or top of a column.

CARTOUCHE: panel or tablet with curved and scrolled surround.

CARYATID: human figure doing duty as a column.

CAVETTO: bold concave moulding, usually a quadrant in section.

CAVO-RELIEF: sunk relief, produced by carving within the boundaries of incisions on a flat surface; as distinct from bas or alto-relief where the carving projects from the plane of the background.

CENOTAPH: lit. an empty tomb; monument commemorating some distant burial.

CHAMBERED TOMB: megalithic grave with central passage and projecting side-chambers.

CHAMFER: edge of a block cut off diagonally.

CHEST-TOMB: structurally a cist or stone box placed over a burial, its outward form reproducing the features of the classical sarcophagus or medieval effigy-base; formerly loosely described as a sarcophagus or altar-tomb.

CHEVRON: heraldic; an inverted V, commonly repeated zig-zag fashion in Romanesque moulding.

CHI-RHO: first two letters of Christ's name in Greek, used as a sacred monogram.

CIPPUS: classical round or square altar adapted to funerary use.

CIST: receptacle for a corpse; a grave lined with wood or stone, as distinct from the portable coffin.

COFFIN: portable receptacle for a corpse in various materials.

COFFIN-SLAB: cover-lid of a coffin; coffin-shaped slab.

COLUMBARIUM: lit. dovecote; family tomb or mausoleum (q.v.) with recesses or loculi for remains.

CONSOLE: see bracket.

COPED STONE: ridged or gabled memorial stone.

CORNICE: projecting moulding crowning a façade, upper part of classical entablature.

COVERED GALLERY TOMB or long cist tomb: megalithic grave with corridor divided into compartments.

CROCKETS: projecting leaf-shapes on sides of spires, pinnacles or gables in Gothic building.

CROSS-FLEURY: (heraldic) cross with arms ending in fleurs-de-lis.

CROSS-PATY: (heraldic) cross with splayed arms.

CRUCKS: curved posts fixed scissor-fashion in primitive timber construction.

CURSUS: long and narrow prehistoric banked enclosure.

DEAD-BOARD: see grave-board.

DENTILS: descriptive term for teeth-like row of blocks decorating a cornice.

DIAPER: medieval repeating pattern usually of formalized flowers enclosed in lattice-work.

DISCOID: wood or stone marker with circular or octagonal head set on a short shaft.

DOLMEN: lit. table stone, an outmoded term for what are now thought to be remnants of megalithic chambered graves, e.g. uprights supporting a lintel.

ENTABLATURE: horizontal members above the columns, consisting of architrave, frieze and cornice, in classical building.

EXEDRA: vestibule, porch, or apsidal recess.

FACE-BEDDED: stones laid with natural strata upright.

FESTOONS or swags: classical decoration of drapery or garlands of fruit and flowers suspended at the ends or looped at regular intervals.

FINIAL: ornamental knob or leaf-like finish to pinnacle or gable.

GABLE: triangular top to end walls of a ridged or gabled roof.

GABLETTES: small gables used in Gothic canopy work.

GRAVE-BOARD: inscribed plank supported by upright posts, a later form of grave-rail; also called bed-head, dead-board, leaping-board (q.v.).

GRAVE-RAIL: inscribed horizontal post or beam supported by upright posts, resembling part of a fence.

GROTESQUE: human, animal or monstrous forms combined with arabesques.

GUILLOCHE: classical pattern of interlacing circular bands, used on mouldings and borders.

HALF-EFFIGY: type of fourteenth century memorial in which an effigy appears to be enclosed in a coffin partly cut away to reveal portions of the figure.

HATCHMENT: square or lozenge-shaped armorial board formerly exhibited at funerals, then hung up in the church.

HENGE: prehistoric burial enclosed by circular bank and ditch.

HIGH CROSS: churchyard or memorial cross set on long shaft.

HIPPED ROOF: ridged roof with sloped ends.

HOGBACK: North country memorial of Danish period imitating a wattled hut decorated with formalized bears or snakes.

HOOD-MOULD: projecting moulding above an arch or lintel.

HOUSE-TOMB: monument showing the components of a building, e.g. base, walls or house-body, rounded or gabled roof.

IMMORTELLES: everlasting flowers; also nineteenth century china replicas of flowers, doves, etc., enclosed in a glass bowl and left as a memento on the grave.

JOURNEYMAN: (from journée) strictly a part-time workman, paid by the day; usually applied to any workman who had served his apprenticeship and was an employee.

LATTEN: copper alloy used for memorial brasses.

LEAPING-BOARDS: see grave-board.

LEDGER: horizontal memorial slab, incised or in low relief.

LUNETTE: semicircular or segmental panel.

MAUSOLEUM: derived from King Mausoleus' great monument at Halicarnassus; a large ornate tomb; now more particularly a family tomb-house.

MENHIR: lit. long stone; an upright prehistoric monolith.

MITCHELLS: local Oxfordshire name for square or diamond-shaped paving slabs sometimes used as memorial ledgers.

NECROPOLIS: lit. city of the dead; a cemetery or burial-ground.

OBELISK: tapering shaft of stone, square in section with pyramidal top (pyramidion); Egyptian in origin but adopted in post-Reformation period as a monumental feature.

OGEE: S-shaped curve, characteristic of late fourteenth century Gothic building and ornament.

OGHAM: Celtic script, its characters composed of lines or notches, usually engraved on the edges of upright stones.

PALMETTE: radially-lobed leaf motif; the usual decoration of the classical acroterion or antefix (q.v.).

PATERA: lit. dish; circular or daisy-like pattern.

PEDESTAL: base of a column or statue.

PEDESTAL TOMB: tall tomb, square, polygonal or circular in section, sometimes built in stages and topped with an urn or finial; or consisting of a chest-tomb supporting a pyramid, obelisk, or similar feature.

PEDIMENT: low triangular gabled end of classical building.

PELTA: crescent-shaped ornament derived from archaic shield.

PILASTER: flat column built against wall face.

PILLOW-STONE: small Anglo-Saxon cross-slab apparently buried on the breast or beneath the head of corpse.

PINNACLE: miniature spire crowning a medieval buttress, usually decorated with finial and crockets, a common feature of canopies and tabernacle work (q.v.).

PLINTH: moulded base of a column or wall.

PODIUM: the platform of a building; or lower part of classical pedestal.

POST-STONE: post-Reformation monumental squared or moulded block, mainly confined to Northern counties.

QUATREFOIL: four-lobed panel or tracery opening in Gothic ornament.

QUOINS: stone dressings or ashlar at the angles of a building.

ROCOCO: latest phase of Baroque style, mid-eighteenth century in England, a hybrid ornament with quasi-Chinese and Gothic motifs.

ROSETTE: conventional flower-head with radiating petals.

RUSTICATION: ashlar masonry with imitative rock-like surface, or deeply recessed joints.

SARCOPHAGUS: lit. flesh-eater, originating from stone used for coffins by the Greeks reputed to absorb flesh of corpses; generally used to describe any ornate stone coffin or coffin-like memorial of classical type, in the form of a couch, altar, arca (q.v.), casket, or bath-tub with rounded ends.

SCABBLING: preliminary roughing-out of the design in stone-carving; hence, scabbled—a roughly pecked or chipped surface.

SCANT: sawn or cleft stone slab prepared for carving.

SERIFS: ornamental terminations to strokes of letters.

SHEELA-NA-GIGS: small figures, probably fertility charms, found on Romanesque churches in Ireland and the West of England.

SOFFIT: underside of an arch.

SPALLING: breaking-off of chips of stone (spalls) in ashlar, often due to pressure, or swelling of internal cramps used for fixing.

SPANDREL: triangular space between arches; or between an arch and its rectangular frame.

STELA: classical gravestone, an upright slender block or slab.

STIFF-LEAF FOLIAGE: misnomer for thirteenth century ornamental foliage with multi-lobed leaves and rhythmic stems.

STRAPWORK: sixteenth and seventeenth century ornament of interlaced bands resembling fretwork, punctuated with rivets or bosses.

STRIKINGS: calligraphic flourishes in which the post-Reformation writing-masters showed their "command of hand".

SWAG: see festoon.

TABERNACLE WORK: medieval architectural tracery and canopies over niches and arcading.

TABLE-TOMB: inscribed slab or ledger raised from the ground by supporting slabs or columns.

TONDO: circular panel.

TREFOIL: triple-lobed leaf; panel of tracery in Gothic building and ornament.

TRIGLYPHS: triple-grooved blocks alternating with square panels (metopes) in classical Doric frieze.

TROPHY: limited originally to weapons, but generally used to describe any cluster of emblems bound together with festoons or ribands.

TRUSS: outmoded term for consoles or scrolled brackets, common on post-Reformation chest or pedestal tombs (q.v.).

TYMPANUM: triangular panel beneath classical pediment; or between lintel and arch in medieval doorway.

TYPE and ANTI-TYPE: correspondences drawn between Old and New Testament events showing the pattern of Christian salvation.

VOLUTE: spiral of the Ionic capital; or spiraliform scroll.

WEEPERS: mourning figures placed on the house-body supporting the medieval effigy.

ZOOMORPHS: stylized animal patterns.

Index of Place Names

The number following fig. references indicates the relevant page

315

General Index